THE SIMPLE ADVENTURES OF A MEMSAHIB

THE SIMPLE ADVENTURES OF A MEMSAHIB

SARA JEANETTE DUNCAN

GYAN

Published by

Gyan Publishing House
5, Ansari Road
Daryaganj, New Delhi-110002
Phone: 011-47034999, 9811692060
E-mail: books@gyanbooks.com

Distribution Network
gyanbooks.com
India, USA, Canada, UK, Australia

ISBN: 978-93-7447-669-7 (PB)

First Published, 1893

2nd Impression 2026

Printed at: Gyan Press, Delhi.

THE SIMPLE ADVENTURES OF A MEMSAHIB
Author: SARA JEANETTE DUNCAN

THEY CAME IN LITTLE STRAGGLING STRINGS AND BANDS.

P. 43.

THE SIMPLE ADVENTURES OF A MEMSAHIB

BY

SARA JEANNETTE DUNCAN

AUTHOR OF

A SOCIAL DEPARTURE, AN AMERICAN GIRL IN LONDON, ETC.

WITH ILLUSTRATIONS BY F. H. TOWNSEND

NEW YORK

D. APPLETON AND COMPANY

1893

LIST OF ILLUSTRATIONS.

THE SIMPLE ADVENTURES OF A MEMSAHIB.

CHAPTER I.

HELEN FRANCES BROWNE was formerly a Miss Peachey. Not one of the Devonshire Peacheys—they are quite a different family. This Miss Peachey's father was a clergyman, who folded his flock and his family in the town of Canbury in Wilts, very nice people and well thought of, with nice, well-thought-of connections, but nothing particularly aristocratic amongst them, like the Devonshire Peacheys, and no beer.

The former Miss Peachey is now a memsahib of Lower Bengal. As you probably know, one is not born a memsahib; the dignity is arrived at later, through circumstances, processes, and sometimes through foresight on the part of one's mamma. It is not so easy to obtain as it used to be. Formerly it was a mere question of facilities for transportation, and the whole matter was arranged, obviously and without criticism, by the operation of the law of supply. The necessary six months' tossing fortune in a sailing ship made young ladies who were willing to undertake it scarce and valuable, we hear. We are even given to understand that the unclaimed remnant, the few standing over to be more deliberately acquired, after the ball given on board for the facilitation of these matters the night succeeding the ship's arrival in port, were held to have fallen short of what they reasonably might have expected. But that was fifty years ago. To-day Lower Bengal, in the cold weather, is gay with potential memsahibs of all degrees of attraction, in raiment fresh from Oxford Street, in high spirits, in excellent form for tennis, dancing, riding, and full of a charmed appreciation of the "picturesqueness" of India.

They come from the East and from the West, and from school in Germany. They come to make the acquaintance of their Anglo-Indian fathers and mothers, to teach the Bible and plain sewing in the Zenanas, to stay with a married sister, to keep house for a brother who is in the Department of Police. In the hot weather a proportion migrate northward, to Darjeeling, or Simla, in the Hills, but there are enough in our midst all the year round to produce a certain coy hesitancy and dalliance on the part of pretending bachelors, augmented by the consideration of all that might be done in England in three months' "Privilege" leave. Young Browne was an example of this. There was no doubt that young Browne was tremendously attracted by Miss Pellington—Pellington, Scott & Co., rice and coolies chiefly, a very old firm—down from the Hills for her second cold weather, and only beginning to be faintly spoilt, when it so happened that his furlough fell due. He had fully intended to "do Switzerland this time," but Canbury, with tennis every Wednesday afternoon at the Rectory, and Helen Peachey playing there in blue and white striped flannel, pink cheeks and a sailor hat, was so much more interesting than he had expected it to be, that Switzerland was gradually relegated five years into the future. After tennis there was always tea in the drawing-room, and Helen, in the pretty flush of her exertions, poured it out. Just at first, young Browne did not quite know which he appreciated most, Helen who poured it out, or the neat little maid in cap and apron who brought it in—it was so long since he had seen tea brought in by anything feminine in cap and apron; but

GOT MIDDLE-AGED LADIES OF WILTSHIRE CUPS OF TEA.

after a bit the little maid sank to her proper status of consideration, and Helen was left supreme. And Helen Peachey's tennis, for grace and muscularity, was certainly a thing to see, young

Browne thought. She played in tournaments while he stood by in immaculate whites with an idle racquet, and got middle-aged ladies of Wiltshire cups of tea; but she was not puffed up about this, and often condescended to be his partner on the Rectory lawn against the two younger Misses Peachey. It made the best sett that way, for young Browne's tennis fluctuated from indifferent bad to indifferent worse, and the younger Misses Peachey were vigorous creatures, and gave Helen all she could do to win with her handicap.

Mr. Browne—we must really get into the way of giving him his title—was not naturally prone to depression, rather the reverse; but when the two Misses Peachey came off victorious he used to be quite uncomfortably gloomy for a time. Once I know, when he had remarked apologetically to Helen that he hoped she would have a better partner next time, and she absent-mindedly returned, "I hope so indeed!" his spirits went down with a run and did not rise again until somebody who overheard, chaffed Helen about her blunder and produced gentle consternation and a melting appeal for pardon. That was at a very advanced stage of these young people's relations, long after everybody but themselves knew exactly what would happen, and what did happen in the course of another week. It was a triviality, it would have had no place in our consideration of the affairs of a young man and woman who fell in love according to approved analytical methods, with subtle silent scruples and mysterious misunderstandings, in the modern way. I introduce it on its merits as a triviality, to indicate that George William Browne and Helen Frances Peachey arrived at a point where they considered themselves indispensable to each other in the most natural, simple, and unimpeded manner. I will go so far as to say that if Helen had not been there—if she had

YOUNG BROWNE'S TENNIS FLUCTUATED FROM INDIFFERENT BAD TO INDIFFERENT WORSE.

spent the summer with an aunt in Hampshire, as was at one time contemplated—one of the other Misses Peachey might have inspired this chronicle. But that is risking a good deal, I know, at the hands of the critics, and especially perhaps at Helen's. After all, what I want to state is merely the felicitous engagement, in July of a recent year, of Mr. Browne and Miss Peachey. Two tender months later, Mr. Browne sailed for India again, with a joyful conviction that he had done well to come home, that somewhat modified his natural grief. Helen remained behind for various reasons, chiefly connected with the financial future of the Browne family, and the small part of Calcutta interested in young Browne found occupation for a few days in wondering what Miss Pellington would have said if he had proposed to her. There was no doubt as to the point that he did not. Calcutta is always accurately informed upon such matters.

The dreary waste of a year and four thousand miles that lay between Miss Peachey and the state of memsahibship was relieved and made interesting in the usual way by the whole Peachey family. You know what I mean, perhaps, without details. Miss Kitty Peachey "etched" Kate Greenway figures on the corners of table napkins, Miss Julia Peachey wrought the monogram P. M. in the centre of pillow-shams with many frills, their Aunt Plovtree, widow of a prominent physician of Canbury, at once "gave up her time" to the adornment of Helen's future drawing-room in Kensington stitch, and Mrs. Peachey spent many hours of hers in the composition of letters to people like John Noble, holding general councils over the packets of patterns that came by return of post. Mrs. Peachey was much occupied also in receiving the condolences of friends upon so complete a separation from her daughter, but I am bound to say that she accepted them with a fair show of cheerfulness. Mrs. Peachey declared that she would wait until the time came before she worried. As to both the wild animals and the climate she understood that they were very much exaggerated, and, indeed, on account of Helen's weak throat, she was quite in hopes the heat might benefit her. And really nowadays, India wasn't so very far away after all, was it? It was difficult, however, even with arguments like these, to reconcile the Canbury ladies to the hardship of Helen's fate, especially those with daughters of their own who had escaped it. Helen listened to the condolences with bright eyes and a spot of pink on each cheek. They brought her tender pangs sometimes, but, speaking generally, I am afraid she liked them.

In six months it was positively time to begin to see about the trousseau, because, as Mrs. Plovtree very justly remarked, it was not like getting the child ready to be married in England, where one would know from a pin or a button exactly what she wanted; in the case of Indian trousseaux everything had to be thought out and considered and time allowed to get proper advice in. For instance, there was that very thing they were talking about yesterday—that idea of getting Jaeger all through for Helen. It seemed advisable, but who knew *definitely* whether it was! And if there *was* an unsatisfactory thing in Mrs. Plovtree's opinion it was putting off anything whatever, not to speak of an important matter like this, till the last moment.

The event redounded to the wisdom of Mrs. Plovtree, as events usually did. It took the Peachey family quite six months to collect reliable information and construct a trousseau for Helen out of it; six months indeed, as Mrs. Peachey said, seemed too little to give to it. They collected a great deal of information. Mrs. Peachey wrote to everybody she knew who had ever been in India or had relations there, and so did several friends of the Peacheys, and the results could not have been more gratifying either in bulk or in variety. As their Aunt Plovtree said, they really could not have asked for more, indeed they would have had less difficulty in making up their minds without quite so much. "*Do* be advised," one lady wrote, with impressive underlinings, "and let her take as little as she can *possibly* do with. It is impossible to keep good dresses in India, the climate is simple *ruination* to them. I shall never forget the first year of my married life on that account. It was a *heart-breaking* experience, and I *do* hope that Helen may avoid it. Besides, the *durzies*, the native dressmakers, will copy *anything*, and do it *wonderfully* well, at about a fifth of the price one pays at home." Which read very convincingly. By the same post a second cousin of Mrs. Plovtree's wrote, "If you ask me, I should say make a special point of having everything in reasonable abundance. The European shops ask frightful prices, the natives are always unsatisfactory, and your niece will find it very inconvenient to send to England for things. My plan was to buy as little as possible in India, and lay in supplies when we came home on leave!"

"In the face of that," said Mrs. Plovtree, "what are we to do?"

Ladies wrote that Helen would require as warm a wardrobe as in England; the cold might not be so great but she would "feel it more." She must take her furs, by all means. They wrote also that when they were in India, they wore nothing more substantial than nun's veiling, and a light jacket the year round. They gave her intense directions about her shoes and slippers—it was impossible to get nice ones in India—they were made very well and cheaply in the "China bazar"—they lasted for ever if one took care of them—they were instantly destroyed by mould and cockroaches when "the rains" came on. She would require a size larger than usual, on account of the heat; she must remember to take a size smaller because she would use her feet so little that they would decrease somewhat, everybody's did. She must bear one thing in mind, they were quite two years behind the fashion in India, so that it would be advisable to date her garments back a little, not to be remarkable. In another opinion there was this advantage, that in taking a fashionable trousseau to India, one could rely upon its being the correct thing for at least two years. The directions in flannel, and cotton, and linen, were too complicated for precise detail, but they left equal freedom of choice. And choice was difficult, because these ladies were all ex-memsahibs, retired after fifteen, twenty, or twenty-five years' honourable service, all equally qualified to warn and to instruct, and equally anxious to do it. They had lived in somewhat different localities in India, ranging from seven to seven thousand feet above the level of the sea, in the Northwest provinces, in the Punjaub, in Southern India, in Beluchistan, and none of them had spent more than an occasional "cold weather" in Calcutta, but this triviality escaped the attention of the Peachey family, in dealing with the matter. India, to their imagination, was incapable of subdivision, a vast sandy area filled with heathen and fringed with cocoanut trees, which drew a great many young Englishmen away from their homes and their families for some occult purpose connected with drawing pay in rupees. So the Peacheys put these discrepancies down to the fact that people had such different ideas, and proceeded to arrange Helen's trousseau upon a modification of all of them. When this was quite done Mrs. Plovtree remarked with some surprise that with the addition of a few muslin frocks, the child had been fitted out almost exactly as if she were going to live in England. There was the wedding dress, which she might or might not wear upon the occasion, it would be indispensable *after*wards; there was the travelling dress chosen primarily not to "take the dust" and secondarily not to show it; two or three gowns of incipient dignity for dinner parties; two or three more of airier sorts for balls—but at this point I must refer you to the ladies' papers. Turn over a few of their pages and you will see Helen's trousseau illustrated with skill and imagination, but with trains, I am bound to add, more prehensile than Helen ever wore, the habit of the Peachey family being to follow the fashions at a safe and unaggressive distance. Among the photographs of the brides which accompany you may even find one fairly like Helen. These young ladies have always struck me as bearing a charmingly subdued resemblance to one another, probably induced by the similarly trying conditions under which their portraits are published. And certainly in the lists of presents appended you will find many, if not all of those that the Rev. Peachey packed with his own clerical hands in large wooden boxes, for consignment to the P. and O., indeed I fancy a discriminating inspection of the advertisements would reveal most of them. As the Rev. Peachey himself would say, I need not go into that.

Helen was the first bride that Canbury had contributed to India, in the social memory. Two or three young men had gone forth to be brokers' assistants or civil servants or bank clerks, and an odd red-coat turned up periodically in the lower stratum of society on furlough, bringing many-armed red and yellow idols to its female relatives; but Canbury had no feminine connections with India, the only sort which are really binding. Helen's engagement had an extrinsic interest therefore, as well as the usual kind, and Canbury made the most of it. There was the deplorable fact, to begin with, that she could not be married at home. Canbury gave a dubious assent to its necessity; everybody had a dim understanding of the exigencies of "leave," and knew the theory that such departures from the orthodox and usual form of matrimonial proceeding were common and unavoidable. Yet in its heart and out of the Peachey and Plovtree earshot, Canbury firmly dissented, not without criticism. Would anybody tell it why they had not gone out together last year? On the face of it, there could be no question of saving. The young man was not in debt, and received a salary of five hundred pounds a year—had not Mr. Peachey's curate married Jennie Plovtree a month after they were engaged on two hundred, and no expectations whatever! Or why, since they had made up their minds to wait, could they not have put it off another year! Surely in two years Mr. Browne might scrape enough together to come home again! Canbury thought it possessed a slight opinion of a young man who could not come after his wife. Privately Canbury upheld the extremest traditions of chivalry, and various among Miss Peachey's young lady friends, quite unconscious of fibbing, confided to each other that "they wouldn't be in Helen's place for anything." In the rectory drawing-room, however, these stringencies took a smiling face and a sympathetic form, sometimes disappearing altogether in the exaltation of the subject's general aspects. Helen was told it was very "brave" of her, and Mrs. Peachey was admired for her courage in letting her daughter go. At which she and Helen smiled into each other's eyes understandingly. Then Canbury began to search the aforesaid advertisements in the ladies' papers for mementoes suitable in character and price, and to send them to the rectory with as hearty wishes for the happiness of the future Brownes as if they had behaved properly in every respect.

CHAPTER II.

TO Mrs. Peachey, one very eonsoling eircumstance eonneeted with Helen's going to India was the good she would probably be able to do to "those surrounding her." Helen had always been "active" at home; she had been the inspiration of work-parties, the life and soul of penny-readings. She often took the entire superintendence of the night sehool. The Canbury branch of the Y. W. C. T. U. did not know how it should get on without her. Besides playing the organ of St. Stephen's, in whieh, however, another Miss Peaehey was by this time ready to sueeeed her. Mueh as Mrs. Peachey and the parish would miss Helen, it was a sustaining thought that she was going amongst those whose need of her was so much greater than Canbury's. Mrs. Peaehey had private ehastened visions, ehiefly on Sunday afternoons, of Helen in her new field of labor. Mrs. Peaehey was not destitute of imagination, and she usually pictured Helen seated under a bread-fruit tree in her Indian garden, dressed in white muslin, teaehing a eirele of little "blaeks" to read the Seriptures. Helen was so sueeessful with children; and so far as being tempted to its ultimate salvation with goodies was eoneerned, a blaek ehild was probably just like a white one. Of course, Helen would have to adapt her induee-ments to eircumstances—it was not likely that a little Bengali eould be baited with a Bath bun. Doubtless she would have to offer them riee or—what else was it they liked so much?—oh yes! sugar-cane. Over the form of these delicacies Mrs. Peachey usually went to sleep, to dream of larger schemes of heathen emancipation which Helen should inaugurate. Mr. Peachey, who knew how hard the human heart could be, even in Canbury, among an enlightened people enjoying all the blessings of the nineteenth century, was not so sanguine. He said he believed these Hindus were very subtle-minded, and Helen was not much at an argument. He understood they gave able theologians very hard nuts to crack. Their ideas were entirely different from ours, and Helen would be obliged to master their ideas before effecting any very radical change in them. He was afraid there would be difficulties.

Mrs. Plovtree settled the whole question. Helen was not going out as a missionary, except in so far as that every woman who married undertook the charge of *one* heathen, and she could not expect to jump into work of that sort all at once. Besides, the people were so difficult to get at, all shut up in zenanas and places. And she did not know the language; first of all, she would have to conquer the language; not that it would take Helen long, for see what she did in French and German at school in less than a year! For her part, she would advise Helen to try to do very little at first—to begin, say, with her own servants; she would have a number of them, and they would be greatly under her personal influence and control. Mrs. Plovtree imparted an obscure idea of Helen's responsibility for the higher welfare of her domestics, and a more evident one that it would be rather a good thing to practice on them, that they would afford convenient and valuable material for experiments. In all of which Mrs. Peachey thoughtfully acquiesced, though in fancy she still allowed herself to picture Helen leading in gentle triumph a train of Rajahs to the bosom of the

Church—a train of nice Rajahs, clean and savoury. That, as I have said, was always on Sunday afternoons. On the secular days of the week they discussed other matters, non-spiritual, and personal, to which they were able to bring more definiteness of perspective, and they found a great deal to say.

A friend of young Browne's had gone home opportunely on six months' leave, and his recently acquired little wife would be "delighted," she said, to wreak her new-found dignity upon Helen in the capacity of chaperone for the voyage out. But for this happy circumstance, Helen's transportation would have presented a serious difficulty, for the Peacheys were out of the way of knowing the ever-flowing and returning tide of Anglo-Indians that find old friends at Cheltenham and take lodgings in Kensington, and fill their brief holiday with London theatres and shopping. As it was, there was great congratulation among the Peacheys, and they hastened to invite Mr. and Mrs. Macdonald to spend a short time at the rectory before the day on which the ship sailed. Mrs. Macdonald was extremely sorry that they couldn't come; nothing would have given them more pleasure, but they had so many engagements with old friends of her husband's, and the time was getting so short and they had such a quantity of things to do in London before they sailed, that—the Peacheys must resign themselves to disappointment. Mrs. Macdonald hoped that they would all meet on board the *Khedive*, but held out very faint hopes of making acquaintance sooner than that. It was a bright agreeable letter as the one or two that came before had been, but it left them all in a difficulty to conjure up Mrs. Macdonald, and unitedly they lamented the necessity. What Mr. Macdonald was like, as Mrs. Plovtree observed, being of no consequence whatever. But it was absolute, and not until the *Khedive* was within an hour of weighing an-

FIELD OF LABOUR.

chor at the Royal Albert Docks, did the assembled Peacheys, forlorn on the main deck in the midst of Helen's boxes, get a glimpse of Mrs. Macdonald. Then it was brief. One of the stewards pointed out the Peachey group to a very young lady in a very tight-fitting tailor-made dress, swinging an ulster over her arm, who approached them briskly with an outstretched hand and a businesslike little smile. "I think you must be Mr. and Mrs. Peachey," she said; "I am Mrs. Macdonald. And where is the young lady?" Mr. Peachey unbent the back of his neck in the clerical manner, and Mrs. Peachey indicated Helen as well as she could in the suffusion of the moment, taking farewell counsels of her sisters with pink eyelids. "But you mustn't *mind* her going, Mrs. Peachey!" Mrs. Macdonald went on vivaciously, shaking hands with the group, "she will be sure to like it. Everybody likes it. *I* am devoted to India! She'll soon get accustomed to everything, and then she won't want to come home—that's the way it was with me. I dare say you won't believe it, but I'm dying to get back! You've seen your cabin?" she demanded of Helen, "is it forward or aft? Are you port or starboard?"

The Peacheys opened their eyes respectfully at this nautical proficiency, and Helen said she was afraid she didn't know, it was down some stairs and one turned to the left, toward the end of a long passage, and then to the right into a little corner.

"Oh, then you're starboard and a little forward of the engines!" Mrs. Macdonald declared. "Very lucky you are! You'll have your port open far oftener than we will—we're weather-side and almost directly over the screw. So much for not taking one's passage till three weeks before sailing—and very fortunate we were to get one at all, the agent said. We have the place to ourselves though, one can generally manage that by paying for it you know—one comfort! How many in your cabin?"

"Three of us!" Helen responded apprehensively, "and it *is* such a little one! And the one whose name is Stitch has piled all her rugs and portmanteaux on my bed, and there's nowhere to put mine!"

"Oh, the cabins in this ship are not small," returned Mrs. Macdonald with seriousness. "She's got a heavy cargo and they're pretty low in the water, if you like, but they're not small. Wait till you get used to it a little. As to Madam Stitch, just pop her bags and things on the floor—don't hesitate a moment. One *must* assert one's rights on shipboard—it's positively the only way! But there are some people to see me off—I must fly!" She gave them a brisk nod and was on the wing to her friends when Mrs. Peachey put a hand on her arm. "You spoke of the ship's being low in the water, Mrs. Macdonald. You don't think—you don't think there is any danger on that account?"

Little Mrs. Macdonald stopped to enjoy her laugh. "Oh dear, no!" she said with vast amusement, "rather the other way I should think—and we'll be a great deal steadier for it!" Then she went, and the Peacheys saw her in the confused distance babbling as gaily in the midst of her new-comers as if a thought of the responsibilities of chaperonage had never entered her head.

"Helen, I believe you are older than she is!" exclaimed the youngest Miss Peachey.

"I don't like her," remarked the second succinctly. "She giggles and she gabbles. Helen, I wish some of *us* were going with you."

"She doesn't seem to mind travelling," said the Miss Peachey with the prospective claim to the title.

"Dear *me*, Helen!" began Mrs. Peachey almost dolorously, "she—she seems very bright," changing her comment. After all they must make the best of it. The Rev. Peachey clasped his stick behind his back, and tapped the deck with it, saying nothing, with rather a pursing of his wide shaven lips, Helen looked after Mrs. Macdonald helplessly, and her family exchanged glances in which that lady might have read depreciation.

"Your roll-up, Helen?" exclaimed Mrs. Peachey.

"Here, mamma."

"You have seven small pieces, remember! *Have* you got your keys? Are you sure you are dressed warmly enough? It will be some time before you get to India, you know!" Mrs. Peachey had suffered an accession of anxiety in the last ten minutes.

They stood looking at each other in the common misery of coming separation, casting about for last words and finding none of any significance, for people do not anticipate an event for a whole year without exhausting themselves on the topic of it. Helen would keep a little diary; she would post it at Gibraltar, Naples, Port Said, and Colombo; and they were to write overland to Naples, and by the next mail to Calcutta, which would reach before she did. These time-worn arrangements were made over again. Helen thought of a last affectionate message to her Aunt Plovtree and was in the act of wording it, when a steward with a yellow envelope inquired of them for "any lady by the name of Peachey." The contents of the yellow envelope had telegraphic brevity. "Good-bye and God bless you! J. Plovtree." Helen read, and immediately took out her handkerchief again. "Just like Jane!" said Mrs. Peachey, sadly, with her eyes full, and Mr. Peachey, to cover his emotion read aloud the hours at which the message had been received and delivered. "Forty-two minutes" he announced "fairly quick!" Helen proposed a walk on the quarter-deck. "The luggage, my dear child!" Mrs. Peachey cried. "We mustn't leave the luggage, with all these people about! James, dear, it would not be safe to leave the luggage, would it! You and the girls may go, Helen. Your father and I will stay here."

AUNT PLOVTREE.

"Oh, no!" Helen returned reproachfully, and clung to them all.

The crowd on the deck increased and grew noisier, people streamed up and down the wide gangway. Cabin luggage came rattling down in cabs, perilously late, the arm of the great steam-crane swung load after load high in air and lowered it into the hold, asserting its own right of way. "That's one of your tin-lined boxes, Helen," exclaimed Mrs. Peachey, intent on the lightening of the last load, "and oh, I'm *sure* it is not safe, dear! James won't you *call* to them that it is not safe!" But the long deal case with "Miss Peachey, Calcutta," in big black letters on it was already describing an arc over the heads of the unwary, and as it found its haven Mrs. Peachey made a statement of excited relief, "I never saw such carelessness!" said she.

A number of ladies, dressed a good deal alike, arrived upon the deck in company and took up a position near the forward part of the ship, where the second class passengers were gathered together, producing little black books. From these they began to sing with smiling faces and great vigour, various hymns, with sentiments appropriate to long voyages, danger, and exile from home. It was a parting attention from their friends to a number of young missionaries for Burmah, probably designed to keep up their spirits. The hymns were not exclusively of any church or creed—Moody and Sankey contributed as many of them as the *Ancient and Modern*, but they were all lustily emotional and befitting the occasion to the most unfortunate degree. The departing missionaries stood about in subdued groups and tried to wave their handkerchiefs. One or two young lady missionaries found refuge in their cabins where they might sob comfortably. The notes rang high and bathed the whole ship in elegy, plaintively fell and reveled in the general wreck of spirits and affectation of hilarity. It began to rain a little, but the ladies were all provided with umbrellas, and under them sang on.

> "While the nearer waters roll,
> While the tempest still is high."

"What idiots they are!" remarked the youngest plain-spoken Miss Peachey when it became impossible to ignore the effect upon Helen's feelings any longer. "As if they couldn't find anything else to sing than *that!*"

"Oh, my *dear*," rebuked Mrs. Peachey, drying her eyes, "we may be sure that their motive is everything that is good." Whereat the youngest Miss Peachey, unsubdued, muttered "*Motive!*"

"H'all this for the cabin, miss?" asked a steward, grasping a hat-box and a portmanteau. "I don't *quite* know 'ow that there *long* box is a-going in, miss. Is it accordin' to the Company's regillations, miss?" Mr. Peachey interposed, with dignity, and said that it was—the precise measurements. It came from the Army and Navy Stores, he was quite sure the size was correct. The man still looked dubious, but when Helen said, regardless of measurements, that she must have it, that it contained nearly everything she wanted for the voyage, he shouldered it without further dissent. He was accustomed to this ultimatum of seafaring ladies, and bowed to it.

Mrs. Peachey began to think that they ought to go down to the cabin and stay beside the luggage, there were so many odd-looking people about; but she succumbed to the suggestion of being carried off; and they all went up on the quarter-deck. Mrs. Macdonald was there—they might see something more of Mrs. Macdonald. They clung to the hope.

They did see something more of Mrs. Macdonald—a little. She interrupted herself and her friends long enough to approach the Peacheys and ask if all Helen's luggage was on board, "wedding presents and all?" jocularly. Mrs. Peachey replied fervently that she hoped so, and Mrs. Macdonald said, Oh, that was all right then, and Was she a good sailor? Oh, well, she would soon get over it. And oh, by the by—departing to her beckoning friends again—it was all right about their seats at table—

Miss Peachey was to sit by them—she had seen the head steward and he said there would be no difficulty. Having thus reassured them, "I'll see you again," said Mrs. Macdonald, and noddingly departed.

The first whistle shrilled and bellowed, and a parting stir responded to it all over the ship. Mrs. Peachey looked agitated, and laid a hand on Helen's arm. "There is no cause for haste, mamma," said the Rev. Peachey, looking at his watch. "We have still twenty minutes, and there is a quantity of freight yet to be got on board." The missionary ladies began a new hymn,

"Oh, think of the friends over there!"

"Only twenty minutes, my love! Then I think we ought really to be getting off! My darling child——"

The whistle blew again stertorously, and the gangway began to throng with friends of the outward-bound. The dear, tender, human-hearted Peacheys clustered about the girl they were giving up—the girl who was going from their arms and their fireside an infinite distance, to a land of palm-trees and yams, to marry—and what a lottery marriage was!—a young Browne. They held her fast, each in turn. "I almost w-wish I w-weren't go—" sobbed Helen in her mother's embraces. "Helen!" said the youngest Miss Peachey sternly, with a very red nose, "you do *nothing of the sort!* You're only too pleased and proud to go, and so should I be in your place!" Which rebuke revived Helen's loyalty to her Browne if it did not subdue the pangs with which she hugged her sister.

At last the gangway was withdrawn and all the Peacheys were on the other side of it. It rained faster, the missionary ladies still sang on, people called last words to their friends in the damp crowd below. A box of sweets was thrown to a young lady on the main deck—it dropped into the black water between the ship and the wharf and was fished out with great excitement. The Peacheys gathered in a knot under their several umbrellas, and Helen stood desolately by herself watching them, now and then exchanging a watery smile. They cast off the ropes, the Lascars skipped about like monkeys, the crowd stood back, slowly the great ship slipped away from the wharf into the river, and as she moved down stream the crowd ran with her a little way, drowning the missionary ladies with hurrahs. In the Peacheys' last glimpse of their Helen she was standing beside little Mrs. Macdonald and a stout gentleman with a pale face, rather flabby and deeply marked about the mouth and under the eyes—a gentleman whom nature had intended to be fair but whom climatic conditions had darkened in defiance of the intention. Mrs. Macdonald tapped the gentleman in a sprightly way with her parasol, for the Peacheys' benefit, and he took off his hat. The Peachey family supposed, quite correctly, that that must be Mr. Macdonald.

CHAPTER III.

HELEN thought the prospect of England slipping away from her in the rain as the ship throbbed down the river, too desolate for endurance, so she descended to her cabin with the unavowed intention of casting herself upon her berth to weep. Miss Stitch was there, however, and Mrs. Forsyth-Jones, who occupied the berth above Miss Stitch's, and the steward, which seemed to Helen a good many, and she retreated.

"Oh, come in!" both the ladies cried; but Helen thought it was obviously impossible. She wandered into the long dining-saloon and sat down in one of the revolving chairs; she watched a fat ayah patting a baby to sleep on the floor, looked into the ladies' cabin and went hastily out again, for already the dejected had begun to gather there, prone on the sofas and commiserated by the stewardesses. Finally she made her way upon deck again, meeting Mrs. Macdonald in the companion-way. "Are you all right?" asked Mrs. Macdonald cheerfully; but, before Helen had time to say that she was or was not, the lady had disappeared.

The deck was full of irresolute people like herself, who sat about on the damp benches or walked up and down under the awning, still with the look of being fresh from town, still in gloves and stiff hats, and land-faring garments. They put their hands in their pockets and shivered, and looked askance at each other, or made vain attempts to extract their own from the steamer chairs that were heaped up astern, waiting the offices of a quartermaster. An occasional hurrying steward was stopped a dozen times by passengers thirsting for information. Barefooted Lascars climbed about their monkey-like business among the ropes, or polished the brasses on the smoking-cabin, or holystoned a deck which seemed to Helen immaculately clean before. She found a dry corner and sat down in it to consider how much more familiar with the ship many of the people seemed to be than she was, and to envy all the accustomed ones. It seemed to Helen that she had better not analyse her other emotions. She wasn't comfortable, but no doubt she soon would be; she wasn't cheerful; but how could anybody expect that? She was restless and damp and unhappy, and it finally became necessary for her to draw young Browne's photograph out of her hand-bag and peruse it in shelter of the *Daily Graphic* for a very long time. After which her spirits rose appreciably. "He *is* a dear!" she smiled to herself, "and he's got a lovely forehead—and in just five weeks I shall see him again—just five weeks!"

Quite an ordinary reflection you see, without a shade of

subtlety, a reflection probably common to engaged young ladies the world over; but I have already warned you under no circumstances to expect anything extraordinary from Helen. It will be my fault if you find her dull, I shall be in that case no faithful historian, but a traducer. I have not known the present Mrs. Browne to be dull, even at the close of a protracted round of Indian social gaieties; but you must not expect her to be original.

The voyage to Calcutta began in this way, and I happen to know that its chief feature of consolation—young Browne's forehead—remained in Helen's pocket, and was constantly bespoken. Especially perhaps in the Bay of Biscay, which fulfilled all its traditions for her benefit. I fear that there were moments, tempestuous moments, in the Bay of Biscay, heightened by the impassioned comments of Miss Stitch and Mrs. Forsyth-Jones, when Helen did not dare to dwell upon the comparative advantages of desiccated spinsterhood in Canbury, and matrimony in foreign parts attainable only by sea. She felt that it would be indiscreet, that she could not trust her conclusions to do credit to her fealty. If it were not for Miss Stitch and Mrs. Forsyth-Jones, Helen reflected, the horrors of the situation would have been less keen; but I have no doubt that each of these ladies entertained the same sentiments towards her two fellow-voyagers. They united, however, in extolling the steward. The stewardess was a necessarily perfunctory person, with the quaverings of forty ladies in her ears at once. The stewardess was always sure she "didn't know, ma'am," and seemed to think it was a duty one owed the ship to go up on deck, no matter how one felt. She was also occasionally guilty of bringing one cold vegetables, if one occurred about thirty-ninth upon her list of non-diners in public. But the steward was a man, and always respectfully cheerful. He could tell exactly why it was the ship rolled in that peculiar manner—owing to the disposition of iron in the hold. He knew just how long they would be in "the Bay," and what sort of weather "she" would be likely to experience during the night; also could predict within a quarter of an hour, the time at which they would land at Gibraltar. He was generally incorrect in every particular, but that made no difference to the value of his sanguine prophecies, while it mitigated the distressful effects of his gloomy ones. And it was always he who brought the first advice that the ports might be opened, who calmed all fear of a possible rat or cockroach "coming up from the hold," and who heralded the ladies' appearance on deck with armfuls of rugs, in the days of early convalescence. They chanted to one another continually how "nice" he was, and how hard he was obliged to work, poor fellow, each mentally determining a higher figure for her farewell tip than she had thought of the day before. This is the custom of ladies the world over who sail upon the seas.

It must be mentioned that Mrs. Macdonald visited Helen's cabin several times in the Bay of Biscay. For her part Mrs. Macdonald was never ill, she simply made up her mind not to be, and in her opinion if Helen would only commit herself to a similar effort she would be all right immediately. The expression of this opinion rather lessened the value of Mrs. Macdonald's sympathy; and the announcement that there was really lovely weather going on above and the ship was beginning to be so jolly, failed to make Helen any more comfortable. "Well, you are funny!" Mrs. Macdonald would say cheerfully in departing, and she said it every day.

Mr. Macdonald remarked that Gibraltar looked much as usual

the morning they steamed under its hostile shadow, and Mrs. Macdonald said that if she wasn't in absolute need of some darning cotton and letter-paper she wouldn't think of going ashore—the place was such an old story. The consideration of darning cotton prevailed, however, and the Macdonalds went ashore, Helen with them. Helen's acquaintance with the Macdonalds had progressed meanwhile. She had learned what not to expect of them, which excluded all but the gayest and airiest and most indifferent companionship, and this facilitated matters between them considerably. It was a little difficult at first. It seemed to this young lady from Wiltshire, brought up among serious traditions of matrimony, that her case, if not herself, ought to be taken a little more importantly, that some impression of the fateful crisis in her life, toward which they were helping to hurry her, ought to be evident occasionally in the Macdonald conduct or conversation. It was only gradually that she came to see how lightly such projects as hers and young Browne's were regarded by these people who were still in the initial stages of their own; how little space she or her affairs occupied in their good-natured thoughts; how invariably she must expect any reference to it to be jocular. During the process Helen had now and then a novel sense of making one of the various parcels which Mrs. Macdonald had undertaken to bring out to friends in Calcutta—a feeling, that she ought properly to be in an air-tight box in the hold, corded and labelled and expected to give no further trouble. She realized, at moments, that she was being "shipped" to young Browne.

They did exactly what everybody does in Gibraltar. There was no time to get permission from the authorities and go through the galleries, there never is. Barring which, the people of the ships find themselves without resource except to drive in the rattle-trap conveyances of the place through its narrow twisting, high-walled over-topping white streets and out past the Spanish market, where everybody buys figs and pomegranates to throw overboard afterwards, and so emerging from the town trot through the sand and the short grass round the mighty gray foot of the Rock, to look up and marvel at the terror of those irregular holes upon its face, and the majesty that it had long before it became conscious with cannon. Helen and the Macdonalds did all this and said just what P. and O. voyagers have said for the last quarter of a century about it. Coming back Mrs. Macdonald bought her darning cotton and her letter-paper at a little shop, whose black-browed proprietor sold photographs and wicked knives, and long pipes as well. Afterwards they all strolled through the Alameda gardens, that cling for life among their verbenas and rose bushes to the sides of the Rock, and finally fell into that fatal corner shop which entraps the unwary with curios. All roads seem to lead to it in Gibraltar, and one knows it by the crowd of speculative passengers that encumber the doorway considering and contrasting desirable purchases. The Spaniards inside are haughty and indifferent, they will abate a shilling or two of their exorbitance perhaps, not more. That is what the Macdonalds said to everybody in an undertone—"You needn't try, they won't come down—it doesn't seem to be worth their while. We used to think they would, but now we don't ask them!" and in the face of this advice of experience the passengers hesitated still more over their ill-shaped Moorish vases, black and red and blue and gilt, their brass and coloured glass hanging lamps from Cairo, their Persian china superficially gilt but beautifully blue. The things that fascinated Helen were curious plaques in relief, all marshy greens, in which the most realistic lizards and toads were creeping about in imitated moss. Miss Peachey would have liked at least four of these, they struck her as so original and clever, until Mrs. Macdonald at her elbow said, in an impressive whisper "*Don't!* You see them in *boarding*-houses in Calcutta!" when she put them reluctantly down, and bought a big bedecked Spanish hat to make a work-basket of, and a large fan, upon which sundry ladies of depraved appearance and very Irish features were dancing a *fandango* instead. I have seen that fan in the present Mrs. Browne's Calcutta drawing-room frequently since. She has it fastened on the wall immediately under a photogravure of *The Angelus*, and she will not take it down.

Between Gibraltar and Naples, Helen observed the peculiarities of the species P. and O. passenger, the person who spends so large a portion of a lifetime shorter than the average, in wondering how much more of this delightful or this abominable weather "we'll have," in the Indian Ocean or the Red Sea. She observed that Miss Stitch arose betimes every morning, and attended the service held by the little pale ritualistic clergyman in the saloon before the tables were laid for breakfast, which struck her as eminently proper, Miss Stitch being a missionary. She also noticed that Mrs. Forsyth-Jones, returning to her husband in Burmah, with three photographs of him in uniform variously arranged in the cabin, had as many small flirtations well in hand, one in the morning, of the promenade sort, with a middle-aged Under Secretary, one in the afternoon, conducted in long chairs, enhanced by sunset, with a Royal Engineer, whose wife was similarly occupied at the other end of the ship, and one in the evening in a secluded corner of the hurricane deck, charitably witnessed by the moon and stars, with a callow indigo planter about the age of her eldest son. Helen thought that the missionary or somebody, some older person, ought to speak to this lady in terms of guarded reproof, and tell her that her conduct was more conspicuous than perhaps she knew; and our young lady from Wiltshire was surprised to observe not only that nobody did, but that Mrs. Forsyth-Jones seemed to be a person of some popularity on board. The Macdonalds, for instance, hung about her chair with solicitude, in the temporary absence of any of the *attachés*. Mrs. Macdonald herself had plenty of "men-friends" as she called them. They buzzed about her, whenever she sat or stood long enough to permit their approach, all day—they were always bringing her rugs, or old numbers of *Punch*, or an orange. But Mrs. Macdonald did not particularize, she was content with a general empire, though she prized that, as anybody could see. Among the throng Mr. Macdonald remained supreme; she expected most attention from him too, and she called him "Mac."

Miss Stitch confided to Miss Peachey her opinion that "the people on board this ship" were more than usually cliquey; but this was not a conclusion that Helen would have arrived at unassisted. She saw about her day after day, lining the long tables and afterwards scattered about easefully on deck, a great many people, some of whom she thought agreeable-looking, and others distinctly the reverse. Miss Stitch seemed to think one ought to know everybody. Helen was sure that a few—a very few—of the agreeable-looking people would do quite well. She did not see at all how Miss Stitch could bring herself to talk to the person who sat next her at table, and wore a large diamond ring on his third finger, and drank champagne every day at tiffin, and said he was travelling for his "'ealth," and pointed most of his remarks with a tooth-pick. Helen thought that even missionary zeal would not carry her so far as that. On the other hand, she found it difficult to understand why everybody, including Miss

Stitch, seemed agreed not to make acquaintance with a soft-eyed, sad-faced lady of rather dark complexion, who talked in a gentle voice with a slightly foreign accent, Helen thought, and was accompanied by three daughters, who much resembled her. They looked very quiet and lady-like to Helen, and she thought the manners of certain boisterous young ladies who polkaed with the ship's officers on a heaving deck after dinner, and whom everybody accepted, suffered by comparison with them. When she was told that their name was De Cruz, Helen privately criticised her fellow countrywomen's attitude. "It must be," she said to herself, "because they are foreign." And so it was—because they were foreign. "About four annas in the rupee," said Miss Stitch about them one day, and told Helen that she would find out what that meant before she had been long in India. But Miss Stitch, M. D., was interested in the welfare, temporal and eternal, only of ladies who were "pure native."

Then one peaceful rainy morning, after a rolling night, Naples lay before them, gathered all about her harbour with Vesuvius gently smoking in the distance. The slippery hurricane deck was full of people looking for Vesuvius, grouped round the single male passenger, who, awakened by the first officer at four in the morning, had seen it spouting fire. Enviable male passenger! Invidious first officer! Out from shore came disreputable Neapolitan companies in small boats, with stringed instruments, who lay under the ship's sides and sang, "Finiculi—Finicula!" in a lavish and abandoned manner, turning up their impudent faces for contributions from the truly musical souls on board. Helen listened, enraptured, to a number of these renditions, after which she concluded that she preferred "Finiculi—Finicula" as she had heard it sung by Mr. Browne, in Canbury, Wilts. After breakfast, the Macdonalds attached themselves to an exploring party for Pompeii, under the guidance of a black-browed Neapolitan, representing Messrs. Cook. Mrs. Macdonald went about in a pretty, new waterproof, with Bulwer's *Last Days* in her hand, telling people she really must go this time, she had been lazy so often before, and it was so awfully cheap with these people—carriages, rail, tiffin and see everything for only thirty francs each! Helen and Miss Stitch stayed behind, the night had been too rough to let them venture on the absorption of so much ancient history, even at this advantageous rate. But later, when the sun came out, the young ladies recovered their spirits sufficiently to cruise adventurously to shore by themselves, to engage a ragged-pocketed "guide" of perhaps thirteen, and a rattling little victoria, pulled by a clinking little pony, with bells upon his collar, and drive about Naples for three delicious hours. I can't say they added much to their stock of information. They had no idea where to go and what to see; but one can always absorb colour and life without a guide-book, happily; and I know, from what she told me afterward, that Helen Peachey did that. They found abundant happiness in the curio shops and much unpalatable fruit in the open market; they filled their rattletrap of a carriage with great bunches of tiny pink roses at a few coppers a-piece, and buried their faces in them. They were told, driving through a grand toppling main street, all draped and garlanded with little glass bells for candles, red, green, and blue, that the King was coming next day. The boy guide told them this. He showed them also the Royal Palace, with all the statues of former kings standing about outside, and the "Grand Café de l'Europe," much embellished by a painter whose art had evidently once found favour with the municipality. In the opinion of the guide, the "Grand Café de

'Europe" was what reasonable people came to Naples to see; he pointed it out many times and with an increasing show of personal admiration. He was a very useful, clever boy the young ladies thought, especially when he took them to the post office and obtained for Miss Stitch a receipt for the registered letter she wanted to send away, in as business-like a manner as if he were in the habit of transmitting large sums abroad daily. "Don' you lossit, for *good*niz sake!" he exclaimed, as he gave her the slip. But I doubt whether he was quite worth the sum he claimed at the water's edge when they departed—the pay of a full-grown, well-fed guide for a whole day, plus a *pourboire*, which they ungrudgingly gave between them.

But I cannot give any more of my valuable space to Mrs.. Browne's reminiscences of that voyage, which must, according to the volumes of them, have lasted a space of about seven months. I believe they were all very gay at Port Said, walking through the single wide China bazaar street of the place, flaming with colour and resonant of musicians in the gambling houses, drinking black coffee on the boulevard, and realizing no whit of Port Said's iniquity. The Suez Canal had no incident but several loathly odors, and then came the long smooth voyage to Colombo and a fantastic glimpse of first cocoanut trees fringing the shores of Ceylon. A great deal here about sapphires and rubies and cat's eyes and little elephants made of ivory and small brown diving-boys, and first tropical impressions, but I must not linger in the chronicling. Then the sail up to Madras, and the brief tarrying there, and the days that came after, short days when everybody packed and rejoiced. At last, one night at ten o'clock, a light that was not a star, shining far through the soft still darkness beyond the bow of the ship, the light at the mouth of a wide brown river that slipped to the sea through the India, Helen would see in the morning, and past the city whither her simple heart had gone before her.

. . . .

Mrs. Macdonald kept out of the way. It was the one considerate thing she did during the voyage. Young Browne, rather white and nervous-looking, came upon Mr. Macdonald first in the turbulent shore-going crowd. Mr. Macdonald was genial and reassuring. "You'll find her over there, old man," said he without circumlocution, "rather back. Better bring her up to Hungerford Street to breakfast yourself." And Helen straightway was found by young Browne in the precise direction Mr. Macdonald had indicated, and "rather back." She always remembers very distinctly that on that occasion she wore a blue Chambray frock and a sailor hat with a white ribbon round it. It is not a matter of consequence, still it might as well be mentioned.

CHAPTER IV.

I HAVE no doubt that the present Mrs. Browne would like me to linger over her first impressions of Calcutta. She has a habit now of stating that they were keen. That the pillared houses and the palm-shaded gardens, and the multiplicity of turbaned domestics gave her special raptures, which she has since outgrown, but still likes to claim. She said nothing about it at the time, however, and I am disposed to believe that the impressions came later, after young Browne had become a familiar object, and all the boxes were unpacked. As they were not married immediately, but a week after the *Khedive* arrived, to give Mrs. Macdonald time to unpack *her* boxes, the former of these processes was an agreeably gradual one occupying six morning and evening drives in Mr. Browne's dog-cart, and sundry half-hours between. Mrs. Macdonald wanted to make the house pretty for the wedding. "Really, child," said she, "you can't be married in a barn like this!" and to that end she drew forth many Liberty muslins, much "art" needlework, and all the decoration flotsam and jetsam of the season's summer sales in Oxford Street. I understand that both the Brownes protested against the plan to have a wedding; they only wanted to be married, they said, of course in the Church, regularly, but without unnecessary circumstance. "People can see it next day in *The Englishman*," suggested young Browne, urged privately to this course by Helen. But it was a point upon which Mrs. Macdonald was inflexible. "Certainly not a *big* wedding," said she, "since you don't want it, but a few people we must have just to see it properly done. What would Calcutta think of you" — reproachfully, to young Browne, "getting the knot tied that way, in a corner! Besides, it will be a lovely way of letting everybody know we are back. *I'll* manage it—I know exactly who you ought to have!"

Thereupon Helen brought out from among her effects a certain square wooden box, and besought that it might be opened. "It's—it's the cake," she explained with blushes; mother thought I ought to bring it—"

"Oh, of course!" exclaimed Mrs. Macdonald briskly; "everybody does. There were five altogether on board the *Khedive.* Let us hope it has carried well!"

They opened the box, and Helen took out layers of silver paper with nervous fingers. "It seems a good deal crushed," she said. Then she came upon a beautiful white sugar bird of Paradise lacking his tail, and other fragments dotted with little silver pellets, and the petals of a whole flower-garden in pink icing. "It has *not* carried well!" she exclaimed grievously—and it hadn't. It was the proudest erection of the Canbury confectioner's experience, a glory and a wonder when it arrived at the Rectory, but it certainly had not carried well: it was a travelled wreck.

"Looks very sorry for itself!" remarked young Browne, who happened to be present.

"It must have happened in that hateful Bay of Biscay!" said Helen, with an inclination to tears.

"Oh, never mind!" Mrs. Macdonald put in airily, as if it were a trifle. "It's easy enough to get another. I'll send a chit to Peliti's this very afternoon. You can use up this one for five o'clock tea afterwards."

"But do you think it won't do at all, Mrs. Macdonald?" Helen begged. "You see the lower tier isn't much damaged, and it came all the way from home, you know."

"I think it ought to do," remarked young Browne.

"My *dear!*" cried her hostess, "think of how it would *look!* In the midst of everything! It would quite spoil your wedding! Oh, no—we'll have another from Peliti's."

"What could one do?" confided Mrs. Browne to me afterwards. "It was *her* affair—not ours in the least. We were getting married, don't you see, for her amusement!" But that was in one of Mrs. Browne's ungrateful moments. And was private to me. Generally speaking, Mrs. Browne said she thought the Macdonalds arranged everything charmingly. The Canbury cake went, however, to the later suburban residence of the Brownes, and was there consumed by them in the reckless moments of the next six months.

I was one of the people Mrs. Macdonald knew the Brownes ought to have, and I went to the wedding, in a new heliotrope silk. I remember that also came out by the *Khedive.* It was in the Cathedral, at four o'clock in the afternoon, full choral service, quantities of flowers, and two heads of departments in the company, one ex-Commissioner, and a Member of Council. None of them were people the Brownes were likely to see much of afterward, in my opinion, and I wondered at Mrs. Macdonald's asking them; but the gown she graced the occasion in would have justified an invitation to the Viceroy—pale green poplin with silver embroidery.

The bride came very bravely up the aisle upon the arm of her host, all in the white China silk, a little crushed in places, which the Canbury dressmaker had been reluctantly persuaded to make unostentatiously. The bridegroom stood consciously ready with his supporter; we all listened to the nervous vows, sympathetically thinking back; the little Eurasian choir-boys sang lustily over the pair. Two inquisitive black crows perched in the open window and surveyed the ceremony, flying off with hoarse caws at the point of the blessing; from the world outside came the hot bright glare of the afternoon sun upon the Maidan, and the creaking of the ox-gharries,* and the chatting of the mynas in the casucrina † trees, and the scent of some waxy heavy-smelling thing of the country—how like it was to every other Indian wedding where a maid comes trippingly from over seas to live in a long chair under a punkah, and be a law unto kitmutgars!

The new Mrs. Browne received our congratulations with shy distance after it was all over. She looked round at the big stucco church with its white pillars and cane chairs, and at our unfamiliar faces, with a little pitiful smile. I had, at the moment, a feminine desire to slap Mrs. Macdonald for having asked us. And all the people of the Rectory, who ought to have been at the wedding, were going about their ordinary business, with only now and then a speculative thought of this. Everybody who really cared was four thousand miles away, and unaware. We could not expect either of them to think much of our perfunctory congratulations, although Mr. Browne expressed himself very politely to the contrary in the valuable sentiments he uttered afterwards in connection with champagne cup and the Peliti wedding cake, on Mrs. Macdonald's veranda.

They had a five days' honeymoon, so far as the outer world

* Native ox-carts. † Australian fir.

was concerned, and they spent it at Patapore. Darjiling, as young Browne was careful to explain to Helen, was the proper place, really the thing to do, but it took twenty-six hours to get to Darjiling, and twenty-six hours to get back, and nobody wanted to plan off a five days' honeymoon like that. Patapore, on the contrary, was quite accessible, only six hours by mail.

"Is it a hill-station?" asked Helen, when they discussed it.

"Not precisely a hill-station, darling, but it's on rising ground—a thousand feet higher than this."

"Is it an interesting place?" she inquired.

"I think it ought to be, under the circumstances."

"*George!* I mean are there any temples there, or anything?"

"I don't remember any temples. There is a capital dak-bungalo."

"And what is a dak-bungalow, dear? How short you cut your hair, you dear old thing!"

"That was provisional against your arrival, darling—so you couldn't pull it. A dak-bungalow is a sort of government hotel, put up in unfrequented places where there aren't any others, for the accommodation of travellers."

"*Unfrequented* places! O George! Any snakes or tigers?"

"Snakes—a few, I dare say. Tigers—let me see; you *might* hear of one about fifty miles from there."

"Dreadful!" shuddered Helen, rubbing her cheek upon George's convict crop. "But what is the *attraction*, dear?"

"The air," responded he, promptly substituting his moustache. "Wonderful air! Think of it, Helen—a thousand feet up!"

But Helen had not been long enough in India to think of

it. "Air is a thing one can get anywhere," she suggested; "isn't there anything else?"

"Seclusion, darling—the most perfect seclusion! Lots to eat—there's always the railway restaurant if the dak-bungalow gives out, capital air, nice country to walk over, and not a soul to speak to but our two selves!"

"Oh!" said Helen. "It *sounds* very nice, dear——" And so they agreed.

It was an excellent dak-bungalow without doubt, quite a wonder in dak-bungalows. It was new, for one thing—they are not generally new—and clean, they are not generally clean. There had been no deserted palace or disused tomb for the government to utilize at Patapore, so they had been obliged to build this dak-bungalow, and they built it very well. It had a *pukka** roof instead of a thatched one, which was less comfortable for the karaits but pleasanter to sleep under; and its walls were straight and high, well raised from the ground, and newly white-washed. Inside it was divided into three pairs of rooms, one in the middle and one at each end. You stepped into one of your rooms on the north side of the house and out of the other on the south side, upon your share of the south veranda. The arrangement was very simple, each pair of rooms was separate and independent, and had nothing to say to any other.

The furniture was simple too, its simplicity left nothing to be desired. There were charpoys† to sleep on, travellers brought their own bedding. In one room there were two chairs and a table, in the other a table and two chairs. There was nothing on the floor and nothing on the walls. There was ample accommodation for the air of Patapore, and no other attraction to inter-

* Made of brick and mortar.

† Native beds.

fere with it. I don't know whether we have any right to accompany the Brownes to Patapore, and to stay with them there; it is certain that we would not be welcome, if they knew it. It is equally certain that nobody else did—they were, as young Browne had predicted, supremely alone. At seven in the morning the old khansamah in charge of the place gave them chota hazri * in the room with the table in it, bringing tea in a chipped brown teapot, and big thick cups to drink it out of, one edged with blue and the other with green, and buttered toast upon a plate which did not match anything. He was a little brown khansamah, with very bright eyes and a thin white beard and a trot—he reminded one curiously of a goat. His lips were thin and much compressed; he took the Brownes solemnly, and charged them only three rupees a day each for their food, which young Browne found astonishingly moderate, though Helen, when she worked it out in shillings and pence, and considered the value received, could not bring herself to agree with this.

After chota hazri they went for walks, long walks, stepping off the dak-bungalow veranda, as Helen said, into India as it was before ever the Sahibs came to rule over it. For they could turn their backs upon the long straight bank of the railway and wander for miles in any direction over a country that seemed as empty as if it had just been made. As far as they could see it rolled in irregular plains and low broken ridges and round hillocks all covered with short, dry grass, to the horizon, and there, very far away, the gray outlines of an odd mountain or two stood against the sky. A few sarl trees were scattered here and there in clumps, all their lower branches stolen for firewood, and wherever a mud hut squatted behind a hillock there grew a tall

* Little breakfast.

castor oil bean tree or two, and some plantains. There were tracks of cattle, there was an occasional tank that had evidently been dug out by men, and there were footpaths making up and over the hillocks and across the stony beds of the empty *nullahs*;* but it was only in the morning or in the evening that they met any of the brown people that lived thereabouts. Then they came in little straggling strings and bands, looking at these strangers from under inverted baskets, appearing from nowhere and disappearing in vague and crooked directions. Helen's husband told her that they were coolies working in coal mines on the side of the railway. There were crows, too, and vultures—the crows were familiar and impertinent, the vultures sailed high and took no notice of them—and that was all. They went forth and they came back again. Helen made a few primitive sketches in her husband's note-book. I do not think she did the country justice, but her sketches seemed to me to indicate the character of her impressions of it. They went forth and they came back again, always to a meal—breakfast, or tiffin, or dinner, as the case might be. Helen liked dinner best, because then the lamps were lighted, and she had an excuse for changing her dress. They partook of these meals with three-tined steel forks, and knives worn down to dagger points, according to the unfathomable custom of the *mussalchi*.† The courses consisted of variations upon an original leg of mutton which occurred at one of their earlier repasts, served upon large cracked plates with metal reservoirs of hot-water under them, and embellished by tinned peas of a suspicious pallor. And always there was *moorghy*‡—moorghy boiled and fried and roasted, moorghy cutlets, moorghy curry, moorghy stew. "Nice old person," said

* Stream beds. † Dishwasher. ‡ Fowl.

Helen, the first time it appeared, "he has given us fowl! Dear old patriarch." "He may or may not be a dear old patriarch," George responded, fixing grim eyes upon the bird, "but he is tolerably sure to have the characteristics of one. You aren't acquainted with the indigenous moorghy yet, Helen. You regard him in the light of a luxury, as if he were a Christian fowl. He isn't a luxury out here upon my word. He stalks up and down all over India improving his muscular tissues, he doesn't disdain to pick from a drain, he costs threepence to buy. She is an inferior creature still. It may be a prejudice of mine, but if there's any other form of sustenance to be had I don't eat moorghy."

"He tastes," said Mrs. Browne after experiment, "like an 'indestructible' picture-book." It was an unwarrantable simile upon Mrs. Browne's part, since she could not possibly remember the flavour of the literature she used to suck as an infant; but her verdict was never reversed, and so one Indian staple passed out of the domestic experiences of the Brownes.

These two young people had unlimited conversation, and one of them a great many more cigars than were good for him. So far as I have been able to discover, by way of diversion they had nothing else. It had not occurred to either of them that the equipment of a honeymoon required any novels; and the dak-bungalow was not provided with current fiction. They covered an extensive range of subjects, therefore, as they thought, exhaustively. As a matter of fact, their conversation was so superficial in its nature, and led to such trivial conclusions, that I do not propose to repeat it. They were very unanimous always. Young Browne declared that if his views had habitually received the unqualified assent which Helen gave them he would have been a member of the Viceroy's Council years before. They could not say enough in praise of the air of Patapore, and when the wind rose it blew them into an ecstasy. Frequently they discussed the supreme advantages of a dak-bungalow for a honeymoon, and then it was something like this on the afternoon of the third day.

"The perfect freedom of it, you know—the being able to smoke with one's legs on the table——"

"Yes, dear. I love to see you doing it. It's so—it's so home-like!" (I think I see the Rev. Peachey with his legs upon the table!) Then, with sudden animation, "Do you know, George, I think I heard boxes coming into the next room!"

"Not at all, Helen. You didn't, I'm sure you didn't. And then the absolute silence of this place——"

"Lovely, George! And that's how I heard the boxes so distinctly." Getting up and going softly to the wall—"George, there are people in there!"

"Blow the people! However, they haven't got anything to do with us."

"But perhaps—perhaps you know them, George!"

"Most piously I hope I don't. But never mind, darling. We can easily keep out of the way, in any case. We won't let them spoil it for us."

"N-no, dear, we won't. Certainly not. But you'll find out who they are, won't you, Geordie! Ask the khansamah, just for the sake of knowing!"

"Oh, we'll find out who they are fast enough. But don't be distressed, darling. It will be the simplest thing in the world to avoid them."

"Of course it will," Mrs. Browne responded. "But I think, George dear, I really must put on my tailor-made this afternoon in case we *should* come in contact with them in any way."

"We won't," replied George, cheerfully lighting another cigar.

To which Mrs. Browne replied without seeming relevance, "I consider it perfectly SHAMEFUL for dak-bungalows to have no looking-glasses."

An hour later Helen flew in from the veranda. "Oh, George, I've seen them: two men and a lady and a black and white dog—spotted! Quite nice, respectable-looking people, all of them! They walked past our veranda."

"Confound their impudence! Did they look in?"

"The dog did."

"None of the rest? Well, dear, which way did they go?"

Helen indicated a south-easterly direction, and the Brownes that evening walked almost directly north, with perhaps a point or two to the west, and did not return until it was quite dark.

The fourth day after breakfast, a stranger entered the veranda without invitation. He was clad chiefly in a turban and loin cloth, and on his head he bore a large tin box. He had an attendant, much like him, but wearing a dirtier loin-cloth, and bearing a bigger box.

"Oh! who is it?" Helen cried.

"It's one of those wretched box-wallahs, dear—a kind of pedlar. I'll send him off. *Hujao,** you!"

"Oh, *no*, George! Let us see what he has to sell," Helen interposed with interest; and immediately the man was on the floor untying his cords.

"My darling, you can't want anything from him!"

* Be off!

"*Heaps* of things—I shall know as soon as I see what he's got, dear! To begin with, there's a lead pencil! So far as I know I haven't a lead pencil in the world. I'll take that lead pencil! Soap? No, I think not, thank you. Do tell me what he says, George. Elastic—the very thing I wanted. And tape? Please ask him if he's got any tape. Tooth-brushes—what do you think, George?"

"*Not* tooth-brushes!" her lord protested, as one who endures. "They may be second-hand, dear."

"*Oh!* No! Here, take them back, please! Ribbon—have you any narrow pale blue? That's *about* right, if you've nothing better. Hooks and eyes are always useful. So are mixed pins and sewing cotton. I can't say I think much of these towels, George, they're very thin—still we shall *want* towels."

Mrs. Browne was quite pink with excitement, and her eyes glistened. She became all at once animated and eager, a joy of her sex was upon her, and unexpectedly. The box-wallah was an Event, and an Event is a thing much to be desired, even in one's honeymoon. This lady had previously and has since made purchases much more interesting and considerably more expensive than those that fell in her way at Patapore; but I doubt whether any of them afforded her a tenth of the satisfaction. She turned over every one of the box-wallah's commonplaces, trusting to find a need for it. She laid embroidered edging down unwillingly, and put aside handkerchiefs and hosiery with a sigh, pangs of conscience arising from a trousseau just unpacked. But it was astonishing how valuably supplementary that box-wallah's stores appeared to be. Helen declared, for instance, that she never would have thought of Persian morning slippers, which she has never yet been able to wear, if she had not seen them there, and this I can believe.

The transaction occupied the best part of two hours, during which young Browne behaved very well, smoking quietly, and only interfering once, on the score of some neckties for himself. And when Helen remonstrated that everything seemed to be for her, he begged her to believe that he really didn't mind—he didn't feel acquisitive that morning; she mustn't consider him. To which Helen gave regretful compliance, for the box-wallah had a large stock of gentlemen's small wares. In the end Mr. Browne paid the box-wallah, in a masterly manner, something over a third of his total demand, which he accepted, to Helen's astonishment, with only a perfunctory demur, and straight away put his box on his head and departed. About which time young Browne's bearer came with respectful inquiry as to which train he would pack their joint effects for on the morrow. This is an invariable terminal point for honeymoons in India.

CHAPTER V.

IT is time, perhaps, to state a few facts about Mr. George William Browne in addition to those which are in the reader's possession already. I have mentioned, I think, that he played tennis badly and was fond of privacy; it runs in my mind also that I have in some way conveyed to you that he is a rather short and thickly built young gentleman, with brown eyes and a dark moustache, and a sallow complexion and a broad smile. Helen declares him handsome, and I never considered him unpleasant-looking, but it is undoubtedly the case that he is very like other young men in Calcutta, also clerks in tea and indigo houses on five hundred rupees a month, with the expectation of partnership whenever retirement or fever shall remove a head of the firm. His tastes were common to Calcutta young men also. He liked golf and polo, and regretted that his pony was not up to the paper-chases; in literature he preferred Clark Russell and the *Pioneer*, with

Lord Lytton for serious moments. He complied with the customs of the Cathedral to the extent of a silk hat and a pair of gloves in the cold weather, and usually attended one service every Sunday, invariably contributing eight annas to the offertory. His political creed was simple. He believed in India for the Anglo-Indians, and despised the teaching and hated the influence, with sturdy reasons, of Exeter Hall. Any views that he had of real importance mainly concerned the propagation of tea in distant markets; but his spare ideas had a crispness that gave them value in a society inclined to be intellectually limp, and his nature was sufficiently cheerful and sympathetic to make him popular, in connection with the fact that he was undeniably a good fellow.

When all this has been said, I fear that Mr. Browne will not appear in these pages with the equipment proper for a young man of whom anything is expected in the nature of modern fiction. Perhaps this, however, is not so important as it looks, which will be more evident when we reflect that in marrying Miss Helen Francis Peachey Mr. Browne performed considerably the greater part of what will be required of him in this history.

That Young Browne's *tulub** was only five hundred rupees a month is, however, a fact of serious importance both to the Brownes and to the readers of these chapters. It must be borne in mind, even as the Brownes bore it in mind, to the proper understanding of the unpretending matters herein referred to. There are parts of the world in which this amount translated into the local currency, would make a plutocrat of its recipient. Even in Calcutta, in the olden golden time when the rupee was worth two invariable shillings and the stockbroker waxed not so

* Pay.

fat as now, there was a sweet reasonableness about an income of five hundred that does not exist to-day. There is no doubt, for one thing, that at that time it did not cost so much to live in a house. At the present time, and in view of the degeneracy of the coin, that luxury is not so easy to compass as it used to be.

The Brownes would live in a house, however. Young Browne, when the matter was up for discussion, stated with some vehemence his objection to the Calcutta system of private hostelries. Helen said conclusively that if they had no other reason for housekeeping, there were those lovely dessert knives and forks from Aunt Plovtree, and all the other silver things from people, to say nothing of the complete supply of house and table linen, ready marked with an artistically intertwined "HB." In the face of this, to use other people's cutlery and table napkins would be foolish extravagance—didn't George think so? George thought so, very decidedly, that was quite a strong point. It must be a whole house, too, and not a flat; there was no autonomy in a flat and no proprietorship of the compound; moreover, you were always meeting the other people on the stairs. By all means a house to themselves—"if possible," added young Browne.

"About what rent does one pay for a house?" Helen inquired.

"You get a fairly good one for three hundred a month, on lease. A visiting Rajah down for the cold weather to try for a 'C. I. E.'* sometimes pays a thousand."

"But we," responded Mrs. Browne blankly, "are not Rajahs, dear!"

"No, thank the Lord," said Mr. Browne, with what struck

* Companion of the Indian Empire.

his wife as unnecessary piety; "and we'll make ourselves jolly comfortable notwithstanding. Nellums—you'll see!" George Browne was always over-optimistic. If those two young people had come to me—but it goes without saying that they went to nobody.

Helen desired a garden, a tennis-court, and, if possible, a cocoanut palm-tree in the garden. She would prefer a yellow house to a pink one, in view of the fact that the houses were all yellow or pink, and she would like a few pillars in front of it—pillars seemed so common an architectural incident in Calcutta that she thought they must be cheap. Mr. Browne particularly wanted air in the house, "a good south veranda," and a domicile well raised above its native Bengal. Mr. Browne was strong upon locality and drains, and the non-proximity of jungle and bushes. Helen bowed to his superior knowledge, but secretly longed that a garden with a cocoanut palm in it might be found in a neighbourhood not insanitary. And so they fared forth daily in a ticca-gharry to inspect desirable addresses.

They inspected many. There was no unnecessary formality about permission to look, no "Enquire of Messrs. So and So," no big key to procure from anywhere. The ticca-gharry* stopped, and they alighted. If the high wooden gates were closed, Mr. Browne beat upon them lustily with his stick, shouting, "Qui hai!" † in tones of severe authority. Then, usually from a small and dingy domicile near the gate, issued a figure hastily, a lean, brown figure, in a dirty dhoty, that salaamed perfunctorily, and stood before them waiting.

"Iska ghur kali hai?" ‡ Mr. Browne would inquire and the figure would answer, "Ha!"

* Hired carriage. † Whoever is! ‡ Is this house empty?

Whereat, without further parley, the Brownes would enter the place and begin to express their minds about it. Generally it invited criticism. If the previous sahib had been but three weeks departed the place had an overgrown look, the bushes were unkempt, the grass ragged; there were cracks in the mortar and stains on the walls; within it smelt of desolation. Helen investigated daintily; it looked, she said, so very "snaky." The general features of one house were very like the general features of another; that is to say, their disadvantages were fairly equal. They all had jungly compounds, they were all more or less tumble-down, all in fashionable Eurasian neighbourhoods, and all at least fifty rupees a month more than the Brownes could afford to pay. Helen found some æsthetic charm, and young Browne some objectionable odour in every one of them. She, one might say, used nothing but her eyes, he nothing but his nose. With regard to the attractions of one address in particular they came almost to a difference of opinion. It was a bungalow, and it sat down flatly in a luxuriant tangle of beaumontia, and bougainvilliers, and trailing columbine. It had a veranda all roundabout, and the veranda was a bower of creeping things. Not only cocoanut palms, but date palms, and areca palms, and toddy palms grew in the corners of the compound with hibiscus bushes all in crimson flower along the wall, a banyan tree in the middle, and two luxuriant peepuls, one on each side, almost meeting over the roof of the house. The walls and pillars of the bungalow were in delicate tones of grey and green; close behind it were all the picturesque features of a native bustee, and immediately in front a lovely reflection of the sky lay in a mossy tank in places where the water was deep enough. The rent was moderate: it had been empty a long time.

"George!" Helen exclaimed, "it has been waiting for us."

George demurred. "It's far and away the worst place we've seen," he remarked.

"I think it's perfectly sweet," his wife maintained.

"If we took it," he returned implacably, "within three months two funerals would occur in this neighbourhood: one would be yours and one would be mine. I don't speak of the mortality among the servants. I'll just ask the durwan* how many sahibs have died here lately. And he asked the durwan in his own tongue.

"He says three in the last family, and it was the 'carab bimar,' which is the bad sickness or the cholera, my dear. What a fool of a durwan to leave in charge of an empty house! If you still think you'd like to have it, Helen, we can inquire——"

"Oh, *no!*" Helen cried. "Let us go away *at once!*"

"I was going to say—at the undertaker's for additional accommodation. But perhaps we had better not take it. Let's try for something clean."

I consider that the Brownes were very lucky in the end. They found a house in a suburban locality where a number of Europeans had already survived for several years, at a rent they thought they could afford by careful managing. It turned its face aside from the street and looked towards the south; sitting on its roof, they could see far across those many-laned jungle suburbs where the office baboo† lives, and whither the sahibs go only on horseback. The palm fronds waved thick there, fringing the red sky duskily when the sun went down. The compound was neglected, but had sanitary possibilities; there was enough grass for a tennis-court and enough space for a garden. A low line of godowns ran round two sides of it, where the servants might live

* Doorkeeper. † Native clerk.

and the pony. Palms and plantains grew in the corners. It was very tropical, and it was inclosed by a wall coloured to match the house, in the cracks of which sprouted every green thing. The house itself was pink, which Helen declared her one disappointment: she preferred the yellow ones so much. Inside it was chiefly light green, stencilled in yellow by way of dadoes, which must have been trying, though Helen never admitted it. There were other peculiarities. The rafters curved downwards and the floor sloped toward the middle and in various other directions. In several places trailing decorations in mud had been arranged by white ants. None of the doors had locks or bolts; they all opened inwards and were fastened from the inside with movable bars. The outermost room had twelve French windows; the innermost room had no windows and was quite dark when its doors were shut. Irregular holes appeared at intervals over the wall for the accommodation of punkah-ropes, each tenant having fancied a different seat outside for his punkah-wallah. Two or three small apartments upstairs in the rear of the house had corners divided off by partitions about six inches high. These were bath-rooms, arranged on the simple principle of upsetting the bath-tub on the floor and letting the water run out of a hole in the wall inside the partition. Most of the windows had glass in them, but not all, and some were protected by iron bars, the domestic conditions inside having been originally Aryan and jealous.

I do not wish it to be supposed from these details, that the Brownes were subjected to exceptional hardships, or took up housekeeping under particularly obscure circumstances. On the contrary, so few people with their income in Calcutta could afford to live in houses at all, that young Browne had his name put up on the gatepost with considerable pride and circumstance. "George W. Browne," in white letters on a black ground, in the middle of an oblong wooden tablet, according to the custom of the place. The fact being that the characteristics of the Brownes' house are common, in greater or less degree, to every house in Calcutta. I venture to say that even the tub of a Member of Council, on five thousand rupees a month, is discharged through a hole in the wall.

Perhaps their landlord was more or less unique. The landlord common to Calcutta is a prosperous Jew, a brocaded Rajah, at least an unctuous baboo fattened upon dhol-bat and chutney. The Brownes' landlord wore a pair of dirty white trousers and a lean and hungry look, his upper parts being clad in yards of soiled cotton, in which he also muffled up his head. He followed them about the place in silent humility—they took him for a coolie, and young Browne treated his statements with brevity, turning a broad British back upon him. I don't think this enhanced the rent; I fancy it would have been equally extortionate in any case. But it was only when Mr. Browne asked where the landlord was to be found that he proudly disclosed his identity, with apologetic reference, however, to the state of his attire. He said that his house had been vacant for many months, and that he had just spent a thousand rupees in repairing it. His prospective tenant accepted the first of these statements, and received the second with open laughter. They closed the bargain, however, and as the landlord occupied an adjoining bustee, and was frequently to be met in the neighbourhood, Mrs. Browne was for some time uncertain as to whether she ought to bow to him or not.

MRS. BROWNE WAS FOR SOME TIME UNCERTAIN WHETHER SHE OUGHT TO BOW TO HIM OR NOT.

CHAPTER VI.

THERE are a number of ways of furnishing a house in Calcutta. I, who have known the ins and outs of the place for twenty odd years, have learned the unsatisfactoriness of all of them, and am prepared to explain. You can be elaborately done up by a fine *belati* upholsterer, who will provide you with spindle-legged chairs in velvet brocade, and æsthetic window curtains with faded pink roses on them, everything only about six months behind the London shops, with prices however considerably in advance. This way is popular with Viceroys. Or you may go to the ordinary shops and get Westbourne Grove sorts of things only slightly depreciated as to value and slightly enhanced as to cost, paying cash—a way usually adopted by people of no imagination. Or you may attend the auction sale that speeds the departure of some home-going memsahib, and buy her effects for a song: but that must be at the beginning of the hot weather, when the migration of memsahibs occurs. Or you can go to Bow Bazar, where all things are of honourable antiquity, and there purchase pathetic three-legged memorials of old Calcutta, springless oval-backed sofas that once upheld the ponderous dignity of the East India Company, tarnished mirrors which may have reflected the wanton charms of Madame Le Grand. Baboos sell them, taking knowledge only of their outward persons and their present utility; and they stand huddled in little hot low-roofed shops, intimate with the common teak-wood things of yesterday, condescending to gaudy Japanese vases and fly-blown coloured prints and cracked lamps and mismatched crockery. Bow Bazar is not always bad and it is always cheap, granting some previous experience of baboo morals, and the proprietors charge you nothing for the poetry of your bargain. They set it off, perhaps, against necessary repairs. This is not a popular way, as the baboos will testify, but it is a pleasing one, and it is the way the Brownes took in the main, supplementing these plenishings with a few from the China Bazar, where a multitude of the almond-eyed sell you wicker chairs and tables.

It is a divinely simple thing to furnish a house in India. It must be cleaned and it must be matted. This is done in a certain number of hours while you sleep, or ride, or walk, or take your pleasure, by a God of Immediate Results, whom you colloquially dub the "bearer," working through an invisible agency of coolies. Then you may go and live in it with two chairs and a table if you like, and people will only think you have a somewhat immoderate hatred of hangings and furniture and other obstacles to the free circulation of air. This you might easily possess to an extreme, and nobody will consider you any the worse for it. I should have added an "almirah" to the list of your necessaries, however. You would be criticised if you had not one or more almirahs. An almirah is a wardrobe, unless it contains shelves instead of hooks, and then it is a tall cupboard with doors. Almirahs, therefore, receive all your personal property, from a dressing-gown to a box of sardines, and it is not possible to live decently or respectably in India without them. But the rest is at your good pleasure, and nobody will expect you to have anything but plated forks and bazar china. Outward circumstance lies not in these things, but in the locality of your residence and the size of your compound. If you wish to add to your dignity, buy another pony; if you wish to enhance it, let the pony be a horse and the horse a Waler. But think not to aggrandize yourself in the eyes of your fellow Anglo-Indians by treasures of Chippendale or of Sèvres, by rare tapestries or modern masters, or even a piano. Dust and the mosquitos and the monsoon war against all these things; but chiefly our inconstancy to the country. We are in conscious exile here for twenty or twenty-five years, and there is a general theory that it is too hot and too expensive to make the exile any more than comfortable. Beside which, do we not pass a quarter of our existence in the cabins of the P. and O.? But I must not digress from the Brownes' experiences to my own opinions.

The Brownes' ticca-gharry turned into Bow Bazar out of Chowringhee, out of Calcutta's pride among her thoroughfares, broad and clean, and facing the wide green Maidan, lined with European shops, and populous with the gharries* of the sahibs, into the narrow crookedness of the native city, where the proprietors are all Baboo This, or Sheik That, who sit upon the thresholds of their establishments smoking the peaceful hubble-bubble, and waiting until it please Allah or Lakshmi to send them a customer. Very manifold are the wants that Bow Bazar provides for, wants of the sahib, of the "kala sahib,"† of its own swarming population. You can buy a suit of clothes there—oh, very cheap—or a seer of rice; all sorts of publications in English, Bengali, and Urdu; a beautiful oil painting for a rupee, a handful of sticky native sweetmeats for a pice. You can have your beard shaved, your horoscope cast, your photo-

* Carriages.

† "Black sahibs," i. e. Eurasians.

graph taken, all at a rate which will deeply astonish you. There is a great deal of noise in the Bow Bazar, coming chiefly from strenuous brown throats, a great deal of dust, a great number and variety of odours. But there the sahib-lok, in the midst of luxury, can enjoy economy—and you can't have everything.

The sellers of sahib's furniture have the largest shops in Bow Bazar, and the heaviest stock; they are important among the merchants; they often speak a little English. The baboo to whom the Brownes first addressed themselves had this accomplishment, and he wore the dual European garment of white duck, and a coat. He was a short baboo, very black, with a round face so expressive of a sense of humour that young Browne remarked to Helen privately that he was sure the fellow had some European blood in him, in spite of the colour—no pukka Bengali ever grinned like that!

"What iss it, sir, that it iss your wish to buy?" he inquired. He spoke so rapidly that his words seemed the output of one breath; yet they were perfectly distinct. It is the manner of the native who speaks English, and the East Indians have borrowed it from him.

"Oh! we want to buy a lot of things, Baboo!" said Mr. Browne, familiarly, "at half your regular prices, and a large discount for cash! What have you got? Got any chairs?"

"Oh yess indeed; certainlee! Will you please to come this way?"

"This way" led through a labyrinth of furniture, new and old, of glass and crockery and chipped ornaments, a dusty haven of dismayed household gods. "What have you got in there, Baboo?" asked young Browne, as they passed an almirah revealing rows of tins and labels.

"Stores, sir,—verree best qualitty stores. You can sec fo' you'self, sir—Crosse an' Blackwell ——"

"Oh yes, Baboo! And how long did you say they'd been there?"

"Onlee *one* month, sir," the baboo replied, attempting an expression of surprise and injury. "I can tell you the name of the ship they arrived in, sir."

"Of coursc you ean, Baboo. But never mind. We don't want any to-day. Let's see the chairs. Now, Helen," he continued, as the baboo went on in advance, "you see what we are subjeet to in this ungodly place. Those pease and gooseberries and asparaguses have probably been in Calcutta a good deal longer than I have. They look like old sojourners; I wouldn't give thcm a day undcr six years. They are doubtless vcry eheap, but think, Helen, of what *might* happen to my inside if you gave me grccn pease out of Bow Bazar!" Mrs. Browne looked aghast. "But I never will, Georgc!" said shc, solemnly. And young Brown made her vow it there and then. "There are two or three deeent European shops here," he said, with unetion, "where they make a point of not poisoning morc peoplc than they ean help. You pay rather largely for that eomfortable assuranee, I believe, but it's worth having. I'd have more faith in the stability of the family, Helen, if you would promise always to go to them for tinned things."

Helen promised effusively, and it is to hcr eredit that she always informed young Browne, before consumption, whenever a domcstie exigeney made hcr break her word.

Thcy climbed up a dark and winding stair that led out upon a flat roof, crossed the roof and entered a small room, borrowed from the premises of some other baboo. "Hold your skirts well up, Helen; it's just the place for eentipedcs," her husband re-

IT'S JUST THE PLACE FOR CENTIPEDES.

marked callously; and Mrs. Browne exhibited a disregard for her ankles that would have been remarkable under any other circumstances.

"Here, you see, sir, all the chairs," stated the little baboo, waving his hand. "I must tell you, sir, that some are off teak and some off shisham wood. Thee shisham are the superior."

"You mean, baboo," said young Browne, seriously, "that the shisham are the less inferior. That's a better way of putting it, baboo."

"Perhaps so, sir. Yessir, doubtless you are right, sir. The less inferior—the more grammatical!"

"Precisely. And now about the prices, baboo. What is your exact overcharge for fellows like this? He's shisham, isn't he? And he's about as sound as any of 'em."

"*Best* shisham, sir—perfeckkly sound—*not* secon' hand—our own make. Feel the weight of thiss, sir!"

"All right, baboo—I know. What's the price?"

"If thee ladee will just sit down in it for a minit shee will see how comfortable itiss!"

"Trifle no longer, baboo—what's the dom?"

"The price off that chair, sir, is *eight* rupees."

Mr. Browne sank into it with a pretence at gasping. "You can't mean that, baboo. Nothing like that. Eight rupees! You're dreaming, baboo. You forget that you only paid two for it. You're dreaming, baboo—or you're joking!"

Hurry Doss Mitterjee smiled in deep appreciation of the gentleman's humour. He even chuckled, with a note of deprecation.

"Ah, no, sir! You will pardon me for saying that is a mistake, sir! In *bissiness* I doo not joke, never! For those chairs I pay *seven* rupees four annas, sir! It iss a small profit but it iss contentable. I doo *not* ask more, sir!"

"This is very sad, baboo!" said Mr. Browne seriously. "This is very sad, indeed! I understood that you were a person of probity, who never asked more than a hundred per cent. But I know the value of shisham chairs, and this is four hundred—Oh, very sad, indeed! Now see heré, I'll give you three rupees apiece for these chairs, and take six."

"Sala'am!" said the baboo, touching his forehead with ironical gratitude and pushing back the chair. "Nossir!"

"You may take them at coss price, sir—at seven four you may take them, and I make no profit: but perhaps I get your custom. Take them—*seven* four!"

Mr. Browne turned away with a slight sigh. "Come along, dear," he said to his wife, "this man sells only to Rajahs and Members of Council."

The baboo ignored the pleasantry this time—the moment had come for action. "*What* do you give, sir?" he said, following them—"for the sake off bissiness, *what* do you give?"

"Four rupees!"

"Five eight!"

"Four eight, baboo—there!"

"Ah, sir, I cannot. Believe *me* they coss five eight to buy!"

"Look here, baboo—I'll give you five rupees apiece for six of those shisham wood chairs, every one as good as this, and I'll pay you when you send them—that's thirty rupees—and not another pice! Helen, be careful of these steps."

"To what address, sir? Will to-morrow morning be sufficient early, sir?"

"George!" exclaimed Helen, as they reached the outer world of Bow Bazar, "what a horrid little cheat of a man! Did you hear him say at first that they cost seven four to make?"

"Oh, my dear," young Browne responded, superiorly. "That's a trifle! You don't know the baboo."

"Well!" said his wife, admiringly, "I don't know how you kept your patience, George!"

Whereat Mr. Browne looked still more superior, and informed Mrs. Browne that the only way to deal with these fellows was to chaff 'em; make up your mind in the beginning that you're going to be done in the eye, and act accordingly. They always score, he added, with true Anglo-Indian resignation.

They bought a table next, from a very fat old gentleman—simply clad—in a beard and a dhoty.* The beard and the dhoty were much the same colour, and both fell so abundantly about his person that it would be difficult to say which was most useful to him as an article of apparel. And his moral obliquity was concealed under more rolls and pads of oily-brown adipose tissue than could often be seen in Bow Bazar. He must have been a rascal, as young Browne said, or being a Hindu he wouldn't have had a beard.

It was a small mahogany dining table, second hand, and its owner wanted twenty rupees for it.

"I *think*," said young Browne, "that the memsahib might give you fourteen!"

The usual humbly sarcastic sala'am—it was a very excellent table—the baboo could not think of parting with it for that.

"All right!" said Mr. Browne, "the memsahib says she won't give more than fourteen, and that's very dear. But I'll make you one offer—just one, mind, baboo! I'll give you fifteen. Now take it or leave it—one word!"

The baboo sala'amed so that his beard swept the ground, and fervently refused.

"Very well, baboo! Now I don't want it at any price, see if you can bargain with the memsahib."

* Cloth for legs.

"*Eighteen* rupees, memsahab!" insinuated the old fellow, "very cheap."

"No, indeed!" Helen exclaimed with indignation, rising to the occasion, "I won't give you any more than fourteen."

"*Chowdrah rupia, memsahib—fo*-teen rupee! But the sahib he offer fifteen!"

"Oh, I don't want it at all now," said the sahib, who stood in the door with his back turned and whistled. "Now you must bargain with the memsahib."

The baboo looked at his customers anxiously for a moment. "For sixteen rupees you take it," he said.

"Don't want it," responded Mr. Browne.

"Alright—for fifteen?"

"Will you give him fifteen, Helen?"

"Certainly not, dear! Fourteen."

"Fifteen the sahib *say* he give!" cried the baboo, his beard wagging with righteous reproach. "Take it for fifteen!" But Mr. and Mrs. Browne had made their way out. The baboo followed reminding and entreating for a hundred yards. They were deaf. Then he wheeled round upon them in front. "Very well, you give me fourteen?" The Brownes went back and left their address, which was weak in them, I consider; but I have no doubt that to this day that bearded baboo considers himself an injured person, and the victim of a most disastrous *bandobust*.*

* Bargain.

CHAPTER VII.

"LET'S have them up!" said Mr. Browne.

Mr. Browne was smoking a cigar after breakfast in his own house. There had been a time when Mr. Browne smoked his morning cigar on his way to office, but that was formerly. The department of the tea interest entrusted to Mr. Browne by his firm did not receive his active personal superintendence to the usual extent during the early months of the cold weather of '91. I am aware of this because my husband is a senior partner. Not that the firm minded particularly—they liked young Browne, and I know that we were rather pleased at the time that he had discovered something in the world besides tea.

The Brownes had been settled some two or three days, and the wheels of their domestic arrangements had been running with that perfection of unobtrusive smoothness that can be fully experienced only in India, so far as I know. The meals had appeared and disappeared as by magic, the rooms had been swept and dusted and garnished while there was no eye to see, their wishes had been anticipated, their orders had been carried out in the night, as it seemed.

"Let's have 'em up!" suggested Mr. Browne, with reference to the mysterious agents of all this circumstance. Helen wanted to see her servants.

"Bear-*er!*" shouted the sahib, young Browne.

"*Hazur!*" * came the answer, in deep tones, from regions below, with a sound of bare feet hastily ascending the stair.

"*Hazur bolya?*" † enquired the bearer in a subdued voice, partially presenting himself at the door.

"Ha!" said young Brown, "*Dekko,* ‡ bearer! You may *sub nokar lao. Sumja? Memsaheb dekna muncta!*" #

"*Bahut atcha!*" ‖ responded the bearer, and retired.

Helen sat up very straight, a little nervous air of apprehension mingled with her dignity. It had been no flippant business in her experience, to interview even a prospective under-housemaid, and presently she would be confronted by a whole retinue. "Why are they so long?" she asked.

"They're putting on their clean clothes, and perhaps a little oil in your honour, my dear. They wish to make as radiant an appearance as possible." And in a few minutes later the Brownes' domestic staff followed its leader into the room, where it stood abashed, hands hanging down, looking at the floor. The bearer made a respectful showman's gesture and awaited the pleasure of the sahib.

* Your honour.

† Your honour called.

‡ Look!

‖ Very good.

\# Bring all the servants. Do you understand? The memsahib wants to see them.

The sahib regarded them quizzically, and softly smoked on, with crossed legs.

"Dear me!" said Helen; "what a lot!"

"They are people of infinite leisure, my dear. The accomplishment of any one thing requires a great many of them. Above all it is necessary that they have peace and long hours to sleep, and an uninterrupted period in which to cook their rice and wash and anoint themselves. You will soon find out their little ways. Now let me explain. They don't understand a word of English.

"The bearer you know. The bearer brought all the rest and is responsible for them. I have no doubt that he is in honoured receipt of at least half their first month's wages for securing their situations for them. He is their superior officer, and is a person of weight and influence among them, and he's a very intelligent man. I've had him four years. In that time he has looked after me very well, I consider, very well indeed. He knows all about my clothes and keeps them tidy—buys a good many of 'em—socks and ties and things,—takes care of my room, rubs me down every evening before dinner,—keeps my money."

"Keeps your *money*, George!"

"Oh, yes! one can't be bothered with money in this country."

"Well!" said his wife. "I think it's quite *time* you were married, George. Go on!"

George said something irrelevantly foolish and went on.

"He's perfectly honest, my dear—entirely so. It would be altogether beneath his dignity to misappropriate. And I've always found him moderate in his overcharges. I took him partly because he had good chits and good manners, and partly because of his ingenuousness. I wanted a man for nine rupees—this chap stood out for ten. By way of argument he remarked that he would probably be purchasing a great many things for the sahib in the bazar—that the sahib might as well give ten in the first place! I thought there was a logical acumen about that that one didn't come across every day, and engaged him on the spot."

"But, George—it's—it's almost immoral!"

"Very, my dear! But you'll find it saves a lot of trouble."

Helen compressed her pretty lips in a way that spoke of a stern determination to adhere to the principles in vogue in Canbury.

"And I wouldn't advise you to interfere with him too much, Helen, or he'll pray to be allowed to go to his *mulluk*,* and we shall lose a good servant. Of course, I'm obliged to jump down his throat once a month or so—they all need that—but I consider him a gentleman, and I never hurt his feelings. You observe the size of his turban, and the dignity of his bearing generally? Well, so much for the bearer—he gets ten rupees."

"I've put it down, George."

"Now the kitmutgar—he's another old servant of mine—the gentleman who has just salaamed to you. You see by his dress that he's a Mussulman. No self-respecting Hindu, as you've read in books of travel which occasionally contain a truth—will wait on you at table. Observe his nether garments how they differ from the bearer's. The B. you see wears a dhoty."

"A kind of twisted sheet," remarked Helen.

"Precisely. And this man a regular divided skirt. The thing he wears on his head is not a dinner plate covered with white cotton, as one naturally imagines, but another form of Mussulman millinery—I'm sure I don't know what. But you're

* Own country.

never to let him appear in your presence without it. It would be rank disrespect.

"He is also an old servant," Mr. Browne went on, "because servants do get old in the course of time if one doesn't get rid of them, and I've given up trying to get rid of this one. He's a regular old granny, as you can see from his face; he's infuriatingly incompetent—always poking things at a man that a man doesn't want when a man's got a liver. But he doesn't understand being told to go. I dismissed him every day for a week last hot weather: he didn't allow it to interfere with him in the least—turned up behind my chair next morning as regularly as ever—chose to regard it as a pleasantry of the sahib's. When I went to England, to get engaged to you, my dear, I told him I desired never to look upon his face again. It was the first one I saw when the ship reached the P. and O. jetty. And there was a smile on it! What could I do! And that very night he shot me in the shirt-front with a soda-water bottle. I hand him over to you, my dear—you'll find he'll stay."

"I like him," said Mrs. Browne, "and I think his conduct has been very devoted, George. And he doesn't cheat?"

"He has no particular opportunity. Now for the cook. This is the cook, I take it. You see he wears nothing on his head but his hair, and that's cut short. Also he wears his particular strip of muslin draped about his shoulders, toga-wise. Also he is of a different cast of countenance, broader, higher cheek-bones, more benevolent. Remotely he's got a strain of Chinese blood in him—he's probably Moog from Chittagong."

"*Tum bawarchi hai, eh?*" *

"*Gee-ha!*" †

* You are the cook?

† Worthy one, yes.

"*Tum Moog hai?*" *

"*Gee-ha!*"

"He is, you see. Most of the cooks are, and all of them pretend to be.

"*Tum sub cheese junta, eh, bawarchi!*" †

"*Gee-ha, hazur! Hum atcha issoup sumja—atcha si'dish sumja, atcha eepudin sumja—subcheese khana kawasti teke sumja! Chittie hai hazur.*" ‡

"He says he's a treasure, my dear, but that's a modest statement they all make. And he wishes to show you his chits; will you condescend to look at them?"

"What are his chits?" Helen inquired.

"His certificates from other people whose digestions he has ruined from time to time. Let's see—'Kali Bagh, cook'—that's his name apparently, but you needn't remember it, he'll always answer to 'Bawarchi!'—'has been in my service eighteen months, and has generally given satisfaction. He is as clean as any I have ever had, fairly honest, and not inclined to be wasteful. He is dismissed for no fault, but because I am leaving India.' H'm! I don't think much of chits! This one probably ought to read, 'He doesn't get drunk often, but he's lazy, unpunctual, and beats his wife. He has cooked for me eighteen months, because I have been too weak-minded to dismiss him. He now goes by force of circumstances!' But it's not a bad chit."

"I don't consider it a very good one," said Helen. "As clean as any I have ever had!"

"That's his profoundest recommendation, my dear! He probably does *not* make toast with his toes.

* You are a Moog? † You know everything?

‡ I know good soup, good sidedishes, good puddings. Everything for dinner I know well. Here are recommendations, your honour.

"People are utterly devoid of scruple about chits," Mr. Browne went on, running over the dirty envelopes and long-folded half-sheets of letter-paper. "I've known men, who wouldn't tell a lie under any other circumstances to—to save their souls, calmly sit down and write fervent recommendations of the most whopping blackguards, in the joyful moment of their deliverance, over their own names, perfectly regardless of the immorality of the thing. It's a curious example of the way the natives' desire to be obliging at any cost comes off on us. Now here's a memsahib who ought to be ashamed of herself—'Kali Bagh is a capital cook. His entrées are delicious, and he always sends up a joint done to perfection. His puddings are perhaps his best point, but his vegetables are quite French. I can thoroughly recommend him to anyone wanting a really first-rate chef.—Mary L. Johnson.' Now we don't want a chef, this man isn't a chef, and Mary L. Johnson never had a chef. I knew the lady—she was the wife of Bob Johnson of the Jumna Bank —and they hadn't a pice more to live on than we have! *Chef* —upon my word. And yet," said young Browne thoughtfully, "I've had some very decent plain dinners at Bob Johnson's."

"But what's the use of chits, George, if people don't believe in them?"

"Oh, they do believe in 'em implicitly, till they find out the horrible mendacity of 'em. Then they rage about it and send the fellow off, with another excellent chit! And one would never engage a servant *without* chits, you know. You see how they value them—this man's date back to '79. Here's a break, two years ago.—What sahib's cook were you two years ago, Bawarchi?" asked Mr. Browne.

"Exactly! I thought so, he paid a visit to his mulluk two years ago—that's his own country. In other words, he got a bad chit from that sahib and was compelled to destroy it. They have always visited their mulluks under those circumstances, for the length of time corresponding to the break. But I guess he'll do—we mustn't expect too much. Twelve rupees."

The cook took his chits back and salaamed. Helen looked as if she thought a great deal more might be desired in a cook, but could not bring herself to the point of discussing it in his immediate presence.

"He seems so very intelligent," she said to herself with a qualm.

"Now then, for the mussalchi! *Tum mussalchi hai*, eh?"

"Gee-ha, hazur!"

The mussalchi wore a short cotton coat, a dhoty, and an expression of dejection. On his head was a mere suggestion of a turban—an abject rag. Written upon his face was a hopeless longing to become a bawarchi, which fate forbade. Once a mussalchi, the son of a mussalchi, always a mussalchi, the bearer of hot water and a dish-cloth, the receiver of orders from kitmutgars.

"Consider your mussalchi, Helen! He is engaged to wash the dishes, to keep the silver clean, and the pots and pans. His real mission is to break as many as possible, and to levy large illegal charges upon you monthly for knife-polish and mops. In addition he'll carry the basket home from the market every morning on his head—the cook, you know, is much too swagger for that! Think he'll do?"

"I don't know," said Helen in unhappy indecision. "What do *you* think, George?"

"Oh we'll try him, and I suppose he'll have to get seven rupees. This is the mallic the gardener—this gentleman with his hair done up neatly behind."

"Nice clean-looking man," remarked Helen, "but oughtn't he to wear more clothes."

"Looks like a decent chap. No, I should say not; I never saw a mallie with more on. You see he's a very superior person, a Brahmin in fact. He wears the sacred string, as well as his beads and his dhoty; do you see it, over his right shoulder and under his left arm. He claims to have been 'twice born.' They're generally of a very respectable *jat* * the mallies."

"He will take care of the garden," remarked Helen.

"As we happen to have a garden, yes. But his business is to producc flowers. You want flowcrs, you engage a mallie. You get flowers. This process of logic is perfectly simple to the native mind. It is nothing but justice and sweet reason. A mallie is a person who causes flowers to appear."

"But where does he get them?"

"Oh, my dear, that is one of the secrets of his profession. But I understand that there's a very wisc and liberal understanding amongst mallies—and quite a number of mallies have gardens attached to them. There's a vcry old story about a mallie's chit which you havcn't heard yet. His departing master gave him an excellcnt character and summed up by saying: 'This mallic has been with me fifteen years. I have had no garden, I have never lacked flowers, and he has never had a conviction.'"

"George—do you mean to say they stcal!"

"Oh, no, my dear! It's a matter of arrangement. This man could never take flowcrs out of another sahib's garden without consulting the other sahib's mallie—that would be very wrong. But we'll see if he can't grow us some for ourselves."

* Casto.

"But the other sahib."

"The other sahib is similarly obliged from somebody else's garden, and doesn't know anything about it. Eight rupees for thc mallie."

Helen put it down with inquietude of spirit.

"Now for the syee, who looks after the pony. I've had the syee two or three years, too. He's a very good servant now, but he used to give me a lot of trouble by pure lazincss. Onee he let a pony of mine get a sorc back, and never told me, and I lieked him. I licked him well, and I eonsider that licking made a man of him. He realized gradually—he's a stupid chap—that it was undesirable to be lieked, especially in the eompound with the other servants looking on, and instead of throwing up his plaee and bringing me before the magistrate for assault, he eoncluded that he wouldn't let it happen again. It never has, and he has respected himself and me more ever sinee."

"Do you often 'liek' them, George?"

"Exeept this once I never have. Neither does anybody else, exeept a few ill-conditioned young eubs, who haven't been out long enough to understand the native and think they can kick him about to advantage. But deeent servants never stay with such men. Indeed they can't get 'em. You've got to have a good charaeter to get good servants, and therc isn't a sahib in Calcutta that hasn't a reputation in the bazar. The bearer knows perfectly well I wouldn't touch a hair of his head, and if the bearer went out with cholera to-morrow I could get half a dozen as good in his plaee. On the other hand, probably all the kitmutgar-lok despise me for keeping such a poor servant as the Kit, and I'd have a diffieulty in getting a better one."

"Curious!" said Helen.

"Yes. The syce, my dear, will desire you to pay for quite

twice as much grain and grass as the pony consumes, and for a time you will do it. Bye-and-bye you will acquire the wisdom of a serpent and cut him accordingly. In the meantime he's bound to have as much sugar-cane on hand as you want to feed the pony with, at a fixed charge of four annas a month. Don't forget that the syce's tulub is eight rupees.

"This very smug and smiling person is the dhoby, the washerwoman. He is an unmitigated rascal. There is no palliation for anything he does. He carries off your dirty linen every week in a very big pack on a very little donkey, and brings it home on the same, beating the donkey all the way there and all the way back. He mismatches your garments with other people's, he washes them with country soap that smells to heaven if you don't watch him. His custom in cleaning them is to beat them violently between two large and jagged stones. He combines all the vices of his profession upon the civilized globe; but I'm afraid you'll have to find out for yourself, dear. Put down the dhoby at ten.

"This excessively modest person is the bheesty, who brings us water every day in a goat-skin. He isn't used to polite society, but he's a very worthy and hard-working sort. He's only a ticca-bheesty. I fancy several people about here use him. You see his sole business in life is carrying water about in goatskins. So we only give him three rupees.

"The sweeper is out on the veranda. Very properly he doesn't venture into our presence. He is of very low caste—does the sweeping and all the menial work, you know. You are never to see or speak to him, or you'll be lowered in the respect of the compound. The sweeper is a very poor sort of person—he is the only servant in the place that will eat the remains of our food. He gets six rupees."

"Is that all?" asked Helen. "I'm sure I don't know them apart."

"That's all, except your ayah, who isn't here, and a *durwan* to keep the door, whom we'll get when we're richer, and a *durzie*

A VERY WORTHY AND HARDWORKING SORT.

to mend our clothes, whom we'll get when they begin to wear out. May they be dismissed now?"

"Oh, yes, *please!*" said Helen, and "*Bahut atcha? Tum jane sucta,*"* remarked her husband, whereat they salaamed and departed in single file.

* You may go.

"But George," said Helen, "they come, with my ayah at eleven, to eighty-five rupees a month! Almost seven pounds! I thought servants were cheap in India!"

"No, dear, they're not; at least, not in Calcutta. And these are the very least we can have to be at all comfortable."

The two Brownes looked at each other with a slight shade of domestic anxiety. This was dispelled by the foolish old consideration of how little anything really mattered, now that they were one Browne, and presently they were disporting themselves behind the pony on the Maidan, leaving the cares of their household to those who were most concerned in them.

CHAPTER VIII.

A WEEK later Helen took over the accounts. In the meantime she had learned to count rupees and annas, pi and pice, also a few words of that tongue in which orders are given in Calcutta. She arose on the seventh morning of her tenure of office rigidly determined that the office should no longer be a sinecure. She would drop curiosity and pleasure, and assume discipline, righteousness and understanding. She would make a stand. She would deal justly, but she would make a stand. It would be after George had gone to office. When he came home, tired with tea affairs, he would not be compelled to rack his brain further with the day's marketing. He would see that the lady he had made Mrs. Browne was capable of more than driving about in a tum-tum and writing enthusiastic letters home about the beauties of Calcutta.

George went to office. The kitmutgar softly removed the blue and white breakfast things. Outside the door, in the "bottle khana," the mussalchi, squatting, washed them in an earthen bowl with a mop-stick. It occurred to Helen that she might as well begin by going to look at the mussalchi, and she did. She looked at him with a somewhat severe expression, thereby causing him dismay and terror. She walked all round the mussalchi, but found nothing about him to criticise. "But, probably," thought she, as she went back to the dining-room, "my looking at him had its moral effect." Then she sent for the cook.

The cook arrived with an expression of deep solemnity, tempered by all the amiable qualities you can think of. He held in his hand an extremely dirty piece of paper, covered with strange characters in Nagri—how little anybody would have thought, when they were designed in the dawn of the world, that they would ever be used to indicate the items of an Englishman's dinner! The cook put a pair of spectacles on to read them, which completed the anomaly, and made him look more benevolent than ever.

"Well, bawarchi," said Helen, ready with pencil and note book, "account hai?"

"Gee-ha, hai!" responded he. Then after a respectful pause, "S'in-beef," he said, "*char anna.*"

"Shin beef," repeated Helen, with satisfaction, "four annas. Yes?"

"Fiss—che * anna. Bress mutton—egrupee, che anna. Eggis—satrah—aht † anna."

"*Seventeen* eggs, bawarchi? When did we eat seventeen eggs? How did we eat seventeen eggs yesterday?"

Mrs. Browne spoke impulsively, in English, but Kali Bagh seemed to understand, and with an unruffled front proceeded to account circumstantially for every egg. His mistress was helpless. But, "to-morrow," thought she earnestly, "I will *see* whether he puts four in the soup!"

The cook went on to state that since yesterday the Browne family had consumed three seers of potatoes—six pounds—at two annas a seer, which would be six annas. "And I don't believe that, either," mentally ejaculated Mrs. Browne, but Kali Bagh continued without flinching. He chronicled salt, pepper, sauce,

* Six. † Eight.

sugar, he mentioned rice, dhal, "garden-isspice," "guava isstew," "k'rats,"* "kiss-miss,"† "maida,"‡ and enough "mukkan"# to have supplied a charity-school. Helen was amazed to find the number of culinary articles which undeniably might have been used in the course of twenty-four hours—she did not consider the long calm evening that went to meditation over the list. When it was finished she found that the day's expenses in food had been exactly eight rupees six annas, or about eleven shillings. Helen had had a thrifty education, and she knew this was absurd. She turned to the flagrant eggs and to the unblushing potatoes, and she made a calculation.

"Bawarchi!" said she, "Potatoes—four annas. Eggs—five annas, *daga*." ‖

"Bahut atcha!" said the cook, without remonstrance. He still had twenty-five per cent of profit.

Helen observed, and was encouraged. She summoned up her sternest look, and drew her pencil through the total. "Eight rupees," she remarked with simplicity, "daga na. *Five* rupees daga," and she closed the book.

Kali Bagh looked at her with an expression of understanding, mingled with disappointment. He did not expect all he asked, but he expected more than he got. As it was, his profit amounted only to two rupees, not much for a poor man with a family. But in after days, when his memsahib grew in general sagacity and particular knowledge of the bazar, Kali Bagh had reason to look back regretfully to those two rupees as to the brief passing of a golden age.

"I will now go down," said Mrs. Browne with enthusiasm, "and look at his pots."

* Carrots.
† Raisins.
‡ Flour.
\# Butter.
‖ I will give.

The compound, as she crossed it, was full of the eternal sunlight of India, the gay shrill gossip of the mynas, the hoarse ejaculations of the crows. A flashy little green parrot flew out of a hibiscus bush by the wall in full crimson flower; he belonged to the jungle. But a pair of grey pigeons cooed to each other over the building of their nest in the cornice of a pillar of the Brownes' upper veranda. They had come to stay, and they spoke of the advantages of co-operative housekeeping with another young couple like themselves, knowing it to be on a safe and permanent basis. The garden was all freshly scratched and tidy; there was a pleasant smell of earth; the mallie, under a pipal tree, gathered up its broad dry fallen leaves to cook his rice with. It was a graphic bit of economy, so pleasantly close to nature that its poetry was plain. "We are the only people who are extravagant in India," thought Helen, as she regarded the mallie, and in this reflection I venture to say that she was quite correct.

The door of the *bawarchi khana** was open—it was never shut. I am not sure, indeed, that there was a door. There were certainly no windows. It is possible that the bawarchi khana was seven feet square, and its mistress was just able to stand up straight in it with a few inches to spare. It contained a shelf, a table, and a stove. When Kali Bagh sat down he used his heels. The shelf and the table were full of the oil and condiments dear to the heart of every bawarchi. The stove was an erection like a tenement house, built with what was left over from the walls, and artistically coloured pink to be like them. It contained various hollows on the top, in one or two of which charcoal was glowing—beyond this I cannot explain its construction to be plain to un-

* Cook-house.

derstandings accustomed to the kitchen ranges of Christianity and civilisation. But nothing ever went wrong with Kali Bagh's stove, the boiler never leaked, the hot water pipes never burst, the oven never required relining, the dampers never had to be re-regulated. He was its presiding genius, he worked it with a palm leaf fan, and nothing would induce him to look at a modern improvement. Kali Bagh was a conservative institution himself, his recipes were an heritage, he was the living representative of an immemorial *dustur.** Why should Kali Bagh afflict himself with the ways of the memsahib!

The bawarchi khana had another door, opening into a rather smaller apartment, otherwise lightless and airless, which contained Kali Bagh's wardrobe and bed. The wardrobe was elementary and hung upon a single peg, the bed consisted of four short legs and a piece of matting. Kali Bagh had reposed himself on it, and was already snoring, when Mrs. Browne came in. He had divested himself of his chuddar and his spectacles, and looked less of a philosopher and more of an Aryan. Mrs. Browne made a rude clatter among the pans, which brought him to a sense of her disturbing presence. Presently she observed him standing behind her, looking anxious. His mistress sniffed about intrepidly. She lifted saucepan lids and discovered within remains of concoctions three days old; she found the day's milk in an erstwhile kerosene tin; she lifted a kettle and intruded upon the privacy of a large family of cockroaches, any one of them as big as a five-shilling piece. Kali Bagh would never have disturbed them. She found messes and mixtures and herbs and spices and sauces which she did not understand and could not approve. The day's marketing lay in a flat basket under the

* Custom.

table. Helen drew it forth and discovered a live pigeon indiscriminately near the mutton with its wings twisted around one another at the joint, while from beneath a débris of potatoes, beans and cauliflower, came a feeble and plaintive "Quack!"

"What is this?" said Mrs. Browne with paler and sterner criticism, looking into a pot that was bubbling on the fire.

"*Chaul hai, memsahib! Hamara khana!*" *

"Your, dinner, bawarchi! All that rice?" And, indeed, therein was no justification for Kali Bagh. It was not only his dinner, but the dinner of the sweeper and of the syce and of the mussalchi, to be supplied to them a trifle below current market rates, and Mrs. Browne had paid for it all that morning. Helen found herself confronted with her little domestic corner of the great problem of India—the natives' "way." But she had no language with which to circumvent it or remonstrate with it. She could only decide that Kali Bagh was an eminently proper subject for discipline, and resolve to tell George, which was not much of an expedient. It is exactly what we all do in India, however, under the circumstances. We tell our superior officers, until at last the Queen Empress herself is told; and the Queen-Empress is quite as incapable of further procedure as Mrs. Browne; indeed, much more so, for she is compelled to listen to the voice of her parliamentary wrangling-machine upon the matter, which obeys the turning of a handle, and is a very fine piece of mechanism indeed, but not absolutely reliable when it delivers ready-made opinions upon Aryan problems. At least I am quite sure that is my husband's idea, and I have often heard young Browne say the same thing.

There was a scattering to right and left when Helen reap-

* It is rice, memsahib; my dinner.

"WHAT IS THIS?" SAID MRS. BROWNE, WITH PALER AND STERNER CRITICISM.

peared in the compound. Her domestics were not dressed to receive her, and they ran this way and that, noiselessly like cockroaches to their respective holes. There seemed to be a great many of them, more by at least half-a-dozen than were properly accredited to the house; and Helen was afterwards informed that they were the *bhai* * of the other servants, representing a fraction of the great unemployed of Asia, who came daily for fraternal gossip in the sun and any patronage that might be going. They were a nuisance, these bhai, and were soon sternly put down by the arm of the law and the edict of the sahib, who enacted that no strange native should be allowed to enter the compound without a chit. "It's the only way to convince them," said he, "that the Maidan is the best place for public meetings."

The quarters of the syce and the pony were the only ones that invited further inspection. The same roof sheltered both of these creatures of service, a thatched one; but between them a primitive partition went half way up. On one side of this the pony was tethered and enjoyed the luxuries of his dependence, on the other the syce lived in freedom, but did not fare so well. The pony's expenses were quite five times as heavy. His food cost more, his clothes cost more, his medical attendance cost more, to say nothing of his requiring a valet. He was much the more valuable animal of the two, though the other is popularly believed in England to have a soul. His wants were even more elaborately supplied than the syce's—he had a trough to feed from, and a pail to drink out of, a fresh bed every night, a box for his grain, and a curry-comb for his skin; while the syce's domestic arrangements consisted of an earthenware pot, a wooden stick, and a rickety charpoy. When he was cold he borrowed

* Caste-brothers.

the pony's blanket, and I never heard of any toilet articles in connection with him. The accommodation was not equally divided between him and the pony, either. The pony had at least twice as much, and it was in better repair.

The pony looked much askance at Helen. He was accustomed only to the race of his dark-skinned servitor. The sahib with his white face and strange talk he associated with the whip and being made to pull an objectionable construction upon wheels from which he could not get away; but a memsahib might be something of inconceivable terror—her petticoats looked like it. Therefore the pony withdrew himself into a remote corner of his stable, where he stood looking ineffably silly, and declined to be seduced by split pieces of sugar-cane or wheedling words.

"*Gorah atcha hai?*" * asked Helen, and was assured that he was very "atcha," that his grain he ate, his grass he ate, his water he ate, and "*cubbi kooch na bolta*——" "he never said anything whatever," which was the final proof of his flourishing condition.

It was getting a little discouraging, but Helen thought that before retreating she might at least inspect the bearer's cow, a cow being a gentle domestic animal, of uniform habits, all the world over. One's own cow is a thorn in the flesh and a source of ruin, in India. She declines to give milk, except to the outside world at so much a seer,† she devours abnormal quantities of food, she is neglected and becomes depraved, being nobody's particular business. But it is impossible to draw lacteal supplies from an unknown source in India. It is paying a large price for cholera bacilli, which is absurd, since one can get them almost

* Is the horse well? † Two pounds.

anywhere for nothing. To say nothing of the depravity of the milk-wallah,* who strains his commodity through his dhoty, and replenishes his cans from the first stagnant tank he comes to. The wise and advisable thing is to permit the bearer, as a gracious favour, to keep a cow on the premises and to supply the family at current rates. It is a source of income to him, and of confidence to you, while the cow does her whole duty in that clean and comfortable state whereto she is called. The bearer, too, is honoured and dignified by the possession of the sacred animal. He performs every office for her himself, though he would scorn to bring a pail of water to a horse, and he is happy to live in the odour of her sanctity. Helen discovered the cow of their establishment tied with her calf outside the best "go-down" in the compound—the largest and cleanest—which she occupied at night. The bearer himself had not nearly such good quarters, and this was of his own dispensation. She wore a string of blue beads around her horns, and munched contentedly at a large illegal breakfast of straw which had been bought and paid for to supply the pony's bed.

"Poor cooey!" said Helen, advancing to attempt a familiarity, but the cow put down her head and made such a violent lunge at her that she beat a hasty and undignified retreat. This was partly on account of the calf, which stood a little way off, but well within the maternal vision, and it was quite an unreasonable demonstration, as the calf was stuffed, and put there to act upon the cow's imagination only. This is a necessary expedient to ensure milk in India from a cow that has no calf of her own; it is a painful imposition, but uniformly successful. The fact is one of reputation, as being the only one invariably

* Man.

rejected by travellers as a lively lie, whereas they are known to swallow greedily much larger fictions than stuffed calves.

From an upper window, shortly after, Helen saw the cow's morning toilet being performed by the bearer. And it was an instructive sight to see this solemn functionary holding at arm's length the utmost end of her tail, and with art and precision improving its appearance.

In the cool of the evening after dinner, the two Brownes sat together in the shadow of the pillars of their upper veranda, and Helen told the story of her adventure in the compound. Overhead the pigeons cooed of their day's doings, the pony neighed from his stable in the expectation of his content. A light wind stirred the palms whcrc they stood against the stars, the smoke of the mallie's pipal leavcs curled up faintly from his roof where hc dwelt beside the gate. Below, in the black shadow of the godowns, easeful figures sat or moved, the subdued tones of their parley hardly came to the upper veranda. They had rice and rest and the comfortable hubble-bubble. And the sahib and the memsahib devised how they might circumvent these humble people in all their unlawful doings, till the air grew chill with the dew, and the young moon showed over their neighbour's tamarind tree.

CHAPTER IX.

MRS. BROWNE'S ayah was a little Mussulman woman of about thirty-five, with bright eyes and an expression of great worldly wisdom upon her small, square, high-boned face. She dressed somewhat variously, but her official garments were a short jacket and a striped cotton petticoat, a string of beads round her neck, silver bangles on her arms and ankles, hoops in her ears, and a small gold button in her right nostril. This last bit of coquetry affected Helen uncomfortably for some time. Her name was Chua, signifying "a rat," and her heathen sponsors showed rather a fine discrimination in giving it to her. She was very like one. It would be easy to fancy her nibbling in the dark, or making unwarrantable investigations when honest people were asleep. When Chua was engaged and questioned upon the subject of remuneration, she salaamed very humbly, and said, "What the memsahib pleases," which was ten rupees. At this Chua's countenance fell, for most of the ayahs of her acquaintance received twelve. Accepting the fact, however, that her mistress was not a "burra memsahib"* from whom much might be expected, but a "chota memsahib"† from whom little could be extracted, she went away content, and spread her mat in the women's place in the mosque and bowed many times to the west as the sun went down, and paid at least four annas to the *moulvi*‡ who had helped her to this good fortune.

* Great memsahib. † Little memsahib. ‡ Priest.

Chua abode in her own house, as is the custom of ayahs with family ties. She was married—her husband was a kitmutgar. They lived in a bustee in the very middle of Calcutta, where dwelt several other kitmutgars and their wives, a dhoby and a number of goats, and Chua walked out every morning to her work. Then home at twelve to cook her food and sleep, then back at four for further duty until after dinner. She never breakfasted before starting in the morning, but she carried with her always a small square tin box from which she refreshed herself surreptitiously at intervals. Inside the box was only a rolled-up betel leaf, and inside the leaf a dab of white paste; but it was to Chua what the hubble-bubble was to Abdul, her husband, a great and comfortable source of meditation upon the goodness of Allah, and the easiest form of extortion to be practised upon her lawful taskmistress.

Helen found great difficulty at first in assimilating this handmaid into her daily life. She had been told that an ayah was indispensable, and she could accept Chua as a necessary appendage to the lofty state of her Oriental existence, but to find occupation for her became rather a burden to the mind of Mrs. Browne. Things to do were precious, she could not spare them to be done by anybody else, even at ten rupees a month with the alternative of improper idleness. Moreover, the situation was in some respects embarrassing. One could have one's ribbons straightened and one's hair brushed with equanimity, but when it came to the bathing of one's feet and the putting on of one's stockings Helen was disposed to dispense with the services of her ayah as verging on the indelicate. Chua was still more grieved when her mistress utterly declined to allow herself to be "punched and prodded," as she expressed it, in the process of gentle massaging in which the ayah species are proficient. Mrs. Browne was young

CHUA.

then, and a new comer, and not of a disposition to brook any interference with her muscular tissues. But the other day she particularly recommended an ayah to me on account of this accomplishment. This to illustrate, of course, not the degeneration of Mrs. Browne's sense of propriety, but of her muscular tissues.

The comprehension and precise knowledge which Chua at once obtained of her mistress's wardrobe and effects was wonderful in its way. She knew the exact contents of every box and drawer and wardrobe, the number of pen-nibs in the writing-case, the number of spools in the workbasket. Helen used to feel, in the shock of some disclosure of observation extraordinary, as if the omniscient little woman had made an index of her mistress's emotions and ideas as well, and could lay her small skinny brown finger upon any one of them, which intuition was very far from being wrong. Chua early induced an admiring confidence in her rectitude by begging Mrs. Browne to make a list of all her possessions so that from time to time she could demonstrate their safety. The ayah felt herself responsible. She knew that upon the provocation of a missing embroidered petticoat there might be unpleasant results connected with the police-wallah and the *thana*,* not only for her but for the whole establishment, and she wished to be in a secure position to give evidence, if necessary, against somebody else. It could certainly not be Chua, therefore, Helen announced, when she communicated to her lord at the breakfast table the fact that her very best scissors had been missing for three days. "Isn't it tedious?" said she.

"Scissors," said young Browne. "Yes, good new shiny sharp ones, weren't they, with Rodgers' name plainly stamped on them —and rather small?"

* Police office.

"All that," lamented Helen, "and embroidery size—such loves!"

"You are gradually coming within the operation of custom, my dear. Steel is the weakness of the Aryan. He—in this case she—will respect your clothes, take care of your money, and guard your jewellery—they all have a general sense of property in its correct relation, but it does not apply to a small pair of scissors or a neat pocket knife. Such things seem to yield to some superior attraction outside the moral sense connected with these people, and they invariably disappear. It's inveterate, but it's a nuisance. One has to make such a row."

AN ACCIDENT DISCLOSED THEM AT THE BOTTOM OF AN IMPOSSIBLE VASE.

"George," said Helen gravely, "why do you say in this case *she?*"

"I think you'll find it was your virtuous maid, my dear. It wasn't the bearer—he has permitted me to keep the same knife and nail scissors now for two years and a half, and the rest of the servants, all but the ayah, are the bearer's creatures, and will reflect exactly his morality in quality and degree. She isn't—

she's an irresponsible functionary, except to you; you'll have to keep an eye on her. However, if we make ourselves patiently and unremittingly disagreeable for a week or two they'll turn up."

"I haven't the Hindustani to be disagreeable in," Helen remarked.

"Oh, you needn't be violent; just inquire at least three times a day, '*Humara kinchi, kidder gia?*'* and look forbidding the rest of the time. Never dream for a moment they're stolen or admit they're lost. It's a kind of worry she won't be able to stand—she'll never know what you're going to do. And she'll conclude it's cheaper in the end to restore them."

I don't know whether the Brownes made themselves as disagreeable as they might about the kinchi, but it was a long time before they were restored. Then an accident disclosed them at the bottom of an impossible vase. Chua, standing by, went through an extravaganza of gratification. Her eyes shone, she laughed and clasped her hands with dramatic effect. "*Eggi bat*" †—would the memsahib inform the sahib and also the bearer that they had been found?—the latter evidently having resorted lately to some nefarious means of extracting from her what she had done with them. Chua had doubtless had an uncomfortable quarter of an hour before her mistress discovered them, and felt unjustly served in it. For the theft was only a prospective one, to be accomplished in the course of time, if it looked advisable. It did not look advisable and Chua reconsidered it, thereby leaving her Mohammedan conscience void of offence.

As soon as she was able to understand and be understood, Helen thought it her duty to make some kindly enquiries about Chua's domestic affairs. Had she, for instance, any children?

* My scissors, where have they gone?

† One word.

"*Na, memsahib!*" she responded, with a look of assumed contempt that could not have sat more emphatically upon the face of any *fin de siècle* lady who does not believe in babies. "*Baba hai na! Baba na muncta,*"* she went on with a large curl of the lip, "Baba all time *cry kurta*†—Waow! Waow! *atcha na,*‡ memsahib!"

"Oh na, ayah! Baba atcha hai," laughed Helen, defending the sacredest theory of her sex.

Chua took an attitude of self-effacement, but her reply had a patronising dignity, "*Memsahib kawasti baba atcha hai,*" said she. "*Memsahib kawasti kooch kam hai na! Ayah ka kam hai! Tub baba atcha na—kooch na muncta!*"#

Chua occupied quite the modern ground, which was exhilarating in an Oriental, and doubtless testified to the march of truth—that babies were only practicable and advisable when their possible mothers could find nothing better to do. Helen was impressed, and more deeply so when she presently discovered that Chua and Abdul, her husband, lived in different houses in the bustee I have mentioned—different huts, that is, mud-baked and red-tiled and leaking, and offering equal facilities for the intrusion of the ubiquitous goat. Chua spoke of Abdul with an angry flash of contempt. In accommodating himself to circumstances recently, Abdul had offended her very deeply. It was on an occasion when Chua had accompanied a memsahib to England with the usual infant charge. She was very sick, she earned a hundred and fifty rupees, she was away three months—"*kali tin mahina,*‖ memsahib!" and when she returned she

* I do not want babies. † Makes crying. ‡ Not good.

\# For the memsahib babies are good. The memsahib has no work to do. The ayah has work. Then babies are not good, she does not want any!

‖ Only three months.

found Abdul mated to another. She was artful, was Chua—her mistress's face expressed such a degree of disapprobation that she fancied herself implicated, and instantly laughed to throw a triviality over Abdul's misconduct. It was a girl he married, a mere child "*baba kamafik,* * memsahib"—fourteen years old. But her scorn came through the mask of her amusement when she went on to state that the house of Abdul was no longer without its olive branch, but that Abdul's sahib had gone away and there was very little rice for anybody in that family. The recreant had come to her in his extremity, asking alms, she said with her curled lip. "*Rupia do-o!*" † she whined, holding out her hand and imitating his suppliance with intensest irony. Then drawing herself up proudly she rehearsed her answer brief, contemptuous, and to the point.

"*Daga na!—Jao!*" ‡

She had invested the proceeds of her journey over the "black water" in a ticca-gharry which lent itself all day long to the Calcutta public under her administration and to her profit. The day after Helen had been thus edified, the ayah did not appear until the afternoon. She had been to law about some point in relation to the ticca-gharry. I can't remember what Mrs. Browne said it was—but she wanted an advance of wages for her legal expenses. She intended to spare nothing to be triumphant—her adversary had trusted his case to a common *vakeel,* # she would have a *gorah-vakeel,* ‖ though they came higher. Her witnesses would be properly paid too—a rupee apiece, and eight annas extra for any necessary falsification at present unexpected. The next afternoon she came late, with a tale of undeserved disaster which she lucubrated with indignant tears, after the man-

* Like a baby.
† Ten rupees.
‡ I will not give! Go!
\# Lawyer.
‖ Literally, horse-lawyer.

ner of her sex. It was not that the magistrate sahib was not fair, he was just as the sun at noon, or that Rahim the gharry-wallah had more witnesses than she—indeed, being a poor man, he had only four—but they were four of the five, unhappily, whose services *she* had engaged. The gharry-wallah had offered them two rupees—a higher bid—and so they spoke *jute bat.** But he would never be able to pay! Oh, it was very *carab!* † and Chua sat in the dust and wrapped her face in her *sari* ‡ and wept again. Later, she informed her mistress that it was possible she might again be absent to-morrow—it was possible that she might come into contact that evening in the street with these defaulting witnesses—violent contact. *It was possible* that if they laughed at her she would strike them, and then—with an intensely observing eye always upon Helen—then her memsahib, in the event of her being carried off to the *thana* for assault, would of course enquire "*Hamara ayah, kidder hai?*" # and immediately take proceedings to get her out. Chua's countenance fell, though with instant submission, when Helen informed her sternly that she would on no account institute such proceedings, and she was deprived even of illegal means of satisfaction, taken with impunity.

It was Chua's aptitude for assault that led to her final expulsion from the service of the Brownes and from the pages of these annals. Her manner toward the bearer had been propitiatory from the beginning. She called him "Sirdar," ‖ she paid him florid Oriental compliments; by the effacement of her own status and personality she tried to establish a friendly understanding with him. She undertook small services on his behalf. She attempted to owe him allegiance as the other serv-

* False talk.
† Bad.
‡ Head cloth.
\# My ayah, where is she?
‖ Head bearer.

ants did. It is impossible to say that she did not press upon him a percentage of her *tulab*, to ensure his omnipotent good will. But Kasi was for some dark reason unreciprocal—young Browne believed he thought she was storming his affections—and at best consented only to preserve an armed neutrality. Whereat Chua became resentful and angry, carried her head high, and exchanged remarks with Kasi which were not in the nature of amenities. The crisis came one afternoon when the Brownes were out.

"I have something to tell you after dinner," said Mrs. Browne significantly later, across the joint.

"And I have something to tell *you*," young Browne responded with equal meaning.

Mrs. Browne had the first word, in order, her husband said, that she shouldn't have the last. She explained that she had found the ayah in tears, quite extinguished upon the floor, the cause being insult. Chua had forgotten at noon the little bright shawl which she wrapped about her head in the streets—had left it upon the memsahib's veranda. Seeing it, the bearer had done a deadly thing. He had not touched it himself, but he had sent for the sweeper—the sweeper!—and bade him *fenk-do* * it to his own unclean place of living. And there, after much search, had Chua found it. Therefore was she deeply abased, and therefore did she tender her resignation. The bearer had behaved *Rajah kamafik!* † and had, moreover, spoken to her in *bat* that was *carab*, very *carab*.

"Yes," said the sahib, judicially, "and the bearer came to me also weeping with joined hands to supplicate. His tale of woe is a little different. He declares he never saw the shawl

* Throw. † Like a lord!

and never gave the order—I've no doubt he did both—but that the sweeper acted upon his own responsibility. And what do you think the ayah did in revenge? She *slippered* him!—all round the compound! The bearer, poor chap, fled in disorder, but couldn't escape. He has undoubtedly been slippered. And in the presence of the whole compound! It's worse—infinitely worse—than having his *puggri* * knocked off in ribaldry. And now he says that though he has served me faithfully all these years, and I am his father and his mother, his honour has been damaged in this place, and he prays to be allowed to depart."

"Slippered him, George! but he's such a big man and she such a little woman! All round the compound! Oh," said George's wife, giving way to unseemly hilarity, "I should like to have seen that!"

"Little termagant! Oh, it was the insult he ran from, my dear—not the blow. That she—an ayah and the wife of a kitmutgar, should have touched him with the sole of her shoe! Don't laugh, dear—they'll hear you, and I'd rather they didn't."

The Brownes held further debate, and took all the circumstances into consideration. Young Browne had evidently arrived immediately at a judicial view of the case, though he professed himself willing to let the bearer go if Helen wanted to retain Chua. "Though in that case there'll be anarchy, my dear, I warn you," said he. The result was a solemn gathering of the servants next morning upon the veranda, addressed by young Browne, while the memsahib sat up straight in another chair and looked serious. He took no evidence, there would have been too much, but he spoke thus:

"There was yesterday a great disturbance in the compound,

* Turban.

which is a shameful thing. Those who thus made great noises, and used bad language and were without self-respect, were the bearer and the ayah. The bearer has served me many years in many places and with many other servants, and I have never before known him to act without shame or to quarrel. The ayah has been known a few weeks only. Both the bearer and the ayah wish to go away. The ayah may go. *Bus!*"*

After this simple and direct delivery no word was said. The servants dispersed to the compound, the bearer, reinstated in his self-esteem and justified before the world, applied himself to forget his wrongs and was more diligent than ever in his master's service. Chua stated to her mistress that if she had any more trouble she would die and the wind would blow through her bones, and many other things in grief-stricken Hindustani which Helen did not understand. But her mistress permitted her this balm to her wounded feelings, that when she departed she left the dishonoured shawl scornfully behind her, having privately received sufficient backsheesh to buy three like it.

* Enough.

CHAPTER X.

CALCUTTA, in social matters, is a law unto herself, inscrutable, unevadable. She asks no opinion and permits no suggestion. She proclaims that it shall be thus, thus it is, and however odd and inconvenient the custom may be, it lies within the province of no woman—the men need not be thought of—to change it, or even to discover by what historic whim it came to be. Calcutta decrees, for example, that from twelve to two, what time the sun strikes straightest and strongest on the carriage-top, what time all brown Bengal with sweet reasonableness takes its siesta, in the very heat and burden of the day—from twelve to two is the proper hour forsooth for the memsahib to visit and be visited. Thus this usually tepid form frequently reaches a boiling point of social consideration, becomes a mark of recognition which is simply perfervid. It is also an unamiable time of day. The cheering effects of breakfast have worn off, and tiffin looms distantly, the reward of virtue. It would be impossible to say for how much malice it is directly responsible. But this is of the gods; we stew obediently, we do not dream of demurring. Another honoured principle is that all strangers, except brides, shall make the first call. Herein is the indolence of Calcutta generous and unreckoning. All new comers, of whatever business, jat, or antecedents, have the fee simple of her drawing-rooms, the right to expect their calls to be returned, and even to feel slighted if no further recognition is made of them. Anybody may tacitly request Calcutta to invite him to dinner, and lay upon Calcutta the disagreeable onus of refusing to do it. Strangers present themselves on their merits; the tone of society naturally therefore becomes a little assertive. There are other methods of indirect compulsion. A man may call—this invariably at mid-day on Sunday—and thereby invite you to leave cards upon his wife, and the lady is aggrieved if you decline the invitation. Calcutta suffers all this. It is the *dustur*.

Mrs. George William Browne of course was a bride, and had made her appearance at church. It was not an imposing appearance, and probably did not attract as much attention as the Brownes imagined; they occupied one of the back seats of a sacred edifice of Calcutta which is known to be consecrated to official circles, and the Brownes were only mercantile. But the appearance had been made, whether or not anybody was aware of it; and Mrs. Browne was assuredly entitled to sit from twelve to two in the days that followed at the receipt of congratulations.

"All Calcutta won't come," remarked young Browne, in a tone of easy prophecy. "But Mrs. Fisher will probably look you up, and Mrs. Jack Lovitt, and the Wodenhamers—I've known the Wodenhamers a long time. And Mrs. P. Macintyre"—the person who undertakes this history—"Mrs. P. is the only lady in the firm just now. She's sure to call."

"Where are the rest, George?"

"One of 'm dead. Mrs. J. L. Macintyre's dead—two of 'em, Mrs. Babcock and Mrs. Walsh, home in England with their babies."

"But, George—all the people who came to the wedding?"

"Out of compliment to the Macdonalds. Yes, they'll probably call—in their own good time. They're very busy making other visits just now, my dear. We mustn't allow ourselves to forget that we're popularly known to be living on five hundred a month. Society bows to five hundred a month—with possibilities of advance—but it doesn't hurry about calling. You see there are so many people with superior claims—fifteen hundred, three thousand a month. It's an original place in that respect—Calcutta. The valuation of society is done by Government. Most people arrive here invoiced at so much, the amount usually rises as they stay, but they're always kept carefully ticketed and published, and Calcutta accepts or rejects them, religiously and gratefully, at their market rates. It's rather an uninteresting social basis—especially from our point of view—but it has the advantage of simplicity. You have a solemn official right to expect exactly what you can pay for."

With which treble cynicism young Browne received a bit of mignonette in his button-hole, kissed his wife, and departed. They were not really much concerned, these Brownes, about the conduct and theories of their fellow-beings at this time. Society was homogeneous, a human mass whose business it was to inhabit other parts of Calcutta, and do it as unobtrusively as possible. Even as a subject for conversation, society was perfunctory, and rather dull. It was a thing apart, it did not menace them yet, or involve them, or tempt them. They had not arrived at a point when anything it chose to concern itself with was important to them. It is charming, this indifference, while it lasts, but it is not intended to endure.

"It is certainly pretty," Helen remarked in a tone of conviction, looking round her little drawing-room. "It's charming!" And it was. The walls were tinted a delicate grey, and the windows were all hung with Indian saris, pale yellow and white.

The fresh matted floor was bespread in places with blue and white dhurries, and a big beflowered Japanese vase in a corner held a spiky palm. There were books and pictures—perhaps neither of the sort to bear the last analysis, but that at a glance didn't matter—and bits of old china, and all Aunt Plovtree's crewel work, and two or three vases running over with roses. There were some comfortable wicker chairs from the China bazaar, gay with cushions after Liberty, and there were all the little daintinesses that accompany the earlier stages of matrimony. Through the windows came in bars and patches the sunlight of high noon, and the rustling of the palms, and the cooing of the doves in the veranda.

"It hasn't much *character*," said Mrs. Browne, with her head at a critical angle, "but it's charming."

The fact is that it expressed cleanliness and the Brownes' income. I fear that Mrs. Browne belonged to that very numerous class of ladies in whose opinion character is a thing to arrange, just a matter to be attended to like the ordering of dinner. If you had asked her what particular character she wanted her room to express I think she would have been nonplussed. Or she might have said, Oh, she wanted it to be "artistic," with a little smile of defiance which would have been an evasion, not to say an equivocation of the matter. Helen Browne was not "artistic," and why she should have wanted her drawing-room to express what she did not understand is one of those enigmas common to the sex, as it flowers from day to day into new modern perplexities.

Perhaps it was much more charming of her to be what she was. It led her, at all events, into no burlesques. Nothing could be less extravagant, for instance, than that she should presently occupy herself, with amused concern and mock despair, in turning over a collection of young Browne's garments with a view to improving them. The bearer brought them to her in a basket, laid them deprecatingly at her feet, and retired, doubtless thinking that though the memsahib might be troublesome in various ways, she had her advantages. She would perhaps destroy the sahib's partiality for old clothes. He himself had struggled with these ancient socks and shirts a long and fruitless time, had cobbled them until his soul revolted, especially when the sahib, observing the result of his labour, had laughed deep laughs. The sahib was in no wise stingy—he would give new harness to the pony and new *kupra* * to the syce, and the bazaar was full of beautiful garments for the apparelling of sahibs, yet persistently and without sense of dishonour he enrobed himself daily thus! It was a painful, incomprehensible eccentricity. Now, perhaps, there would be a new order of things, and a chance for a little reasonable *dusturi.*† And Kasi spent the rest of the morning discussing contracts in the bazaar.

To his wife, however, young Browne was obliged to be explanatory, and even apologetic, upon this point. He had to tell her it was a way they had in India of sticking to their old things—it was only the most hideous swells that ever got anything new. You couldn't keep up with the fashion in India anyhow—the thing was to be superior to it altogether. Oh, she wouldn't have him discard that hat; he'd had that hat four years, and he was attached to it. If he might be allowed to keep it another year or two the shape would very likely "come in" again. Surely he wasn't inexorably condemned to a new coat. It would take years to make another as comfortable as

* Clothes. † Profit.

that, and it was only a bit ragged in the cuffs. But Helen was inflexible over the shortcomings of her husband's wardrobe, as it is the first duty of the ladies of Anglo-India to be, and young Browne shortly paid one penalty of matrimony in being reclad at vast expense, and suffered much contumely in consequence from his bachelor contemporaries. This morning Helen smiled over her basket with content and entertainment.

"What aren't shreds are patches," said she to the pigeons. "Dear me! Fancy having married a person who hasn't been properly mended since he left England." The pigeons replied with suitable sympathy. There was a roll of wheels under the porch, and the bearer brought up cards, "Mr. and Mrs. John Lawrence Lovitt."

"Bearer," said Helen, mistress of the situation, "all these things *lejao!* * Memsahib *sala'am do.*" †

"*Bahut atcha,*" ‡ said the bearer, whisking them away as he went. Not for worlds would Kasi have allowed his master's dilapidations to become public. And Mrs. Jack Lovitt tripped up.

"How d'ye do, Mrs. Browne?" she said. "I hope I haven't come too soon. Some one told me you'd been seen—somewhere—church, I suppose. People always do go to church at first, in Calcutta. After a while you won't—at least not so regularly. It gets to be rather a bore, don't you know, either morning or evening. In the morning it takes it out of you so that you haven't energy to receive your callers, and in the evening—well, if you go in for Sunday tennis you're too much done for church. But perhaps you won't go in for Sunday tennis."

Mrs. Lovitt sank into a chair and crossed her knees so that one small high-heeled boot stuck out at a sharp and knowing

* Take away. † Give greeting. ‡ Very good.

angle. She was a very little person, and she wore a very smart gown, though it was only a spotted cotton, and a very small bonnet. Her long-handled parasol had an enormous bow on it, and her small hands were buttoned up in an excessive amount of kid. She had a tiny waist, and her dress fitted her with an absurd perfection. There was a slight extravagance about Mrs. Jack Lovitt everywhere. No one could describe her without saying "very" and "exceedingly" a great many times. Her thin little face hadn't a shade of colour—it was absolutely pale, and there were odd little drawn lines about it that did not interfere with its particular kind of attractiveness. She wore a *pince nez* astride her small, sharp features, and when she sat down it dropped into her lap quite as if it belonged to a man of fashion.

Helen said, with a conscious effort not to be priggish, that she didn't think she would go in for Sunday tennis.

"Oh," said Mrs. Lovitt, smiling tolerantly, "don't believe in it, I suppose? Neither did I when I came out. You'll soon get over that. You'll begin virtuously by doing it for your husband's sake, and by and by you'll find that kind of prejudice doesn't thrive in India. I played with your husband the last Sunday before you came out. The other side completely smashed us up; I don't think your husband was in his usual form."

"Oh, I dare say he was," said Helen, smiling; "he doesn't play a very strong game."

"Oh, I wasn't either. I played abominably. But, of course, I blamed it all upon him; I declared his nerves were affected—on account of you, you know. He *admitted* there might be something in it," and Mrs. Lovitt laughed casually. "He says you're a tremendous swell at it," she continued inquiringly.

Helen protested, and Mrs. Lovitt went on to say that it didn't matter much how one played anyway, for tennis was certainly going out—everybody went in for golf now—links all over the place. Did Helen go in for golf, and had she done any cricket before she left England? Mrs. Lovitt had a cousin, Stella Short, who was in the Wilbarrow Eleven. Perhaps Helen had seen her photograph—it had been in all the ladies' papers.

"What do you think of the climate, Mrs. Browne?"

Helen said she thought it perfectly delightful; she found the glare a little trying.

"Oh, *glare!* Wait till the hot weather comes. It's all very well now and will be till March, but the hot weather's simply beastly; and in the rains—well, in the rains you feel exactly like a dead rat."

"That must be an extraordinary feeling," Helen responded, with some astonishment at the directness of the lady's similes.

"It *is*—rather! I suppose you're going to see the Viceroy's Cup won this afternoon?"

"Yes," said Helen, "are you?"

"Very much so! I'm one of those happy people who have got a tip. Jimmy Forbes gave me mine. You don't know Jimmy. He and I are great chums—we're always out together." Mrs. Lovitt spoke with virtuous candour. "He's an awfully *pucca* * sort of fellow, is Jimmy—you'll like him when you know him. He's a great friend of my husband's, too," Mrs. Lovitt added. "Jack thinks a lot of him. And he's very knowing about horses. How do you get on with the servants? They'll stick you no end at first—of course you know that. When I began I used to pay three rupees for a leg of mutton. It used to cost us two hundred a month more than our income to live!"

"Dear me!" said Helen. "Wasn't that very inconvenient?"

* Genuine.

"Inconvenient as the—as possible, sometimes, till Jack got his promotion. Now we manage all right."

"Have you any children, Mrs. Lovitt?" Helen ventured, as the bearer brought up another card.

"Children! Bless me, no, I should think not!" replied Mrs. John Lawrence Lovitt. "But I've got the littlest black-and-tan in Calcutta. Jimmy Forbes gave him to me. You must come and see him. Hello, Kitty Toote, so you're on the rampage! Good-bye, Mrs. Browne; don't let her prejudice you against Calcutta. She's always running it down, and it's the sweetest place in the world!"

Mrs. Toote made polite greetings to Mrs. Browne. "You know it isn't really," she said, disposing her tall figure gracefully among the cotton cushions of Helen's little sofa. "But of course it depends upon your tastes." Mrs. Toote had fine eyes, and an inclination to *embonpoint.* Her expression advertised a superior discontent, but there was a more genuine suggestion of gratified well-being underneath which contradicted the advertisement. "It's really awfully frivolous here," Mrs. Toote remarked. "Don't you think so—after England?"

"How can I possibly tell—so soon?" said Helen.

"No, I suppose not. Personally, I wouldn't mind the *frivolity.* The frivolity's all right—if there were only anything *else*, but there isn't."

"Anything else?" Helen inquired.

"Yes, anything really elevating, you know—anything that one could devote one's self to. I haven't a word to say against frivolity; I like it myself as well as anybody," said Mrs. Toote with engaging *naïveté*, "but there ought to be something behind it to back it up, you know." Mrs. Toote spoke as if she were objecting to dining exclusively upon ortolans. But the objection was a matter of pure dietetic theory. In practice, Mrs. Toote throve upon ortolans.

"Nobody reads," said Mrs. Toote.

"Nobody?" asked Helen.

"Nobody that *I* know—except novels, of course."

"And you prefer other kinds of books," Helen said, impressed. "More solid reading?"

"Oh, I enjoy a good novel," Mrs. Toote conceded; "but I don't think people ought to confine themselves to fiction. There's biography and philosophy, and—and social economy. All very interesting—to me."

"Which are your favorite authors?" asked Helen, with deference.

Mrs. Toote thought a minute. "John Stuart Mill," said she, "is a very fine writer. My husband has all his books. So is Herbert Spencer; we have all his, too. So is Sir Henry Cunninghame. *Have* you read *The Chronicles of Dustypore?*"

"I'm afraid not," said Helen. "Is it very good?"

"Oh, awfully. You *must* read it. Then, of course, there's Kipling. I'm devoted to Kipling."

"Do you think he's nice?" asked Mrs. Browne, doubtfully.

"I think he's everything. And I must say for the people here they do read their Kipling. But they don't talk about him. I don't believe they know the difference between Kipling and anybody else."

"Perhaps," Helen ventured, "they're tired of him."

"That's just where it is. How could anybody get tired of Kipling! You'll find plenty of gaiety in Calcutta, Mrs. Browne; but you won't find much—culture!" And Mrs. Toote lifted her eyebrows and twisted her lips into a look of critical resignation.

"Aren't there any societies?"

"Oh, if you mean the Asiatic, that's for scientists and people of that sort, you know, and they read awful papers there about monoliths and ancient dynastics and things. You can't consider that the Asiatic represents any popular tendency. *I* don't know anybody that's fond of Sanskrit. Of course," Mrs. Toote continued, "I'm speaking generally, and I mean particularly the women out here. There are some clever men in the departments, naturally. One or two of them are my greatest friends, and it *is* refreshing to talk to them."

"But are the ladies *all* frivolous?" Helen asked.

"Oh, dear, no!"

"And the unfrivolous ones—what do they do?"

"They mess about charities, and keep their husbands in their pockets, and write eternal letters to their children in England. I've less patience with them than with the other kind," Mrs. Toote avowed.

"Well," said Helen, smiling, "I'm not very literary, so I daresay it won't matter much to me."

"Then you'll either go in for society or philanthropy—that's the way everybody ends up. You are going to the Drawing-Room next Thursday?"

"I think so."

"Well, immediately after you must write your names down in the Government House books. Then they ask you to everything, you see. Don't put it off," advised Mrs. Toote, on the point of departure. "Don't put it off *a day*."

In a quarter of an hour the Wodenhamers came—Colonel and Mrs. Wodenhamer, a large lady and a generously planned gentleman. The smallest and slightest of Helen's wicker chairs creaked ominously, as Colonel Wodenhamer sat down in it with an air of asserting that he wasn't the weight you might think him. As to Mrs. Wodenhamer, her draperies completely submerged Helen's cotton cushions upon the sofa. Colonel Wodenhamer had mutton-chop whiskers and a double chin and a look of rotund respectability that couldn't be surpassed in Hyde Park on Sunday. He was not a fighting colonel, and in the adding up of commissariat accounts there is time and opportunity to develop these amplitudes. Mrs. Wodenhamer matched him more perfectly than is customary in the odd luck of matrimony, and had a complexion besides, which the Colonel couldn't boast. The complexion spread over features generously planned, and a smile that contained many of the qualities of a warm sunset, spread over both. Helen wondered in vain to which of Mrs. Toote's two social orders they belonged, for as soon as Colonel Wodenhamer had explained how it was he had come to call on a week-day—Colonel Wodenhamer made this a point of serious importance—Mrs. Wodenhamer led the conversation into domestic details. It wandered for a time among pots and pans—enamelled ones were so much the best—it embraced all the servants, took a turn in the direction of the bazaar, and finally settled upon *jharruns*.

"You'll find them *so* troublesome!" said Mrs. Wodenhamer.

"I don't know what they are," said Mrs. Browne, reflecting upon the insect pests of India.

"Don't you, really! It's a wonder you haven't found out! They're towels or dust-cloths—anything of that sort. Almost every servant must have his *jharruns*. You have no idea how they mount up."

"I suppose they must," returned Helen, and turned to Colonel Wodenhamer with intent to venture something about the weather.

"I don't see how you've got on without them so long!" Mrs. Wodenhamer remarked, glancing round with involuntary criticism. "I assure you I give out weekly in my house no less than five dozen—five *dozen!*"

"That's a great many," Helen agreed. "A very fair passage, I believe, Colonel Wodenhamer—thirty-one days."

"It's just a question whether they're better made in the house," Mrs. Wodenhamer went on placidly; "I don't know that I wouldn't advise you to go to the Women's Friendly—they work very neatly there."

"For the *jharruns*. Oh, yes!" said Helen. "The captain's name? I'm *afraid* I forget, Colonel Wodenhamer. He was a little man."

"They wear out so frightfully fast," his lady remarked.

"P. and O. captains? But consider the life, my dear!"

"*Jharruns*, John! Mrs. Browne really shouldn't begin with less than six dozen."

"I must see about them at once," Helen said. "I'm sure they are very important."

"The whole comfort of your life depends upon them," her visitor replied, rather ambiguously, and at that moment Mrs. Macdonald came up, and the conversation became so general that nobody noticed Mrs. Wodenhamer's being lost in thought. As she and her husband rose to go, "Your house is smaller than mine," said Mrs. Wodenhamer, "I forgot that. I think"—conscientiously—"you *might* do with four dozen."

Neither could Helen bring Mrs. Macdonald under Mrs. Toote's classification, for Mrs. Macdonald certainly did not give one the idea of a serious person, and yet she talked a great deal about committees. Mrs. Macdonald expressly advised Helen to "go in for" philanthropy, and in the next breath declared that of eourse she and young Browne must get themselves put up at the Saturday Club, where a proportion of Calcutta banded itself together for purposes of dancing and amateur theatricals, tennis and light literature. It was puzzling, this combination of good works and fashionable recreation, until Mrs. Macdonald explained, the explanation being inferential.

"You see," said Mrs. Macdonald, "you must take up something, you know, and then you will get to be known, and it will make all the differenee. Of eourse if you came out as the wife of a major-general or a commissioncr or a bishop it wouldn't matter—you could bc independent. But as it is," eontinued Mrs. Maedonald with delicate vagucness, indicating the Brownes' five hundred a month, "it would be bctter for you to take an interest in something, you know. There's the Home for Sailors' Orphans—Mrs. Leck and Mrs. Vondcrmore—they're not very important, though. And there's Lady Blebbin's Hindu Widow Institutc—that's overcrowded now. I believe thc very best thing for you"—with an incrcase of business-like emphasis—"would be the East Indian Self-Hclp Soeicty! Mrs. Walter Luff runs that, and she's just thc woman to appreciate anybody fresh and energetie like you! I've got influenee thcre too—I'll get you nominatcd."

"But," said Helen, in some dismay, "it's not at all likely that I should be able to be of any usc."

"Use? Of course you will. You'll be driven to death, but if Mrs. Walter Luff takes you up, you won't mind that! Besides," said Mrs. Maedonald with an cffcct of awakcned conscienee, "the East Indian Self-Helps do a lot of good. You're interested in the East Indians, aren't you—the Eurasians?"

"I don't know them when I see them," said Helen. "I always eonfuse them with the Jews and the Greeks."

"Oh, well, you soon will. As a rule they're awfully poor, you know, and give us a lot of trouble in Calcutta. Dear me!" Mrs. Macdonald ejaculated, looking round, "how pretty you are! But if I were you I'd have a Mirzapore rug for the middle of the floor; it makes the room so much richer, you know—shows up everything. And you ought to get two or three good engravings—there are some lovely new French things at Thacker's—only fifty rupees each. Go and see them. But I must be off," said this sprightly lady, and Helen was presently again alone, with a delicate disappearing odour of jessamine and her reflections.

I dropped in that morning too, after all the rest; but it is not essential to the progress of this narrative that you should be allowed to gather from my conversation the sort of person that I am.

CHAPTER XI.

IT was clearly impossible to attend Her Excellency's Drawing-Room in a tum-tum. The Brownes discussed it with fulness and precision at some length. Most people resident in Calcutta would have arrived at this conclusion more rapidly; but as young Browne said, he had never taken a wife to a Drawing-Room before, and a fellow always went to the levées in his tum-tum.

"It's that awful silk tail of yours that's the difficulty, dear," said he. "It might get wound up in the wheels, or Lord knows what. Couldn't you take it in a parcel and put it on when you get there?"

I can safely leave Helen's response to the imagination of all femininity.

"Then," said young Browne, "it must be a ticca," and Helen sighed compliance, for she hated ticcas.

So does all Calcutta, except the baboos. The ticca is an uncompromising shuttered wooden box with a door in each side and a seat across each end. Its springs are primitive, its angles severe. When no man has hired the ticca, the driver slumbers along the roof and the syce by the wayside. When the ticca is in action, the driver sits on the top, loosely connected with a bundle of hay which forms the casual, infrequent *déjeuner* of the horses. The syce stands behind, and if the back shutters are open he is frequently malodorous. There may be some worldly distinction between the syce and the driver, but it is imperceptible to the foreign eye. I have never been able to decide which is the more completely disreputable of the two. Their rags flutter in competition. There is more variety among the horses. They are large and gaunt and speckled. They are small and lean and of one colour. They are fly-bitten, unkempt, knock-kneed, vicious, and nasty. They have bad and vulgar habits. Some of them have seen Australia and better times, but it is not evident in their manners. Some of them have been country-bred for so many generations that the original animal has almost disappeared, leaving a stricken and nondescript little representative that might more fitly be harnessed to a wheelbarrow, if wheelbarrows lent themselves to harness. The ticca-gharry horse is always ridiculous when he is not pitiful; his gait under pressure is a gallop, and his equipment is made out in places with pieces of rope and other expediencies. The baboo loves the ticca-gharry because the baboo knows not mercy and gets a long ride, yea and seven of his kind with him, for threepence. Calcutta people hate it for reasons which are perhaps obvious. And for another. The ticca-gharry directly aids and abets Government in its admirable system for the valuation of society, represented, as has been seen, by the Accountant-General. A person who habitually drives in a ticca-gharry is not likely on the face of it to be in receipt of more than a very limited income, and is thus twice gazetted as not being a particularly desirable person to know. It is evident therefore that when the Brownes decided to go to the Viceregal Drawing-Room in a ticca they bowed to circumstances.

"Only *don't* get one, George," said Helen, plaintively, "with a pink rosette on its ear."

There were a few, a very few, other ticca-gharries in the

crowd of vehicles that blocked the street leading to Government House, and presently they all found themselves unaccountably in the rear of the line that was made to preserve order and prevent aggression. The stately landaus, the snug broughams and the smart victorias rolled naturally into their places in front. The British policeman whether in Hyde Park or Imperial India, knows his duty. So that Mr. and Mrs. Browne were not the first who alighted under the wide porch and made their way with more trepidation than they allowed to appear, into the crimson-carpeted precincts of the Burra Lord Sahib.

"Where shall I meet you after—after it's over, George?" asked Helen coming out of the cloak-room, very pretty in her soft white silk and the fresh Wiltshire colour that showed in her cheeks and proclaimed her newly "out."

"Oh I'll find you—I'll be waiting with the other men outside the door. Good-bye, dear. Don't be nervous!"

"I *am* nervous," said Mrs. Browne. "But I don't propose to show it. Good-bye!" and Mrs. Browne followed in the wake of other shimmering trains that were being marshalled from corridor to corridor on their way to the Throne Room, where Their Excellencies, doubtless very bored, were returning bows to the curtseys of all feminine Calcutta. How very fine those trains were, some of them. How elaborate and marvellous—how effective! And indeed they had come forth straight from Bond-street, many of them, for this very occasion, and therefore, why not? What use, pray, in being wives and daughters of thousands a month in the land of exile, if measures could not be sacredly kept in England and "decent things" got out at least once a year! And how the trains of thousands a month rejoiced in their contrast with others representing a smaller *tulub.* I do not speak of Helen's, for hers was a flowing credit to the Canbury dressmaker and quite up to date, but of gowns of an elder fashion and another day that showed themselves with delightful *naïveté* among the glittering creations of the season. They had seen, some of them, a great many December dissipations; they had been carefully packed away through a great many hot weathers and monsoons; they smelt of camphor; there was a quaintness in their very creases. One or two of them even told of trousseaux, Helen thought, that must have come to India in the old sailing days, round Cape Horn. Doubtless this new little memsahib felt amused in her trim feathers, but I have worn creases and smelled of camphor myself in my day, and I could have told her that with five sons at college and a daughter at school in England, one becomes necessarily indifferent to the fashions, even if the daughter does spend the holidays with an aunt in the country, free of expense. But of course one can't forecast one's own camphor and creases, and Helen Browne may never have any.

The dames who waited or who didn't wait their turn at the various barriers that regulated the road to Viceroyalty were chiefly imported English ladies of the usual pale Anglo-Indian type and pretty, either intrinsically or with the prettiness that comes of being well spoilt. Most of them had curtseyed formally to Their Excellencies every December for several years, yet they were quite as happily a-tremble as the brides or the *débutantes*—the brides of next season.

"I suppose," Helen overheard one little woman remark with animation, "Their Excellencies won't *bite!*" But she continued to behave as if she thought they would. There were also a few ladies who had not been imported. These were noticeable for a slight and not unbecoming Oriental duskiness under the powder, an unusual softness and blackness of eye, and an oddity of inflection that struck Helen as so pretty and "foreign." These ladies usually wore the feathers in their hair—the three feathers that compliment Royalty—of the same hue as their gowns, pink or blue or perhaps yellow, which was doubtless a survival of some lavish and tropical taste for colour that may have been peculiarly their own. The Ranees and the Maharanees made no attempt to subdue the gorgeousness of their natural instincts, but showed undisguisedly in purple and gold and eccentric gems, disposed according to the fashion that best liked them; and it was Helen's lot to proceed into the Viceregal presence immediately behind a Mohammedan lady of enormous proportions, who represented matrimonially a great Nawab, and did it wholly in crimson satin.

Their Excellencies stood upon a daïs, near enough to the Throne chair to suggest their connection with it. There were two stately lines of the Body-Guard, imperturbable under the majesty of their turbans; there were five or six A.-D.-C.'s, and secretaries in uniform with an expression of solemn self-containment under their immature moustaches. And there were, gathered together at Their Excellencies' right, the ladies of the Private Entrée. These ladies were the wives of gentlemen whose interests were the special care of Government. It was advisable therefore that their trains should not be stepped on, nor their tempers disarranged; and they had been received an hour earlier, with more circumstance, possibly to slower music, different portals being thrown open for the approach of their landaus—they all approached in landaus. If you stay in India long enough, Government will see that you get the Private Entrée before you go, as a rule. That is if you are a person of any perseverance, and have objected with sufficient stolidity to getting out of anybody else's way. This is not invariably the case, however, or John Perth Macintyre, my husband, with his success in tea and the knowledge of Indian commerce he has got in the last twenty years, would have been in the Viceroy's Council long ago, and Mrs. Macintyre's landau approaching with proper distinction in consequence, which it never has. I have no objection whatever to this coming out in print, for everybody knows that we wouldn't take it now. Moreover I daresay it is one reason why I always notice that the ladies of the Private Entrée are disposed to giggle slightly and otherwise forget the caste of Vere de Vere, as they look on upon the curtseys that come after. On this occasion, though Helen Browne was much too nervous to observe it, they were politely convulsed—of course with cast-down eyes and strained lips, and in the manner of good society—at the genuflections of the Mohammedan lady in red satin. I have no doubt one wouldn't observe this to the same extent if one were amongst them.

When it was over it had been very simple. The first A.-D.-C. had handed Helen's card to the second A.-D.-C., and so on, until it reached the Military Secretary who stood at the end, and he had read distinctly aloud from it the perfectly inoffensive description, "Mrs. George Browne." Whereat Mrs. George Browne had gone down several unsteady inches first before one Excellency, and then before the other, not at all able to observe the kindly smile with which they encouraged her unreliable equilibrium. After which she followed the other ladies whose ordeal was over, with hurrying footsteps and much relief through sundry tall pillared apartments to the corridor where Mr. George Browne awaited her, and took his arm with the greatest satisfaction she had yet experienced in its protection.

Everybody repaired to the ball-room, where, after the last agitated respects had been received, Their Excellencies also appeared, and Helen had the opportunity of taking a lesson in social astronomy, and learning if she chose, how that there is one glory of the sun and another glory of the moon, and how dark and unamiable those regions may be where the sun and the moon shine not. Also how an A.-D.-C. may twinkle as a little star in the firmament, and how a Lieutenant-Governor may be the centre of a brilliant constellation. Helen noticed a subtle difference between Their Excellencies and the rest, and put it down in her admiring innocence to aristocratic lineage or some such vague reason. As a matter of fact they were the only people in the room who did not directly or indirectly suggest a life-long interest in pay and promotion, which is quite enough to make a most vital difference, a most violent contrast, though it must take some years to discern this. The pay of a Viceroy is magnificently absolute, and you can't promote him. I believe that is arranged by Her Majesty, in order that he may have time to think about other things. This may look a trifle caustic, but the Perth Macintyres have out-stayed five Viceroys in Calcutta, and I have found that number at least to be quite human. Although it is a serious fact that the more one comes in contact with them the less one is struck with any idea of their common fallibility, and the more one is inclined to refer to His Excellency as a very superior mind, and to Her Excellency as "a perfectly charming woman," without cavil. The last two Viceroys for instance have seemed to me to be much more valuable acquaintances than their predecessors. Can it be that circumstances—chiefly viceregal dinners—have thrown us more together?

Little Mrs. Macdonald, sitting alone upon a sofa in a corner, welcomed the Brownes with effusion.

"Do let me go half shares in your husband for a while," she

said to Helen, making room for them. "Mine has gone off with Mrs. Toote, and I know what *that* means. Half an hour's desertion at least."

"What did he go for?" asked young Browne.

"Because Mrs. Toote is charming."

"Do you think so?"

"Don't *you?* I thought all the men grovelled before Mrs. Toote!"

"I don't grovel," said young Browne. "I think she's a bit of a humbug."

"But she *has* good eyes," Mrs. Macdonald protested.

"Lovely eyes," Helen chimed.

"Though *I wish* she wouldn't spoil them with charcoal the way she does," remarked Mrs. Macdonald with amiable unction. "She doesn't *need* to, you know."

"How do you *do*, Captain Delytis?" and Mrs. Macdonald bent very much forward on the sofa in recognizing a young man in blue lapels, who suddenly reined himself in as it were, responded profoundly to her salutation, and then hurried on. "That's Captain Delytis," she informed Helen. "One of the A.-D.-C.'s. Such a dear! He called on me twice last cold weather, and I was *darwaza bund* each time. Wasn't it a shame!"

"I wouldn't be too remorseful," remarked young Browne, not without malice. He had found Mrs. Macdonald *darwaza bund* frequently, and had all a black coat's aversion to the superior charms of blue lapels. "A.-D.-C.'s have a way, you know, of finding out first."

"Don't be nasty, George Browne," responded Mrs. Macdonald, "besides in this case it doesn't apply, for Captain Delytis told me himself how sorry he was. I daresay they have to resort to that sort of thing occasionally though, poor things. They have so much to do."

"Do!" remarked young Browne, with the peculiar contempt mercantile pursuits so often inspire for the army and the civil service in Calcutta. "They order dinner, I believe."

"They have charge of the invitations to everything, so you'd better just make him properly civil to them," said Mrs. Macdonald, turning to Helen, who responded, with perfectly feminine appreciation of the advice, that she would indeed.

"I wonder," continued Mrs. Macdonald thoughtfully, "why Mrs. Alec Forbes didn't see me just now. Did you notice her? —that tall woman in the pompadourish gown that passed just now. They say she's getting too swagger to see lots of people now that the Simlaites have taken her up so tremendously, but she's generally as sweet as possible to me. They tell a funny story about Mrs. Forbes and Mrs. Perth Macintyre—you've seen Mrs. Perth Macintyre: perhaps you can imagine how patronising and interfering the old lady is! Well, it was when Mrs. Forbes first came out, and Calcutta wasn't at all disposed to take to her—a little of the tar-brush, you know, and that doesn't go down here. But everybody liked Alec Forbes, and she had a lot of money, and people came round. Mrs. Perth Macintyre decided to come round too, and one night at dinner, when people were discussing this very function, she undertook to encourage Mrs. Forbes about it. 'I daresay you'll be a bit timid, my dear,' said she, 'but you'll just have to go through it like the rest of us.' 'Oh,' said Mrs. Forbes casually, 'I daresay its nothing to St. James's!' Mrs. Perth Macintyre was sat on for once—*she* had never been presented at home. Wasn't it good?"

"I can't see what earthly difference it made," said young

Browne, but his wife could, and turned another page in Part II., Feminine: of the Book of Anglo-India.

"Why, George," she said presently, "who's that?" her husband having emitted a gruff "How do!" as a gentleman passed them.

"That? Oh, nobody much! Sir William Peete."

"What did Sir William get his K for?" asked Mrs. Macdonald. "I've forgotten."

"For trimming up Calcutta the time some Royalty or other came out. He made a very good municipal milliner, got out a most unusual amount of bunting. They had to recognise it. The man who drained the place got nothing, so far as I remember."

"George, you don't like him," Mrs. Browne remarked astutely.

"Oh, yes, I do, for two months in the year, when he likes me. They occur in the rains. Then he's passionately fond of everybody who will speak to him. For the rest of the time he's exclusively occupied with Sir William Peete and a few other people of similar standing."

"What *do* you mean?" asked Mrs. Macdonald.

"About August and September," young Browne continued suavely, "Sir William comes out in boils—comes out copiously. He gets 'em on his neck and on his face and in the middle of his forehead. He becomes an awful spectacle. He fawns on his fellow-beings then. As soon as they leave him he returns to the sublime consideration of the social eminence of Sir William Peete. Boils are the only known method of reminding him that he belongs to the human race, so Providence takes it."

Mr. Macdonald came up at this moment and carried off his wife, leaving these young Brownes alone on the sofa in the corner of the room, looking on. They seemed to themselves as they sat there to have drifted into some tranquil place from which they could watch the steady current passing, the current that changes every year and yet is always the same, of English life in India. The old, old ambitions, the stereotyped political aims, the worn competitions, the social appraisements—how they have repeated themselves through what illustrations of the great British average, even in my time! How little more than illustrations the men and women have been, as one looks back, pictures in a magic lantern, shadows on a wall! Good illustrations, though sharp reflections of the narrow conditions they lived in, solemn warnings to those that are so eager to come after, if only the glamour of India left people with eyes to see. How gay they were and how luxurious, and how important in their little day! How gorgeous were the attendants of their circumstance, on the box with a crest upon their turbans—there is a firm in Calcutta that supplies beautiful crests. And now—let me think!—some of them in Circular Road Cemetery—cholera, fever, heat—apoplexy; some of them under the Christian daisies of England—probably abscess of the liver; the rest grey-faced Cheltenham pensioners, dull and obscure, with uncertain tempers and an acquired detestation of the climate of Great Britain. And soon, very soon, long before the Brownes appear in print, the Perth Macintyres also will have gone over to the great majority who have forgotten their Hindustani and regret their khansamahs. Our brief day too will have died in a red sunset behind clustering palms, and all its little doings and graspings and pushings, all its pretty scandals and surmises and sensations, will echo further and further back into the night.

Of course the Brownes did not moralize thus unpardonably. Why should they? They sat in their corner and looked at the brilliant scene before them, and young Browne talked with more or less good-natured cynicism about everybody he saw, and Helen quite failed to understand why George should take such ridiculous views of things. And by and by they went down the broad stairs, past the brown men that stood aside in their garments of crimson and gold, and the Browne's ticca-gharry rolled home with as light-hearted a sahib and memsahib as left Government House that night. As they had forgotten all about refreshments it was perhaps fortunate that they were able to find two mutton cutlets cold from the hands of Kali Bagh and some biscuits and marmalade, when they arrived, which afforded them keen satisfaction. They could still, poor dears, with the solace of a cold cutlet enjoy seeing the world go by.

CHAPTER XII.

I HAVE hinted, perhaps broadly, how the Government of India assists society in determining the Values of People. But this is not wholly done by columns of figures prepared with great accuracy in the Accounts Department, it is much facilitated by the discriminating indication of official position. I feel that official position should have capitals too—in India it always has. Government determines it profoundly, awfully, and with a microscope. It affixes a tag to each man's work and person describing him and all that he does. There is probably an office for the manufacture of these, and its head is doubtless known as the Distributor-General of Imperial Tags to the Government of India. With all his own time and energy at his disposal for the purpose he might arrange a designation for himself even more striking than that. He would date his letters from the Imperial Tag Office, and they would be composed by the Sub-Assistant-Deputy-Distributor, who would dictate them to one of the various gentle and oleaginous baboos who are content to sharpen pencils and permit their white nether draperies to fall round tall office stools for moderate remuneration without tags. In the hot weather the Distributor-General would go to Simla and the Assistant-Distributor would act for him, indulging prematurely in the airs which are attached to the office of his superior—borrowing his tag as it were, for the time. And so the days of the Distributor-General of Imperial Tags to the Government of India, and those of the lady who is made comfortable under the same title would be days of great glory and importance, except perhaps those which he spends in England on furlough, when he would be obliged to leave his halo behind him, with his bearer, to be kept in order. After an absence of a year or two the halo is apt to be found a little large, but in such cases it is never cut down, the head is allowed to expand.

I don't know of the actual existence of such an office in Calcutta, for as I have stated, Mr. Perth Macintyre has never had occasion to apply for a tag—they are comparatively uncommon in what the Simla element is pleased to call the mercantile community here—but if it does not exist I am at a loss to understand how they get on without it. Somewhere and somehow the solemn work of such a Department goes on under the direction of Heaven, and whether gentlemen in Government service wear their tags upon their watch-chains or keep them in their pockets, they are all tagged.

It makes a notable difference. It gives Calcutta for admiration and emulation a great and glorious company, concerning whom the stranger, beholding their red-coated chuprassies and the state which attends them, might well inquire, "Who, who are these?" Then one who knew—and everybody knows—might make answer, "These are the Covenanted Ones. These are the Judges of the High Court and all those who dispense the law of the Raj, the Scions of the Secretariat and other Departments, such people as commissioners and Collectors who are in authority throughout the land, the Army! Bow down!" The stranger would then remember the old saying in the mouths of women concerning these, "Three hundred a year dead or alive," with reference to pensions, which at one time was distinctly the most important quotation in the matrimonial market for India.

Thereafter follow the great multitude of the Uncovenanted Ones, the men whose business is with education, and science and engineering, and the forests and the police, whose personal usefulness dies with them, probably because they get less pay and less furlough while they live. The human heart is deceitful above all things, and desperately wicked, and it has lately entered into the Uncovenanted kind of human heart to cavil at this arrangement. It has had the audacity to suggest that it is just as homesick, that it suffers just as much from the climate, and that its work is just as indispensable as can possibly be the Covenanted case. I believe the matter is with the Secretary of State, where so many other matters have tender and indefinite safe keeping. Meanwhile there are certain positions of lustre among the Uncovenanted also, but they are few to count and difficult to attain. It is safe to say that a large proportion of the Uncovenanted Ones keep their tags in their pockets.

I have heard it stated that an expert can tell a Covenanted from an Uncovenanted individual by his back, given a social occasion which would naturally evoke self-consciousness. In the case of their wives, one need not be an expert. Covenanted shoulders are not obviously whiter or more classically moulded than the other kind, but they have a subtle way of establishing their relations with Government that is not to be mistaken even by an amateur. The effect cannot be described, and may be obtained only by contrast. You look at Uncovenanted shoulders, and you will observe that they fall away. You consider a pair of mercantile ones, and however massive and richly girt, you will notice that they suggest a slight depreciation of themselves. It is only the Covenanted neck that can assert itself with that impressive unconsciousness that comes from the knowledge of constant homage—bones, one might say, or no bones. This is in accordance with the will and intention of the Government of India, and therefore is as it should be. It is the Raj that has accorded this lady her consideration, therefore in no quarter is it withheld. The feet of such a one are stayed upon a rock; it has never been hers to pick her anxious way among the quicksands of ordinary social advance. Her invitations are secure. She is acquainted with the number and magnitude of them, she might almost demand them under a specific regulation. I have never heard anybody discuss her brains. She occupies a position which an intellect no doubt adorns, but not indispensably. Her little frivolities are the care of the Government that holds her in the hollow of its hand. Society declines to be Pharisaical about them, and asks her to dinner just the same. The shifting aristocracy of England affords nothing like her security, her remarkable poise. It is difficult to understand how, in spite of all this, she can be as charming as she occasionally is.

It was in my mind to say much sooner that the Brownes were going out to dinner. They had gone out to dinner on several occasions already among the people who had known young Browne before he was married, but the occasions had been informal, the invitations worded "quite quietly," and there had been no champagne. This was to be a "burra-khana," with no lack of circumstance. The invitation ran thus:—"My dear Mrs. Browne—Will you and your husband give Mr. Peckle, Mr. Cran and myself the pleasure of your company at dinner on Tuesday the 27th, at eight o'clock?—Yours sincerely, J. L. Sayter."

"Old Sayter!" remarked Mr. Browne. "It's a chummery,

Nell. They called, the lot of them, that Sunday we went up the river."

"A chummery—that's a lot of bachelors living together," said Helen.

"Not necessarily bachelors—Sayter's a bachelor, Cran and Peckle are both married men, wives in England. It's two years since Mrs. Cran went home, and Mrs. Peckle's never been out, so far as I know. In fact, we've only got Peckle's bare word for the existence of a Mrs. Peckle; maybe it's a fiction in self-defence."

"George!"

"And I don't know that he doesn't invent the little Peckles. To hear him groan over their expenses you'd think there was a new one every year, and you know that's manifestly—"

"GEORGE!"

"I was going to say improbable. But I dare say there are a lot of 'em. Peckle goes home once in three or four years and refreshes his memory as to number and size. After that he always has a fit of economy and puts down a horse or two."

"Poor things!" said Helen, pensively, "an old bachelor and two grass widowers! How wretched their lives must be! Why, if I had to go home for my health, dear, I can't imagine what would become of you!"

"Y—yes! No, indeed, darling! But you sha'n't go!" An interruption foolish but inevitable. "As to those old fellows—well, you'll see. It's rather a swagger chummery, very decent men," young Browne went on, "and therefore, my dear," with mock resignation, "they'll give us all sorts of unholy indigestibles to eat, and your husband will have liver of the most frightful description for a week."

"Liver," however, very seldom ensues in the early days of

matrimony, and Helen, unacquainted with this domestic bane, laughed it to scorn. It was her unconscious belief that the idylls of the Brownes could not suffer from such a commonplace.

Mr. Sayter wore a civil tag of considerable size; the other two men were brokers. Mr. Sayter's tag was not offensively

MR. SAYTER.

conspicuous, was not in fact to be seen at all unless one took the trouble to observe it by inference. I mean that a critical estimate of Mr. Sayter's manner would discover the tag; it might be detected behind his attitude and his aphorisms and the free way in which he lifted his voice upon all things. Perhaps it was only observable in the course of time and the progress of one's acquaintance with tagography. At first sight Mr. Sayter was a little grey gentleman with a look of shrinking modesty and a pair of very bright eyes. Indeed Mr. Sayter bore himself almost with humility, his shoulders had a very unaggressive slope, and he had a way of casting down his eyes as he talked to you which did not suggest a lofty spirit. Custom, however, proved Mr. Sayter's modesty to be rather like that of the fretful porcupine, his humility to take amused superior standpoints of opinion, and his eyes to be cast down in search of clever jests that were just the least bit wicked. All of which, in Anglo-India, subtly denotes the tag. The untagged or the undertagged are much more careful how they behave.

Mr. Sayter came down to meet them in the hall and give Mrs. Browne his arm up stairs, as is the custom in this place. Helen observed that the wall was very white and high and undecorated, that the floor was tiled with blocks of marble, and that the stairs were of broad polished mahogany. In her host she saw only the unobtrusive Mr. Sayter with a reassuring smile of characteristic sweetness anxiously getting out of the way of her train. Young Browne, temporarily abandoned, followed them up discreetly, and at the top Mrs. Browne was introduced to a Calcutta dinner-party waiting for a Calcutta dinner.

Among the various low-necked ladies Helen was pleased to recognise Mrs. Wodenhamer. The presence of Mrs. Wodenhamer at a dinner given even participially, by Mr. Sayter, indicates as well as anything the inalienable privileges connected with the wife of a Commissariat Colonel; but that is by the way. It is perhaps enough to say that the other ladies were various, one or two young and rather flippant, one or two middle-aged and rather fat, verging toward Mrs. Wodenhamer; all very

MR. SAYTER GAVE MRS. BROWNE HIS ARM.

agreeably dressed, except Mrs. Wodenhamer, who wore crimson and black; all extremely self-possessed, all disposed to be easily conversational. I might itemize their husbands standing about in degrees of eminence and worldly plethora fairly proportioned to their waistbands, and sharing the proud consciousness of having contributed a wife to the occasion. I ought to mention also Mr. Cran and Mr. Peckle, though I need not dwell on Mr. Cran's bearded baldness, or Mr. Peckle's rosy expansiveness, as it is quite unlikely that you will have occasion to recognise them out of their own house. They followed Mr. Sayter down stairs with Mrs. Wodenhamer and the lady who most resembled her, when the sound of the gong came up. Helen, as the bride of the occasion, went down on Mr. Sayter's arm.

"Well, Mrs. Browne," said Mr. Sayter presently, giving her an amiable glance from his soup, "what do you think of us? Now I know what you're going to say," he continued, holding up a bit of crust in a warning manner. "You're going to say that you haven't been here long enough to form an opinion, or words to that effect. I'm perfectly right, ain't I?"

Helen admitted that her answer might have been "something like that."

"But you don't mean it, you know. Really and truly, if you think a minute, you'll find you don't mean it. You've got a lovely opinion of us, all ready for use, in this last month. And very proper too. The very first thing everybody does here is to form an opinion of Anglo-Indians. It can't be postponed, it's involuntary. Besides, it's a duty. We appeal to the moral side. We call out, as it were, for condemnation. Isn't that so, Wodenhamer?"

"Isn't what so?" said that gentleman. "Certainly. *Na!*

peg do,"* to the kitmutgar who wanted to give him champagne.

"You should have been listening. I decline to begin again. I was trying to convince Mrs. Browne that India is the only country in the world where people can be properly applied to for their impressions before they leave the ship—the way they do in America with travellers of distinction. But there's no use asking Wodenhamer. He's never been to America, and when he does travel he goes incog. to avoid these things."

Colonel Wodenhamer's mutton-chop whiskers expanded in recognition of the joke, "People know it when *you* travel," he said.

"That's sarcastic of you, Wodenhamer, and naughty and unkind. I think he refers, Mrs. Browne, to the fact that I was gazetted for duty in Assam last month, and just a fortnight and three days after I came back the *Briton* announced that I was going. Do you know the *Briton?* Capital paper in many respects, but erratic occasionally in matters of considerable importance. Delicious paper for description of ball dresses. I revel in the *Briton's* ball dresses."

"Who d'you think does that sort of thing for them?" Mr. Peckle inquired. "Some lady, I suppose."

"No indeed, Mr. Peckle," volunteered one in grey bengaline and gold embroidery, on the other side of the table. "It's Captain Dodge, if you please! I know, because at the Belvedere dance on Friday he came and *implored* me to tell him what colour Lady Blebbins was wearing. It was hyacinth and daffodil faille—the *simplest* thing, but he was awfully at a loss, poor fellow! And afterwards I saw him put it down on the back of his dance-card."

* Whisky and soda.

"I daresay they pay for such things," Mr. Peckle remarked.

"I fancy Dodge gets a polo pony out of it," observed Mr. Cran.

"I didn't give that man Dodge credit for so much imagination," said Mr. Sayter. "I wonder if I could induce him to put me in! I'd like to be treated poetically in the newspapers, for once. But I'm afraid he won't," Mr. Sayter continued sadly, "because I can't wear mull muslin—isn't that what you call it?" to Helen. "I can't wear it because I should suffer from the cold, and yet the baboos do! That's queer, you know. The baboo is vain enough already, and I'm not vain at all; yet Heaven permits the baboo to disport himself in the sweetest gossamer and threatens me with fever and rheumatism if I should even think of such a thing!"

"But surely, Mr. Sayter," Helen interposed, "nobody suffers from the cold *here!*"

"Oh, my dear lady! You don't know! The cold is the one thing we can't get acclimatized to in India! To-night it would be Arctic if we weren't dining. *Kitmutgar, bund caro darwaza!** We'll have a fire up stairs afterwards."

"A *fire!*" said Helen in astonishment.

"Yes. And then we'll be comfortable. He can leave all the doors and windows open, you know, so that you can take a severe cold if you want to. Although this is a country governed by a merciless despotism we don't compel people to keep well if they'd rather not."

"I can't imagine anybody suffering from the cold in Calcutta!" Helen declared. "Why, to-day the thermometer stood at eighty-three!"

"Oh," said Mr. Sayter, "how I envy you.—What! no Roman

* Shut the door.

punch! You are still warm, you still believe in the thermometer, you still find the baboo picturesque—I know you do! Thank Heaven, I continue to like Roman punch—I retain that innocent taste. But I've been cold," said Mr. Sayter, rubbing his hand, with a shiver, "for years. For years I've had no faith in the thermometer. For years I've been compelled to separate the oil from the less virtuous principles in the baboo. It's very sad, Mrs. Browne, but you'll come to it."

"I say, Sayter," remarked young Browne, who was singularly without respect of persons, considering that he lived in Calcutta, "I can't have you frightening my wife about what she'll come to in Calcutta. I don't want her to develop nervous moral apprehensions—based on what *you've* come to!"

Mr. Sayter's chin sank into his necktie in official deprecation of this liberty on the part of a junior, and a mercantile one, but he allowed himself to find it humorous, and chuckled, if the word does not express too vulgar a demonstration. He leaned back and fingered his empty glass.

"Mrs. Browne," he said deliberately and engagingly, "will come to nothing that is not entirely charming." And he smiled at Helen in a way which said, "There, I can't do better than that." As a matter of fact he could, and Helen, as she blushed, was blissfully unaware that this was the kind of compliment Mr. Sayter offered, though not invidiously, to the wives of mercantile juniors.

"Moral apprehensions," repeated Mr. Sayter slowly.—"*No!* I've had you for ten years,"—he apostrophized the kitmutgar—"you've grown grey in my service and fat on my income, and you don't know *yet* that I never take anything with a hole in it like that—and pink vegetables inside the hole! Mrs. Browne, I'm glad you refrained. That's the single thing Calcutta dinners teach—the one great lesson of abstinence! I was very clever and learned it early—and you see how many of them I must have survived. But talking of moral apprehensions, I know you're disappointed in one thing."

"No," said Helen, promptly; "I like everything."

"Then you haven't anticipated us properly—you haven't heard about us. You ought to be very much disappointed in our flagrant respectability."

"But I like respectability," Helen replied, with honesty.

"Oh! There, I'm obliged to consider that you come short again, Mrs. Browne. You're not in sympathy with the age. I don't. I'm very respectable myself, but that's not my fault. I've never had the good luck to be married, for one thing; and that, in India, is essential to a career of any interest. But I was once quite an exceptional, quite an original, character on that account, and I'm not any more. *Those* were the good old times. And to see a beautiful, well-based, well-deserved reputation for impropriety gradually disappear from a social system it did so much to make entertaining is enough to sadden a man at my time of life."

"Really," said Helen; and then, with a little bold shivering plunge, "Were the people out here formerly so very—incorrect?"

"Oh, deliciously incorrect! Scandals were really artistic in those days. I often wish I had preserved more of them; my memory's getting old too. I find myself forgetting important incidents even in those concerning my most intimate friends. And how people spent their money then! Big houses—turned into boarding-houses now—heaps of servants, horses—entertained like princes! Nowadays people live in flats, and cut the cook, and save to the uttermost cowrie, so they can retire a year earlier to drink beer with impunity and eat mutton chops with a better appetite in England. Ignoble age! People—these respectable people—go home second-class now, too, and pretend to be comfortable. Disgraceful, I call it."

"There isn't the money there used to be, Sayter," protested Mr. Peckle. "In those days a man got a decent *tulub*, and carried it away in a bag. And the vile rupee was worth two shillings."

Mr. Peckle helped himself to pistachios, and passed the port.

"I believe that explains it!" and Mr. Sayter pressed his lips knowingly together. "It never occurred to me before. Economy and scandals don't go together. Make a man economical, and he becomes righteous in every other respect. So Government's to blame, as usual. I think, in view of this, we ought to memorialise Government to drop the income-tax. You would sign, wouldn't you, Mrs. Wodenhamer?"

"Yes, indeed," Mrs. Wodenhamer returned, placidly. "Government ought to get the income-tax out of those rich natives. I think it's a shame to make *us* pay."

"Quite right, Mrs. Wodenhamer! These, Mrs. Browne, are called promotion nuts! They're useful to effect the permanent removal of your superiors from office. Very nice and very deadly. You must be sure to have them when you ask any of Browne's firm to dinner. No, I've a prejudice against them ever since they were once offered to me in a pudding. I've a sad association with them, too." And Mr. Sayter looked grave.

"Indeed!" said Helen, not quite sure whether she ought to make her tone sympathetic.

"Yes, they always come on just as the ladies are leaving," twinkled Mr. Sayter; and Helen became aware that Mrs. Wodenhamer was looking at her with ponderous significance. There was the usual gracious rustle, and presently the ladies were comfortably and critically ensconced in the drawing-room, sipping their coffee, at various distances from the indubitable fire. The conversation was not very general. Mrs. Wodenhamer discussed something in a suppressed voice on the sofa, with the lady who approximated her. Helen wondered if it were *jharruns*. There was apparently some sympathy between the grey bengaline and gold embroidery and a cream crêpe de Chine and pearls, with very yellow hair. A little incisive lady in black who happened to be nearest to Helen, asked if she didn't think for three *men* the room was awfully pretty. Helen said she did, indeed; and the little lady in black continued, with an entirely unnecessary sigh, that men certainly *did* know how to make themselves comfortable, there was no doubt about that. Did Mrs. Browne ever see anything more exquisite than that water-colour on the easel? Mr. Peckle had just bought it at the Calcutta Art Exhibition; Mr. Peckle was a great patron of art and that sort of thing, but then he had to be; he was a director, or something.

"My husband says," remarked Helen, with lamentable indiscretion, "that there isn't any art in Calcutta."

"*Does* he? Oh, I think that's a mistake. There's Mrs. Cubblewell, and Colonel Lamb, and Mrs. Tommy Jackson. Mrs. Tommy paints roses beautifully, and I do a little on satin myself!" Then, as if it were a natural outgrowth on the subject, "What *is* your husband here, Mrs. Browne?"

"He's in Macintyre and Macintyre's."

"Oh, *yes!*"

Whereafter there fell a silence, during which the little lady in black seemed to be debating young Browne's probable connection with the firm of Macintyre and Macintyre—it sometimes made such a difference—but before she had properly made up her mind the gentlemen appeared, and there ensued that uncertain form of conversation which betrays the prevalent desire that somebody should "make a move."

Somebody made one finally, before Mr. Sayter actually yawned. The Brownes drove home rather silently in their ticca-gharry.

"Well?" said young Browne interrogatively, chucking his wife tenderly under the chin in a moonlit space of Chowringhee.

"I was thinking, George," said she, "that I didn't see any photographs of their wives about the room."

"No," said young Browne.

CHAPTER XIII.

INDIA is a country of ameliorations. The punkah is an amelioration. So is the second-rate theatrical company from Australia, notwithstanding its twang. So, for those who like it, is the custard-apple. It is our complaint that our ameliorations are too numerous and too obvious. It is painful to us that they should obscure everything else in the vision of the travelling public, and suggest themselves as the main facts of an idyllic existence which runs sweetly among them to the tinkle of the peg and the salaams of a loyal and affectionate subject race—which they do. When the travelling public goes back and represents this to be the case in the columns of the Home Press we do not like it. The effect is that we are embittered, and the single one of us who is clever enough writes the ballad of "Paget M. P." This is natural and proper. We are none of us constituted to see our trifling advantages magnified, and our tragic miseries minimised, especially in the papers, without a sense of the unpardonable obtuseness of the human race. I do not intend to be drawn into personal anathema in this chapter though. It will always be so. The travelling public will continue to arrive and tarry during the months of November, December, January, and February, and to rejoice in the realisation of all they have ever read in the Sunday School books. The travelling public will continue to prefer its own impressions. In British journalism and Great British Parliamentary opinion there will always be a stodgy impracticability which the returned Anglo-Indian can never be strong enough to influence. We are a little leaven, but we cannot leaven the whole lump.

We die too soon. Besides, it is easier and more comfortable to philosophise when one is going home next hot weather for good. I am content, as I write, to think of my ameliorations even with gratitude, and will only say what so many have said before me, that a protracted residence under ameliorations is necessary to the full understanding of how grievous a thing an ameliorated existence may be.

The Brownes were not contented with what Nature does for us in this way in the cold weather—green peas and cauliflowers, red sunsets, oranges and guavas at twopence a dozen. Ever since the evening they dined with Mr. Sayter they had been of opinion that the only people whose existence was properly ameliorated in Calcutta were the people with the joy of a fireplace in their houses. As a family young Browne declared they were entitled to a fireside—it was monstrous that they should lack such an elemental feature of the domestic habit. True they had a "siggaree," a funnel-shaped pot of charcoal, like everybody else—the kitmutgar made toast with it and the bearer dried damp sheets over it—but one couldn't be comforted at the risk of asphyxiation, and besides, it smelled. There was nothing else, and the Brownes felt that they could not accustom themselves to gather in a semicircle round a tall Japanese vase, or a blank space in a white wall fifteen feet high, for anything like cheerful discourse. They considered that the enduring bliss which they seemed to have taken with the house lacked this one thing only. It was impossible to persuade the Spirit of the Hearth to make himself comfortable in a flower-pot.

It was also impossible to build a chimney—their local tenure being of that brief and uncertain kind which is popular in Calcutta. A long lease is not desirable when a neighbourhood may develop typhoid any day, when beams may take to dropping any night, when one may want six months' leave just at a season which is unpropitious for sub-letting. All these conditions obtain in Calcutta, and any of them might be the Brownes'! Besides, a chimney would cost rupees incalculable.

There were alternatives, however. The Brownes went to the ironmonger's to look at them. They were disposed to take an alternative if it could be had at a moderate price. Most of those they saw were connected with a length of stove pipe which went through the wall, some of them were decoratively tiled, some involved a marble mantel, and they all required an outlay which, for a matter of pure sentiment, seemed large to the Brownes.

"For forty-nine weeks in the year," remarked young Browne gloomily, "it would have to be stored."

"Wouldn't it rust?" inquired Helen.

"Inches!"

"I don't think we can depend on being able to make a new hole in the wall every time we move," Mrs. Browne suggested. "The landlord mightn't like it."

"We could always arrange to fill it up with purple glass when we leave. If we did that the baboos would encourage our perforations. So much do they love coloured glass that they paper it on one side, and thus dissimulate."

Helen thought this ingenious, but it did not alter the fact that the tiled temptations were expensive. Then the ironmonger's young man, rising to the situation, suggested a kerosene stove. You purchased a kerosene stove, he said, and there it was, your inalienable property, or words to that effect. It didn't require no fittings, nor yet being built into the wall. It would go with you anywheres, it didn't want a stove pipe nor yet a hole. It didn't go in for being to say decorative, not exactly, but then see how cheerful it was. You never knew till you tried how cheerful kerosene could be! The young man gave them to understand, moreover, that its mechanism could be comprehended by a child or a punkah wallah. And they had no idea to what extent it would reduce the consumption of coal. The Brownes listened attentively, and when the young man paused and rested one elbow against a patent punkah machine in his exhaustion, young Browne made a scientific observation of the stove. He turned one wick up and the other down. "Seems to work all right," he said to Helen.

"Perfectly, sir," said the ironmonger's young man.

Young Browne looked at him curiously. "You haven't been long out?" he remarked.

"No, sir. Only three weeks, sir. I came from this department in William W'itely's, sir."

"I remember," said Mr. Browne, "they do like to sell things there. Three months in Calcutta and you won't care a blow."

"That so, sir?" the young man returned, smilingly. "I 'ope not, sir, for the sake of business."

"It is. What do you think of this thing, Helen? Shall we have it sent up?"

"It would be nice for toffee," said Helen. "And I'm sure I can make toffee cheaper than the cook does. I dare say it would save us a lot in toffee, George."

"I'm sure it would. And it's only thirty-five rupees—about two pounds seven, at the current rate of exchange. It isn't just my ideal of a fireside, but it seems the best we can do." And the next morning the kerosene stove arrived on the heads of four coolies, at the Brownes' suburban residence.

The night was propitiously and comfortably cold. As they drove home from tennis at Mrs. Jack Lovitt's, muffled up in the

MRS. LOVITT.

striped flannel jackets with which Calcutta protects itself from the inclemency of the weather after tennis, Helen declared, with the kerosene stove in anticipation, that it was really almost piercing. "It's a pity, though, George," she said regretfully, "that we were *quite* in such a hurry about buying the stove, for I was telling Mrs. Lovitt about it, and she said she was so sorry she didn't know we wanted one—we could have had theirs, and it's in perfect order, for ten rupees."

"Oh, next cold weather," returned her lord, "we'll have the pleasure of selling ours for ten rupees instead. It comes to much the same thing, you see."

It is almost impossible to persuade a sahib of Calcutta to take his domestic accounts seriously. If his natural proclivities are in that direction, he is usually not to be respected.

The Brownes had a hump for dinner, and a hump costs a rupee and several annas. Nevertheless they hurried through it, the more speedily to avail themselves of their unaccustomed luxury in kerosene, to "cluster round the cheerful blaze," as George Browne put it, which stood solemnly between two long windows in the drawing-room awaiting a match. Entering, they found the bearer, the kitmutgar and the mallie kneeling about it, with varied expressions of concern, the machine still grim and black, in the midst of a pervasive odour of kerosene. The Brownes felt palled. It was not what they had expected.

"*Bilcul na hona sucta*,"* said the bearer, rising and surveying the thing as if it were an obdurate Hindu deity.

"What does he say?" inquired Mrs. Browne. Mrs. Browne was always inquiring what the bearer said. Mr. Browne was rapidly becoming a peripatetic hand-book of Hindustani. He implored his wife to have a *munshi*,† and Helen thought it would be delightful but sternly declined on the score of economy. So young Browne had no surcease.

* Simply it may not be! † Instructor.

"*Albut hona sucta!*"* said he, going upon his own knees before the refractory divinity. Helen stood by with superior interest and knitted brows, after the manner of women.

"*Dya-silai* HUM *ko-do!*"† enunciated the sahib.

Deep relief became visible upon the faces of the bearer, the kitmutgar, and the mallie. The sahib was omnipotent.

Mr. Browne presently discovered that the wicks had dropped into the oil reservoirs. He proceeded to take the newly imported fireside upon his lap, so to speak, and unscrew it, his wife remarking meanwhile that she supposed it was quite safe. He rescued the wicks, but Helen has since mournfully given me to understand that certain of the garments he had on were never tenable afterwards.

Then they applied a match to engender the sacred fire upon their hearth, and it was engendered in two long narrow flames that flared up in yawning tin chasms on either side and sent before them a wreathing blackness of smoke which escaped rapidly through the holes on the top for the saucepan and the gridiron.

"It *is* cheerful," said Helen insistently. "But it seems to need a stove pipe after all," she added, in doubt.

"Not at all," said her husband, "only to be turned down." So he turned it down to a wavering blue and yellow line, and closed the doors.

"Finish *hai?*" inquired the bearer, and the sahib said yes, it was finished, so the bearer, the kitmutgar and the mallie repaired to the simpler solaces of sentimental organisations less subtly devised than ours.

These two exiled Brownes drew up chairs and tried to feel at least anticipative appreciation. There were two round trans-

* Without doubt it may be! † Give ME the matches.

parent holes in the doors through which they could see a reflection of their glowing hearth. They leaned towards it and spread out their hands. Young Browne remarked, with a chill smile, that it was certainly warmer than it had been. They pulled their chairs closer together, in order, I have no doubt, to impede the heat that might escape into other quarters of the room. Helen slipped her hand into her husband's, and together they looked thoughtfully into the depths of the burning wick. I think the way in which they must have regarded this thing, which was to mean for them the essence of home life in an unhomelike country, and the warm glow of home love caught and held where it is reputed apt to stray abroad, was not altogether laughable though. In fact——

"*Nellie!*" exclaimed young Browne, and had occasion to bring his chair closer still There was a moist contact of cheeks and a succession of comforting silences. The kerosene stove continued to burn excellently, but was disregarded.

"It looks like some kind of—of engine, doesn't it, George?" Mrs. Browne recovered herself sufficiently to say.

"Yes. Beastly thing!" concurred young Browne in further disparagement. Then they began to observe the effect of the heat on the varnish. It took the form of a hot penetrative unpleasant smell that radiated from the kerosene stove into every quarter of the room.

"I expect it will wear off," said young Browne gloomily, "but we'd better put the thing out in the compound every night until it does."

It has never worn off, however. Helen, with responsible memory of the thirty-five rupees, used it conscientiously all last cold weather. She did serious and light-minded cooking with it while she suffered the delusion that she was Kali Bagh's superior

—inevitable but short—and she made almost enough toffee upon it to justify its expense, if it had been necessary to subsist upon toffee. Whenever anything could be done with it the Brownes did it. They had it lighted to welcome their return from burra-khanas and Government House dances, and on one occasion Helen sat for half an hour before it in her most cherished gown, under a shower of softly falling black flakes of carbonized kerosene without being aware of it—the result of an injudicious lighting and forgetting on the part of the bearer. Many an evening they sat in its presence making efforts at hilarity and trying to forget the odours of varnish and kerosene—in the end they always confessed it inadequate. It had a self-contained moroseness, it never snapped or sparkled or died down. When they went to bed they turned it out. Through its two round eyes it mocked their homesick effort after the cheer of other lands. The bearer admired it and took pride in setting it alight. But the Brownes regarded it with feelings that grew constantly more "mixed." It made no ashes and gave no trouble, and when they didn't want it it was not there—all of which seemed additional offences.

The old kite that surveyed them always through the window from his perch in the sago palm beside the veranda said nothing, but if they had been intelligent they might have heard the jackals that nightly pillaged the city's rubbish heaps, howling derision at the foolishness of a sahib who tried to plant his hearth-stone in India.

CHAPTER XIV.

MRS. BROWNE was not permitted to know any of her immediate neighbours, which she thought unfortunate. It was a pity in a way, and yet not a great pity, for if I know anything about Helen Browne she would not have been able to assimilate her neighbours comfortably. Unless they live with the great and good in Chowringhee, it is often difficult for Calcutta people to do this. It is said that the missionaries manage it, but about this no one is certain, for between Calcutta people and the missionaries there is a great gulf fixed. Calcutta interprets the missionary position with strict logic. It was not Calcutta —Calcutta proper—that the missionaries came out, second class, to establish intimate spiritual relations with, but the heathen. Calcutta is careful, therefore, not to interfere in any way with this very laudable arrangement; the good work must not be retarded by any worldly distraction. Calcutta contributes to it, in her own peculiar way, by allowing the missionaries the fullest possible opportunity for becoming acquainted with the heathen. If one does not readily suspect the self-denial in this, it is because one is predisposed against society—it is perhaps because one has been snubbed.

I cannot say with accuracy, therefore, whether a missionary in Mrs. Browne's place would have known Radabullub Mitterjee, Bahadur, who lived next door to the west; doubtless she would have made attempts, at least, to introduce herself to the ladies who divided the matrimonial dignities of his establishment; but it did not occur to Helen that there was any opening for such advances upon her part. Even the slits of windows which commanded the Browne compound were generally shut and always iron-barred; no dangerous communication from an unveiled memsahib who ate with her husband could get in there. It was a little narrow, silent, yellow house, too tall for its width, much overgrown with heavy-hanging trees, and it stood a long way back from the road, looking out on a strip of compound, through a glass door, purple in places and green in places, and altogether brilliant to behold. The strip of compound was a marvel of rectangular crookedness. It was a good deal taken up with a tank, a long narrow tank covered with a generous green slime, dug rather sidewise. The rest of the place was divided into small sharp-angled-beds with rows of stones. They were very much at odds with each other, and nothing grew in them but a few ragged rose-bushes, and flagrant things that came of their own accord. Almost every evening R. Mitterjee, Bahadur, went out to drive. The Brownes used to meet him in the broad Red Road that cleaves the Maidan, where the landaus, and victorias, and tum-tums of Calcutta amuse themselves by passing and repassing, and bowing to each other, in the pleasant part of the day, before the quick darkness comes and sends them all home to dinner. Nobody bowed to Radabullub, and he bowed to nobody, though assuredly no sahib drove in so resplendent a gharry as his. It was built on the most imposing lines, with ornamentation of brass, and a beautiful bunch of flowers painted on either door-panel. And it was pulled by two of the most impetuous prancing steeds in silver mounted harness, that the soul of a Bahadur could desire. The silver mountings were very rusty, and the prancing steeds lamentably weak in their fore legs, but the soul of a Bahadur is not perturbed by little things like that. Radabullub leaned back behind them superciliously, folding his arms over his tight silk coat of pink brocade, or twisting his moustache. With his embroidered yellow turban at a certain angle, this Bahadur was a killing fellow—very much a man of the world indeed, but not enough to know a good horse when he saw it, or to be able to drive it if he did, or to understand what earthly difference it made to a sahib how his servants were dressed. His own sat behind in a cluster—he had more of them than any sahib—in turbans of the colours they most fancied, and alike only in the respect that they were all dirty and down at heels, if the expression, in a shoeless case, is properly applied. But when it was necessary to prepare the way none shouted louder or ran faster than the servants of Radabullub Mitterjee, who probably thought that there ought to be a sensible difference between the apparel of a syce and pink brocade, and approved it. Radabullub did not always drive in the Red Road alone. Sometimes the cushion beside him was occupied by a very small and high-shouldered edition of himself, encased in blue satin with gold edgings. This Bahadur in embryo folded his arms like his father and looked at the Red Road with equal superciliousness; indeed, I fancy he took much the same views of life generally. They are early inherited in Bengal.

But the ladies, the Mesdames Mitterjee, when they issued forth from the little silent yellow house, which they did but seldom, went most securely in charge and under cover, and Mrs. Browne might look in vain for any glimpse of their fascinations

THE LADIES WENT MOST SECURELY IN CHARGE AND UNDER COVER.

behind the purple curtains of their palanquins, as they passed her gate.

I don't know the name of the people on the other side, and neither does Mrs. Browne. They seemed to live a good deal in the veranda in an untidy way. Helen could always command a man asleep there in pyjamas from her drawing-room window, up to eleven o'clock in the morning. They paid no more attention to their compound than Radabullub did, but they had a leggy bay colt tied up there upon which the family lavished the tenderest affection. When the Brownes drove home in the early darkness from tennis, they could usually see a casual meal going on through an open window at which the discourse was very cheerful and general, the men in shirt-sleeves, the ladies posed negligently with their arms upon the table. There was a baby, a cracked piano, and a violin in the house, but the baby had a good constitution and went to bed at eight o'clock, and it did not seem to the Brownes, as they listened to the songs their neighbours sang after dinner, that the piano was very much out of tune. They were old old songs that everybody knew, sung with great spirit and energy, chiefly in chorus, and Mrs. Browne's slipper kept time to them with great enjoyment. A boisterous old song in Calcutta was a pleasant anomaly and struck through the mango trees like a voice from home. The hearts of the Brownes warmed towards their neighbours as they smote the languid air with "Do ye ken John Peel with his coat so gay?" and as it came again and again, Mr. and Mrs. Browne smiled at each other and joined softly in the chorus, being comforted thereby. It was rather an additional attraction that these harmonies grew a little beery later in the evening. Young Browne could drink beer in Calcutta only under pain of his own later displeasure—a bitter thing for an Englishman.

They were jockeys, these neighbours of the Brownes'—from Australia very likely, with the last batch of Waler horses. They belonged to the class Calcutta knows collectively, as a sub-social element, that nevertheless has its indeterminate value, being white, or nearly so, as a rule. The aristocracy of the class is probably represented by the commissariat sergeants and the local police, and I have no doubt it observes its rules of precedence, though it is unlikely that Mrs. Browne's neighbours had much regard for them. On certain days of the year Calcutta makes brief acquaintance with "Light Blue and Canary," or "Green Pink Sleeves," but his wife and baby go on, one might say, without official sanction of any sort; they are permitted. So it doesn't matter to anybody what Light Blue and Canary's Christian name is—his cap and sleeves are enough. Occasionally the reporters are obliged to find it out when Light Blue and Canary breaks his wretched neck and half ruins a beautiful horse, and the public have to be informed of it. Then his friends dress Light Blue and Canary in mufti and bury him early next morning in Circular Road Cemetery, and there is the most annoying confusion when both he and his horse have to be scratched for the afternoon's races. As to the wife and baby under these circumstances, they still go on, it is supposed.

I regret to say that the Brownes were bounded on the north by a bustee. It is not necessary to explain that a bustee is an unsavoury place, the word has a taste and a smell of its own. One is always aware of the vicinity of a bustee, chiefly because of the bovine nature of the fuel it consumes. It is impossible to put it less vulgarly than that. All over Calcutta, in the cold weather, there hangs at set of sun a blue cloud of smoke with an acrid smell. It offends the nostrils of the very Viceroy, yet it is not in the power of any municipal Commissioner to put out the fires that send it up. It curls through a thousand roofs, the tiled roofs of the country, representing much humble comfort and many humble dinners, and every morning on the Maidan you may see ugly old women stooping to collect the material for it. Bustees, moreover, are never drained. They and their inhabitants fester comfortably through the long blue and green Indian days unconscious that their proximity does not enhance rents.

Mrs. Browne found her bustee neighbours more approachable. Her dressing-room window overlooked the place and gave her a point of speculation which she enjoyed quite shamelessly. A young papoia tree flourished in a corner of the roof she looked down upon, and various forms of vegetables fringed it. It was the daily promenade of the family cock, and occasionally a black goat took the air there. The cock flew up, but the goat always made use of the family staircase. The family lived mostly in the yard—three old women and five babies. The old women wore various kinds of rags, the babies were uniformly dressed in a string. The biggest baby carried the littlest about, astride her hip, and they all played together in one corner, where they made marvels in mud, just as children who wear clothes do. The old women scolded them severally and collectively, especially when they came and teased for breakfast with pathetic hands upon their little round stomachs. The oldest of the old women cooked the breakfast, and she would not have it hurried. She cooked it in a single pot that stood on a mud fireplace in the middle of the yard, squatting before it, feeding the flames with one hand and stirring the mess with the other. Helen could see what she put in it—rice, and more rice, and yellow dhol, and last of all pieces of fish. As she cooked the woman looked up at Helen now and then and smiled, amused that she should be interested in so poor an occupation—a memsahib! And the babies, when they discovered her, stood open-mouthed and gazed, forgetting the pot. In the house they divided it upon plantain leaves, a popular dinner service in Bengal; and when the babies issued forth again, in file, their appearance was quite aldermanic. The old women perhaps reposed, the sun grew hot on the window-ledge, and Helen thought of other things to do. In the evening, though, when the hibiscus bushes threw long shadows across the garden path, and Helen waited for her lord by the gate as a bride will, the babies came round through devious lanes to assert themselves as the same babies of the morning and eligible for pice. Helen felt an elementary joy in bestowing it, and the babies received it solemnly, as entirely their due, with little salaams for form's sake. There was tremendous interest on both sides, but beyond the statement that the babies lived in the little house, and the memsahib in the big one, conversation was difficult, and Helen thought with concern of the vocabulary that would be necessary in order to teach them about man's chief end. They came every day to watch the going forth of the Brownes in the tum-tum, and made a silent, open eyed, admiring little group beside the gate, at which the pony usually shied. Then young Browne would crack his whip in the air very fiercely indeed, and address them in language that sounded severe, though it had no perceptible effect. Even the babies in Bengal accept the sahib as a blustering, impolite person of whom nobody need be afraid.

And then opposite, across the weedy road and the stagnant ditch, a riotous Rajah resided, in a wonderful castellated place with four or five abandoned acres around it. The Rajah was very splendid and important. He had a slouching guard at his gate with a gun, who probably bullied the dhoby; and when he went abroad in the evenings, four badly uniformed horsemen, and no less, pranced uncertainly behind his carriage. The Rajah gave entertainments to European gentlemen of circumstance, whereat I do not think any single variety of food or drink procurable in Calcutta was omitted; but ladies did not participate, except, of course, those who contributed to the entertainment—the ladies of the nautch, or those of a stray theatrical company whose performances the Rajah fancied. In return the Rajah was invited to evening parties at Government House, where he appeared in a turban and diamonds, supremely oiled and scented, stood about in corners with his hands behind his back, and never for an instant dreamed in his disdainful Hindu soul of eating at the Viceroy's supper-table. At the end of the cold weather he went back to his own state, where he sat on the floor and hatched treason against the British with both majesty and comfort. In the evening his domain was dotted with the cooking-fires of his people, who made a sort of tented field of it. The wind blew the smoke across the Brownes' compound, causing young Browne to use language uncomplimentary to Rajahs, and that was all they ever had to do with this one.

I mention the local isolation of these young people because it is typical of Calcutta, where nobody by any chance ever leans over anybody else's garden gate. Doubtless this has its advantages—they are probably official—but Helen, not being official, found it cramping.

There was always the garden, though; she had that much liberty. The garden had begun with the Brownes, it was a contemporary success. There had been desolation, but you have heard how they engaged a mallie. Desolation fled before the mallie by daily degrees, though he was seldom seen in pursuit of it. When gardeners work in Christendom, this one sought repose and the balmy hubble-bubble, or bathed and oiled and ate in his little mud house under the pipal tree. It was very early in the morning, at crow-caw one might say in poetic reference to the dawn in India, that the mallie scratched and scraped along the garden beds with his wonderful little trowel, and spoke to the flowers so that they sprang up to answer him. When the shadow of the house fell on the hibiscus bushes he came out again, and slaked the hot beds with water from the tank in many buckets. Here and there he stooped over them like a glistening brown toad-stool, but Helen never knew what he did or his reason for doing it—that was hid with the mallie-lok.

As to the garden, there was not a tropical seed in it, they were all English flowers, which made the mallie's excellent understanding with them more remarkable, for they spoke a different language. It was not much of a garden, there was absolutely no order or arrangement—it would have worried me—but the Brownes planted a vast amount of interest and affection and expectation in it; and it all grew. There were such nasturtiums as Helen longed to show her mother, there were phloxes white and purple, pansies too, and pinks, and not a quiet corner but was fragrant with mignonette. A row of sunflowers tilted tall against the side of the house, and they actually had corn-bottles, and balsams and daisies. Violets too—violets in exile, violets in pots, with the peculiar property that violets sometimes have in India, of bringing tears to the eyes if one bends over them.

The Brownes began by counting them—the first pansy-bud was an event, and I have heard references between them to "the day the sunflower came out." They chronicled daily at breakfast: "Two nasturtiums and a pink," "two pinks, three nasturtiums, and the monthly rose," with great gratulation, while I am convinced neither of them looked twice at the fine bunch I sent round occasionally from my garden while their garden was growing. It grew so fast, their garden, that presently, if you met them in society, they could talk of nothing else. It was new to them, this friendly solace of the flowers of home. One would have thought it specially invented for their honeymoon, whereas the rest of us demanded it every cold weather, as regularly as the punkah on the fifteenth of March. Mrs. Browne used to go about saying what a wonderful amount of comfort one could get out of a verbena, if it were only the right colour, without the slightest suspicion of the triteness of the remark; and young Browne would show you his home-grown button-hole, as if no other man in the place possessed one. It was eminently good for them, as it is for all of us. To some of us, you know, England at last becomes a place where one dies daily of bronchitis, and is obliged to do without a kitmutgar; but this never happens if every cold weather one plants one's self round about with English flowers. They preserve the remnant of grace which is left in the Anglo-Indian soul, and keep it homesick, which is its one chance of salvation. Young Browne seldom said anything cynical in the garden, and as for Helen, it was simply Canbury to her. She could always go down and talk of home to her friends in the flower-beds, who were so steadfastly gay, and tell them, as she often did, how brave and true it was of them to come so far from England, forgetting, perhaps, that from a climatic point of view nasturtiums like heathendom. And in the evening the smoke of the hubble-bubble was lost in the fragrance of the garden.

Mrs. Browne says that if I am writing about their compound, I ought not to omit to mention the fowl-yard, which was situated at one end of it, near the stable. It was another experiment in economy—the cook used such a quantity of eggs that the Brownes saw no reason why they should not be produced on the premises. So they enclosed a fowl-yard and stocked it, and the cock vied with the crows in informing them of the earliest hint of daylight. But the Brownes do not now advise the keeping of fowls on the ground of economy; they say, indeed, that only the very rich can afford to keep them. It seems that the syce kindly supplied their food out of the pony's gram, charging the deficit to the memsahib, who also paid liberally for barley, a visionary provision at which her birds had never a pick. They were, notwithstanding, sound healthy hens, and the marvel was that they did not lay—except an egg or two a week for pure ostentation. Kali Bagh was doing a good business with the rest, supplying them to Mrs. Browne at full market rates, and to Mrs. Green Pink Sleeves at about half, to secure her custom. The hens in the meantime clucked cheerfully, and Helen was in a parlous state when in the end they had to be cut off untimely and stewed. "But with ruin staring us in the face," she said, "what else could we do!"

This will serve as an explanation to posterity, if any should inquire why it was that toward the end of the nineteenth century in Bengal only Members of Council were in the habit of keeping hens.

CHAPTER XV.

THE cold weather is not a season of unqualified delight in Calcutta, in spite of the glorious coming of the Raj into his winter palace, and the consequent nautch. The cold weather has its trifling drawbacks. The mosquitoes and the globe-trotters are so bad then, that some people have been known to prefer the comparative seclusion they enjoy when the thermometer stands at 103° in the shade, when the mosquitoes have gone to the Hills, pursuing the fat of the land, and the globe-trotters to northern latitudes seeking publishers.

It may be set down as an axiom that the genus globe-trotter is unloved in Calcutta. It may also be set down as an axiom that it is his own fault, for reasons that may appear. But there are globe-trotters and globe-trotters, and of some the offence is venial—nothing more, perhaps, than that they make the hotels uncomfortable, and put up the price of native curiosities. And some are amusing in their way, and some bring English conversation with them; and I have known one to be grateful for such poor favours as he received, but he was not a globe-trotter that took himself seriously. It is also possible, I believe, if one lives in India long enough, to come across a globe-trotter who is modest and teachable, but we have been out here only twenty-two years, and I am going home without having seen one.

The Parliamentary globe-trotter represents the species which has impressed itself most upon Anglo-India. He has given a character and a finish, as it were, to the whole genus. He has made himself so prevalent and of such repute that, meeting any stalwart stranger of cheerful aggressive countenance at His Excellency's board, we are apt to inquire amongst ourselves, "of what district?" hoping for reasons private to Anglo-India, that it may not be a Radical one. The initials "M. P." have become cabalistic signs. They fill us with the memory of past reproaches, and the certainty of coming ones. They stand for much improper language, not entirely used in India. They inspire a terrible form of fear, the apprehension of the unknown, for the potentials of the globe-trotting M. P. are only revealed in caucus, the simple Anglo-Indian cannot forecast them. Regularly with December he arrives, yearly more vigorous, more inquisitive, more corpulent, more disposed to make a note of it. We have also noticed an annual increase in his political importance, his loquacity, and his capacity to be taken in, which he would consider better described as ability to form an independent opinion. At this moment we are looking forward to the last straw in the shape of Lord Randolph Churchill.

Mr. Jonas Batcham, M. P., was not so great a man as Lord Randolph Churchill when he arrived in Calcutta last cold weather; what he may have become since, by the diligent use of his Indian experiences and information collected "on the spot," I have no means of knowing. George Browne's father was one of Mr. Batcham's constituents, and this made Mr. Batcham willing to stay with the Brownes while he was inspecting Calcutta, and collecting advice to offer to the Viceroy. He kindly put up with them for several weeks, and when he went away he gave four annas to the sweeper.

Mr. Batcham occasionally described himself as one of the largest manufacturers in the north of England, and though the description leaves something to be desired, it does suggest Mr. Batcham. He was large, imposing in front, massive in the rear. He was gray-whiskered, of a rubicund countenance, of a double chin. He wore a soft felt hat a little on one side, and his hands in his pockets, a habit which always strikes me as characteristic of a real manufacturer. He was very well informed—they all are. He had a suave yet off-hand manner, a business-like smile, a sonorous bass voice, and a deep, raging and unquenchable thirst for facts.

Mr. Batcham was very much aware of his value to the Brownes as a new arrival from England—a delicate appreciation of himself, which is never wanting to a globe-trotter. Mr. Batcham blandly mixed himself up with the days when people came round the Cape in a sailing-ship, or across the sands of Suez on a camel, and invested himself with all the sentimental interest that might attach to a fellow-countryman discovered in the interior of Bechuanaland. A generous philanthropic instinct rose up and surged within him as he thought, in the midst of his joyful impressions of the tropics, how much pleasure his mere presence was probably imparting. He almost felt at moments as if he had undertaken this long, arduous, and expensive journey in the interest of the Brownes as well as those of his constituents.

The great concourse of his kind in the hotels, the telegrams in the morning's *Englishman*, the presence of overland cheese, the electric light, and the modern bacteriologist, should have rebuked this pretension somewhat, but it is doubtful if anything could do that. "I saw both your parents before I sailed," said Mr. Batcham, in liberal compensation, as it were, for his first dinner, "and left them quite well." And when young Browne replied that since then he was sorry to say his mother had had a bad attack of bronchitis, however, by the last mail they had heard she was getting over it, the damper was only momentary, and Mr. Batcham proceeded to inform them that Parnell was dead.

Oh, he was sufficiently communicative, that Batcham, sufficiently willing to impart his impressions, as expansive, by the time they got to the joint, as ever you liked. He had a certain humorous perception of what was expected of him. As a "globe-trotter," he was familiar with the expression, and applied it to himself jovially without shame. The perception was incomplete, and therefore did not make Mr. Batcham uncomfortable. However, he understood perfectly that globe-trotters as a class were frequently and prodigiously taken in. Acting upon this, Mr. Batcham made his incredulity the strong point of his intelligence, and received certain kinds of information with an almost obvious wink. That very first night at dinner, he proclaimed himself to the Brownes a person who could not be imposed upon—useless to try. "Coming down from Benares," said Mr. Batcham, "I travelled with a couple of men who said they were indigo planters, and so they may have been for all I know. Anyhow they spotted me to be a globe-trotter—said they knew it by the kind of hat I wore—and then they proceeded to fill me up about the country. One fellow said he didn't own a yard of indigo land himself; always got the peasants to grow it for him; and the other went into some complicated explanation of how blue indigo was got by squeezing green leaves. All sorts of yarns they told me. How the natives wouldn't eat factory sugar, because they believed it defiled in the preparation, but preferred drain water to any other. How a Hill woman would make nothing of carrying me on her back a thousand feet steady climbing. How in the part of the country we were going through, it was so hot in June that men had servants to drench them with water in the middle of the night regularly. I saw they were enjoying it, so I let them go on—in fact I rather drew them out, especially about indigo. Took it all in and cried for more, as the babies do for patent medicine. Then when we got out at the station here I said, 'Thank you gentlemen, for all the "information" you have given me. It has been very entertaining. Of course you will understand, however, that I don't believe a word of it. Good morning!' I fancy those two indigo planters will hesitate before they tackle their next globe-trotter. I never saw men look more astonished in my life."

"I should think so!" exclaimed young Browne; "what they told you was wholly and literally true."

Mr. Jonas Batcham looked at his host with a humorous twinkle. "Don't *you* try it on," said he.

Although Mr. Batcham found it advisable to shed so much of the light of his countenance upon the Brownes, as I have said, it was native India that he came to see and report upon. And to this end he had read one or two of the most recent publications on the subject, works produced, that is to say, by our very most recent visitors, smoking from the London press before their authors' names were dry in the Bombay hotel register. These volumes had given Mr. Batcham comprehensive ideas of native India, and he knew that between Cape Comorin and Peshawur were lying two hundred and fifty million people urgently in need of his benevolent interference. They were of different races, religions, customs, and languages—Mr. Batcham had expected to find that and had equipped himself for it by learning the names of almost all of them. He was acquainted with several of their gods, he knew that Ganesh had an elephant's head, that Kali loved the blood of goats, and that Krishna was the source of all things. He was aware also that it was not proper to speak of Mohammedan rajahs or Hindoo sheiks, and he had informed himself upon the subject of Eastern polygamy. Mr. Batcham was a person of intelligence who did not travel without preparing his mind, and though according to his own modest statement there was still a great deal that he didn't know about India, it was open to an appreciative person to doubt this. In one direction Mr. Batcham had prepared his mind with particular care, so that the very slightest impression could not fail to be deep and permanent—in the direction of the wrongs, the sufferings, the grievances under British rule, of his two hundred and fifty million fellow subjects in India. Upon this point Mr. Batcham was tender and susceptible to a degree that contrasted singularly with his attitude towards the rest of the world, which had never found reason to consider him a philanthropist. This solicitude about his Indian brethren was the more touching perhaps on that account, and the more remarkable because it found only cause for grief and remorse in the condition of native India. Any trifling benefits that have accrued to the people through British administration—one thinks of public works, sanitation, education, courts of justice, and so forth—Mr. Batchám either depreciated or ignored. We had done so little, so "terribly little," as Mr. Batcham put it, compared with what we might have done, and of that little so much had been done badly! Daily Mr. Batcham discovered more things that had been neglected, and more things that had been done badly. He looked for them carefully, and whenever he found one he wept audibly and made a note of it. Time would fail me, as the preacher says, to recount all the iniquities that came under Mr. Batcham's observation during the weeks he spent in India, and I am unworthy to describe the energy and self-forgetfulness with which he threw himself into the task of "investigating" them, always with the most copious notes. There was the fact that both opium and country spirit were sold to the innocent Hindu, not only with Government cognisance but actually under Government regulations, the outrage to every Briton's conscience being that revenues were derived therefrom. The Government fattened, in Mr. Batcham's graphic figure, upon the physical misery and moral degradation of its helpless wards. Mr. Batcham searched his mind in vain to find a parallel to this, strange as it may seem in connection with his accurate acquaintance with the amount of excise paid by his brother philanthropists in British beer. The position of the Government of India was monstrously unique. If Mr. Batcham were the Government of India, he would scorn to fill the treasury with the returns of vice. Mr. Batcham would tax nothing but virtue and the pay of Government servants. And though Mr. Batcham was not the Government of India, was he not entitled from his seat in the British House of Commons and the depth of his righteous indignation, to call the Government of India to account? For what else then did Jonas Batcham, M. P., one of the largest manufacturers in the north of England, with little time to spare, undertake this arduous and expensive journey to the East? Oh, there were many things that grieved him, Mr. Batcham, many things to which he felt compelled to take exception, of which he felt compelled to make a note. He was grieved at the attitude of the Government towards the native press in the matter of seditious and disloyal editorials, scattered by thousands under shelter of the vernacular

MR. JONAS BATCHAM, M.P.

amongst an ignorant and fanatic population. Mr. Batcham did not wish to see this practice discouraged. The liberty of the press Mr. Batcham considered the foundation stone of the liberty of the subject—let the people raise their voice. Grieved also was Mr. Bateham at the cold shoulder turned by Government to the Indian Congress—that noble embodiment of the struggles and aspirations of a subject people. Mr. Bateham thought that all native movements, movements that marked progress and emancipation, should be warmly encouraged. The suspicion of intrigue was an absurd one, and this was not merely a matter of opinion with Mr. Bateham. He had it from a native gentleman prominently connected with the Congress. Mr. Batcham had brought a letter of introduction to the native gentleman—Mr. Debendra Lal Banerjee—and Mr. Debendra Lal Banerjee had given him such an "inside" view of the methods and aims of the Congress as gratified Mr. Bateham exceedingly. Mr. Batcham found Mr. Debendra Lal Banerjee the soul of hospitality, very appreciative of Mr. Bateham's illustrious position, anxious to gratify Mr. Bateham's intelligent curiosity by every means in his power, and brimming over with loyalty and enthusiasm for the institutions which Mr. Batcham represented. And when Mr. Debendra Lal Banerjee declared, in admirably fluent English, that the Congress was inspired by the single thought of aiding and upholding, so far as lay in its humble power, the administration of the British Government—to which every member felt himself personally and incalculably indebted—Mr. Bateham rejoined audibly, begged Mr. Debendra Lal Banerjee to believe that he was proud to be his fellow-subject, friend, brother, and made a copious note of it.

Naturally, under these circumstances, Mr. Batcham would find a very severe grief in the relations existing between European and native society here, and naturally he could not find words to express his indignation at the insolent and indifferent front of his fellow countrymen towards the people of India.

"All," said Mr. Batcham, "on account of a brown skin!" He could not understand it—no, he could *not* understand it! But if Mr. Batcham could not understand it, he could do what lay in his power as a person of generous sympathies and high moral tone to alleviate it, and he threw himself into the task. Mr. Debendra Lal Banerjee gave him no invitation which he did not accept, offered him no opportunity which he did not profit by. He drove with Mr. Debendra Lal Banerjee, he accompanied him to the races, to the native theatre, to the English theatre, to the Kalighat, to the Botanical Gardens, to various interesting religious and family festivals among Mr. Debendra Lal Banerjee's immediate social circle; also, on occasions upon which the Brownes made immoderate thanksgiving, he dined with this Indian gentleman and his emancipated wife, who was allowed to appear in public, where she smiled a great deal and said nothing whatever. Mrs. Debendra Lal Banerjee had not been very long emancipated, however, and it was in complimenting his Indian friend upon having so charming a lady to be his companion and helpmeet, as Mr. Batcham put it, that he observed the first and only slight chill—it is impossible for Indian gentlemen to freeze—in Mr. Debendra Lal Banerjee's responses. If Mr. Batcham could have known how Mrs. Debendra Lal Banerjee was pinched for that compliment!

I suppose that the entertainment and education of Mr. Jonas Batcham, M. P., could hardly have cost Mr. Debendra Lal Banerjee less than four or five hundred rupees when he added it up, but if he had the least desire to see disaffection and sedition properly encouraged among his countrymen, or took the smallest satisfaction in the aggravated annoyance and embarrassment of the Government of India by Her Majesty's most loyal Opposition, he must have felt that he had done much to further these things, and considered the money well invested. Mr. Jonas Batcham, the incredulous, certainly left his hands so brimful of native hypothecations that it would have been impossible to lodge another lie in him anywhere. Urbane, impressively self-satisfied, and well oiled for work, Mr. Jonas Batcham, M. P., being towed homeward down the river Hooghly, was a sight which must have brought tears of pious thanksgiving to the eyes of his amiable native friend upon the wharf. Nor was Mr. Debendra Lal Banerjee without his private reward. Mr. Batcham, in departing, clasped him figuratively to his capacious bosom, and told him movingly that if ever he came to England the Batchams would hasten collectively to do likewise. Mr. Batcham's wife and family and friends would await that event with an impatience which Mr. Banerjee must make as brief as possible. Nothing would give Mr. Batcham greater pleasure than to receive Mr. Banerjee in his home and show him over his "works," or perhaps—jocularly—to take him to a sitting of the House to hear his humble servant badger the Secretary of State. And Mr. Banerjee responded suitably that simply to hear the eloquent addresses of his honourable friend would be amply sufficient to induce him to undertake the journey, and that to witness the domestic happiness of this honourable friend would be only too much joy—he was unworthy. And they parted in mutual dolours. I anticipate, however, Mr. Batcham is not gone yet.

CHAPTER XVI.

I HAVE not yet mentioned the one matter of all the grievous matters that came under his observation in India, about which Mr. Batcham was particularly grieved. So bitterly, so loudly, and so persistently did he grieve about this, that one might almost have thought he came out for the purpose, absurd as it may seem. I cannot do better than describe it in Mr. Batcham's own terms as "the grinding of the faces of the poor, through our culpable neglect in failing to provide India with the humane limitations of a Factories Act." For years past English labour had been thus happily conditioned, and who could measure the benefit to the toiling millions on whose behalf the law had been made! It was incalculable. As a matter of fact the only result of its operation, which could be computed with accuracy, was to be found in the out-turn of the mills. There Mr. Batcham knew to a yard how valuable the Factories Act was to the operatives; but this was not a view of the question upon which he dwelt much in India. While he was with us indeed all practical considerations were swallowed up, for Mr. Batcham, in the contemplation of the profundity of our iniquity in allowing the factories of this country pretty much to manage their own affairs. He did not even permit himself to consider that the enormous product of Indian looms, together with the cheapness of the cost of production, was having a prejudicial effect upon the market. He certainly never mentioned it. His business was with the poor, the down-trodden, the victims of the rapacity of the capitalist, as much among her Majesty's subjects on India's coral strand as in the crowded tenements of Manchester or Birmingham. His duty towards these unfortunates was plain, and heaven forbid that he should think of anything but his duty!

And so Mr. Batcham lamented high and low over the woes of the unprotected factory "hand" in India. He began his lament as soon as ever he was informed—though he knew it before—that protection did not exist; on the face of it, oppression must then be rampant. He himself was in the trade, he knew the temptations of the capitalist, and he would not go so far as to say that, if a wise and just law did not prevent him, the exigencies of the market would never lead him to be—inconsiderate—toward his *employés*. Reflect then upon the result of almost unlimited power in the hands of the Indian manufacturer!

This being Mr. Batcham's pronounced opinion, even before he gave his personal attention to the subject of Indian manufactures, his investigations naturally had the effect of heightening it—one might say they were undertaken with that object. They did not heighten it, however, as satisfactorily or as definitely as Mr. Batcham could have wished. After inspecting a cotton factory in Bombay, a woollen factory in Cawnpore, a jute factory in Calcutta, he found that the notes left too much to the imagination; and it would be useless to appeal to the imagination of the House; the House was utterly devoid of it. True, he had seen hundreds of operatives working in miserable nakedness under the unpitying eye of a Eurasian overseer; but then it was certainly very warm, and the overseer had not been sufficiently considerate to kick any of them in Mr. Batcham's presence. They certainly began early and worked late, but then they ate and slumbered in the middle of the day, chewing betel for casual delectation the rest of the time. Something might possibly be done with that if he were careful to avoid dwelling upon the siesta, and he would be sorry to lay stress upon any trifling amelioration in the condition of these poor wretches. Mr. Batcham pondered long upon the betel-nut, but saw no salvation there. If it could be proved that these miserable beings were compelled to resort to an injurious stimulant to keep their flagging energies up to the incredible amount of labour required of them—and Mr. Batcham had no doubt whatever that this was the case—it might be useful to cite the betel-nut, but there seemed to be a difficulty about proving it. The only tangible deplorable fact that Mr. Batcham had to go upon, was that the pay of a full-grown operative, not a woman or a child, but a man, was represented by the shockingly incredible sum of eight annas—eightpence!—a day! When he heard this Mr. Batcham thought of the colossal wages paid to factory hands in England and shuddered. He was so completely occupied in shuddering over this instance of the rapacity of the Indian manufacturer, that the statement of what it cost the same operative to live according to the immemorial custom of his people—about five shillings a month—entirely escaped his observation. In the stress of his emotion Mr. Batcham failed to notice one or two other facts that would have tended to alleviate it, the fact that a factory operative is paid twice as much as a domestic servant and three times as much as a cooly, though the cost of life weighs no more heavily upon him than upon them. The fact that he often works only two or three months of the year at gunny-bags, and spends the rest of his time in the more leisurely and congenial scratching of his fields, and above all, the fact that in India the enterprises of the foreigner accommodate themselves—not of philantrophy but of necessity—to the customs of the country. It is not the service of the sahib, with his few thousand personal establishments, his few hundred plantations and shops, his few dozen factory chimneys rising along the Hooghly, tainting the sea breeze of Bombay, that can revolutionise their way of life for two hundred and fifty million people with whom custom is religion and religion is more than rice. But Mr. Batcham had no heart to be comforted by such trivialities. He made emotional notes, dwelt upon the "eight anna daily pittance," and felt a still more poignant private grief that there was no cause for louder sorrow.

At first Mr. Dabendra Lal Benerjee was inclined to assure his honourable friend that there was not the slightest need for any beneficent interference with the condition of his humble compatriots, to praise but to deprecate Mr. Batcham's enthusiasm in the matter, and to point out that the only true and lasting elevation of her Majesty's most loyal subjects in India must be brought about through that much maligned and little understood body, the Indian Congress. But it was a very, very short time indeed before Mr. Debendra Lal Banerjee found himself in full union with the noble aims of this British benefactor. He had only to learn—and he learned very quickly—that his sympathy would be appreciated, to bestow it with all the gushing fulness of which the Bengali soul is capable, and Mr. Debendra Lal Banerjee's sympathy was invaluable to Mr. Batcham. It disclosed points of weakness in the Indian factory system that would otherwise have escaped his observation to this day, and suggested interpretations which no simple-minded Briton would have thought of alone. And it divined Mr. Batcham's dissatisfaction that he could not be more dissatisfied with remarkable accuracy.

In taking measures—Bengali measures—to secure the sympathy of the travelling British M. P. with the grand progressive movement of Bengali patriotism, it is highly advisable to discover as soon as possible whether he has any little "movement" of his own in contemplation which might receive a slight impetus with advantage. It is then generally possible to combine the two, to arrange reciprocal favours, to induce the globe-trotting potentate to take "broader views." Mr. Debendra Lal Banerjee put the whole of his time, and a vocabulary which no English dictionary could improve, at Mr. Batcham's disposal, to convince him that this factory grievance was one of the first which the Indian Congress would press upon the ear of the Raj, once it had an official right to make suggestions to that honourable organ. Although Mr. Banerjee quite agreed with Mr. Batcham that it would be inadvisable to wait until that happened, he would like Mr. Batcham to understand how close the interests of the British manufacturer lay to the bosom of the Indian Congress—though of course Mr. Banerjee designated them as the wrongs of the native operatives. In the meantime, however, his honourable friend was naturally restless, naturally desired to lend his own helping hand to the cause he had at heart. Mr. Banerjee was overcome by the sublimity of Mr. Batcham's devotion, and suggested a little evidence acquired personally. If it were possible for Mr. Batcham to *converse* with any of these unfortunate people!

"It's the terrible disadvantage of not knowing the language!" responded Mr. Batcham, in a tone which suggested that the language ought to be supplied to Members of Parliament. "I *have* conversed with 'em through another man, but it was very unsatisfactory. Couldn't get anything definite. The fact is, Mr. Banerjee, the other man was an Anglo-Indian, and I've no doubt the poor wretches suffered from a sort of unconscious intimidation!"

Mr. Banerjee shook his head. The head had a black silk hat on it, and shook as impressively as it might have done in Lombard street or Westminster. "I fear," said Mr. Banerjee, "that it is unhappily but too probable." Then he raised his eyebrows in a sadly submissive way, took out his pocket handkerchief and used it in a manner which suggested—very respectfully—a general deprecation of Anglo-Indians. Mr. Banerjee must have used it, I think, for this purpose. I doubt whether he is even yet sufficiently deteriorated by our civilisation to take out his handkerchief seriously

"Above all things," added Mr. Banerjee, thrusting his fat hand into the breast of his tightly-buttoned frock coat, and wrapping himself up in the situation, "above all things it is indispensable that your evidence shall be unbiassed in every particular. There is no doubt, I deplore to tell you, that here in India the poor and the needy amongst us will sometimes be wrongly influenced by the fear of being deprived of the staff of life. I have even known cases where, under unjust and reprehensible intimidation, *perjury*"—Mr. Banerjee's tone suggested, "I hardly expected you to believe it!"—"has been committed!"

"Dear me, I dare say," said Mr. Batcham, "that happens everywhere."

But Mr. Banerjee had more than sentimental reflections upon the moral turpitude of his fellow Aryans to contribute to the difficulty of his honourable friend. He had given his honourable friend's difficulty the very fullest attention. He had chased it through the most private labyrinth of his mind, where he had come into sudden and violent contact with Ambica Nath Mitter. And in the joyful shock of collision with Ambica Nath Mitter, Debendra Lal Banerjee had said to himself, "Why didn't I think of him before?"

"There is a very intelligent young man in my office," said Mr. Banerjee, "who was formerly employed as clerk in a jute mill here. I think he would most willingly obtain for you any grievances you may require." Mr. Banerjee spoke absent-mindedly, reflecting upon the qualifications of Ambica for the task.

"The statement of them," corrected Mr. Batcham.

"The statement of them—precisely, yes. Young Mitter has had all facilities for observing the oppression in the factories, and I have no doubt it made a deep impression upon his excellent heart. He speaks English also fairly well. I will send him to you."

"I should like very much to see Mr. Mitter," Mr. Batcham remarked. "Mitter, you said?"

"It will not be necessary to remember his name. Call him 'Baboo'; he will answer to plain 'Baboo.' I am sure he will remember well about the oppressions."

"I should be even better pleased," said Mr. Batcham, "if he brought two or three of the oppressed with him."

"I think he could also do that," replied Mr. Banerjee without hesitation.

Then Mr. Banerjee went away and explained Mr. Batcham's difficulty to Ambica Nath Mitter. Considering how discreetly Mr. Banerjee explained it, the sympathetic perception shown by Ambica Nath Mitter was extraordinary. It might possibly be explained by the fact that they both spoke Hindustani. At all events, Mr. Banerjee dismissed the young man of the excellent heart with the comfortable feeling that Mr. Batcham's difficulty would be solved quite inexpensively.

Two days after, Ambica presented himself at the residence of the Brownes, accredited to Mr. Batcham by Mr. Debendra Lal Banerjee. Mr. Browne had gone to office, Mrs. Browne had gone to shop. Mr. Batcham, ruddy and expansive in the thinnest of flannels, occupied a large portion of the small veranda alone. The time was most fortuitous, and Mr. Batcham received Mr. Banerjee's labour with an agreeable sense of freedom for the most searching investigations. Having well breakfasted, digested the morning paper, and fully smoked moreover, Mr. Batcham was in the mood for the most heartrending revelations.

Ambica was a prepossessing young man, Mr. Batcham thought. His lustrous long black hair was brushed smoothly back from a forehead that insisted on its guilelessness. His soft brown eyes were timid but trustful, and his ambient tissues spread themselves over features of the most engagingly aquiline character. He was just at the anti-protuberant stage of baboodom, there was no offence in his fatness. He wore spotless muslin draperies dependent from either shoulder, and his pen behind his ear. In his rear were three others much like himself, but less savoury, less lubricated, less comfortable in appearance. They impressed one as less virtuous too, but this was purely the result of adversity.

Mr. Batcham began by asking "Mr. Mitter" to sit down, which Mr. Mitter did with alacrity. Never in his life had Mr. Mitter been asked to sit down by a sahib before. Then Mr. Batcham took out his note-book and pencil, and said impressively to Mr. Mitter that above all things these men must understand that they were to tell the truth, the whole truth, and nothing but the truth with regard to the matters upon which he was about to question them. Then he questioned them.

Perhaps it is unnecessary to go into Mr. Batcham's questions. They were put with the fluency and precision of a man of business. Ambica Nath Mitter understood them perfectly, and ex-

IN HIS REAR WERE THREE OTHERS MUCH LIKE HIMSELF.

plained them admirably. They elicited exactly what Mr. Batcham wanted to know. His fat, red hand trembled with avidity as he set down fact after fact of the most "painful" description—or possibly it was agitated by an indignation which Mr. Batcham doubtless could not wholly suppress. And, indeed, the recital of the wrongs which these three miserable men had suffered under the cruel hand of the tyrannical sirdar,* and the indifferent eye of the callous sahib, would have moved an even less susceptible heart than that of a British manufacturer in the same line of business. One had been beaten with stripes—he showed Mr. Batcham the weal on his shoulder, and Mr. Batcham touched it, for the sake of the dramatic effect of saying so afterwards. Another had been compelled to work four hours a day overtime for a week without a piec of extra pay; the third had humbly begged for a day's leave to attend the burning of his grandmother, and when he returned had been abruptly and unjustly dismissed—the sahib had said he wished to see his face no more. It was useless to complain; the factory sahibs would cut their wages, and the other sahibs did not care. They were all poor men; they could not buy the law. At this point Mr. Batcham grew quite feverish. He unbuttoned his shirt-collar, and interspersed his notes with interjection-points. "This is better," he said to himself—"I mean worse, than I expected." The interview took a long time—quite three-quarters of an hour—but Mr. Batcham was distinctly of the opinion that it had not been misspent. And when Mr. Batcham closed his note-book, and said to Mr. Mitter that this was a very sad state of things, but that would do for the present, his three down-trodden Indian fellow-subjects knelt weeping and kissed the uppers of Mr.

* Native manager.

Batcham's broad British boots, invoking the secular blessings of heaven upon this "protector of the poor." Mr. Batcham had to shuffle his feet under his chair so suddenly that he nearly dislocated one of his knees. "Don't!" said he, "pray don't, not on any account!" And he raised them with his own hands, very nearly mingled his tears with theirs, and immediately afterwards made a most dramatic note of it.

Mr. Batcham had not breakfasted the next morning in fact, he was looking at his watch and wondering why the Brownes were always so confoundedly late with their meals when his bearer came up and inquired whether the sahib would see again the three "admi" * he had seen the day before, they waited below in the compound. Breakfast was still ten minutes off, and Mr. Batcham said he would go down. He went down, received the men with affability, and learned through his English-speaking bearer that they had been the victims of great injustice at the hands of Ambica Nath Mitter. This one, it seemed, had persuaded them to come to the sahib and leave work for the day on the promise not only of paying them their day's wages, but of making the matter right with the sirdar at the factory. Instead of which, he had paid them only half a day's wages, and when they returned that morning they found themselves dismissed. Therefore, knowing the heart of the sahib that it was full of mercy, they had come to cast themselves at his feet. They were all poor men, a very little would satisfy them—two rupees each perhaps.

"That's six rupees!" said Mr. Batcham seriously, "two rupees each would keep you for nearly a month in idleness. You can get employment much sooner than that." Mr. Batcham

* Persons.

knitted his philanthropic brow. "I'll see you after breakfast," he said, as the kitmutgar came to announce it.

The question of his duty in the matter of the six rupees so agitated Mr. Batcham that he consulted young Browne about it at the breakfast-table, and that is the reason why it is I, and not Mr. Batcham, who recount his experience with Ambica Nath Mitter to the public. Young Browne heard his guest politely and sympathetically through before he ventured to express an opinion. Even then he deferred it. "I'll have a look at your factory-wallahs," said young Browne. Presently he sent the bearer for them, who came up with two. The other, he said, had been taken with a sudden indisposition and had gone away.

Young Browne put up his eye-glass—he sometimes wore an eye-glass, it was the purest affectation—and looked at the victims of British oppression in India as they stood with their hands behind them in acute discomfort, twining and untwining their dusty toes. As he looked, a smile appeared under the eye-glass, which gradually broadened and broadened until it knocked the eye-glass out, and young Browne laughed until the tears came into his eyes. "It's too good!" said young Browne brokenly. "It's *too* good!" and laughed again until Mr. Batcham's annoyance became serious and obvious and it was necessary to explain.

"I don't know what these men may have learned *incidentally* about jute," said he wiping his eyes, "but that's not their occupation, Mr. Batcham, I—I happen to know their faces. They're both umidwallahs in Watson and Selwyn's, indigo people, next door to our place."

"Dear me, are you *sure?*" asked Mr. Batcham with a judicial contraction of his eyebrows. "What is an umidwallah?"

"Umid means hope—a man of hope. They come and ask to work in the office as a favour, and don't get any pay, expecting

THE OTHER HAD BEEN TAKEN WITH A SUDDEN INDISPOSITION AND HAD GONE AWAY.

to be taken on in case of a vacancy. These scoundrels have been in Watson and Selwyn's for the last year. I venture to state they've never been inside a jute mill in their lives."

"Tumera kam, k'on hai?" * asked young Browne mockingly of one baboo.

The baboo cast down his eyes nervously and said, "Wasson Sewwin company *kapas, sahib*," † and the other to the same question made the same answer. They were crushed and sorrowing baboos suffering under a cruel blow of fate. Why should it have been granted to only one of them to conclude to be indisposed at the right moment?

I am afraid the savage Anglo-Indian instinct arose in young Browne and caused him to tease those baboos a little that morning. It was very wrong of him doubtless, and then it led to the destruction of a number of Mr. Batcham's most interesting notes, which is another regretable fact. But the only person who really suffered was Ambica Nath Mitter. Mr. Batcham, of course, thought it his duty to inform Mr. Debendra Lal Banerjee of the whole unfortunate affair, and Mr. Debendra Lal Banerjee, in a white heat of indignation, which lasted several days, dismissed Ambica.

"How could I repose further trust in a man like that!" said Mr. Banerjee to Mr. Batcham. Besides, privately, Mr. Banerjee thought Ambica grasping. Mr. Banerjee had entirely intended that out of the five rupees Ambica received from him, the "factory wallahs" should be paid in full.

* Your work, what is it? † With Watson Selwyn Company.

CHAPTER XVII.

SOCIALLY, as I have said, Mr. Batcham represented one of our cold weather phenomena. They remain phenomena, the globe-trotters, notwithstanding the regularity of their reappearance, flashing like November comets across the tranquil Anglo-Indian mind, which refuses to accustom itself to one class of its heavenly visitors any more than to the other. It is inaccurate, however, to use any figure of speech which represents Mr. Batcham as a meteoric body. He had his prescribed orbit—it is all laid down in Murray—and he circled through it, revolving regularly upon the axis of an excellent digestion with great gravity of demeanor. When he appeared upon Calcutta's horizon, Calcutta could only put up a helpless eyeglass and writhe wearily until the large red luminary dipped again in the west. Then for a week it set at nought and mocked him. Then it unanimously forgot him, and was only reminded of his unnecessary existence afterward by the acerbity of the *Englishman's* comments upon his intelligence, which was entirely deserved.

It was interesting to watch Mr. Batcham in the process of forming an opinion of Anglo-Indian society; that is, of making his observations match the rags and tags of ideas about us which he had gathered together from various popular sources before coming out. They were curious, Mr. Batcham's impressions, and they led him into even greater discreetness of conduct than would naturally be shown by one of the largest manufacturers of the North of England, of sound evangelical views and inordinate abdominal development, travelling in search of Truth. In the doubtful mazes of the flippant Anglo-Indian capital Mr. Batcham felt that it behoved him to wrap the capacious mantle of his virtue well about him and to be very heedful of his walk and conversation. He kept a sharp eye open for invitations to light and foolish behaviour on the part of possible Mrs. Hawksbees and Mrs. Mallowes whom he met at Government House, and he saw a great many. When Lady Blebbins asked him if Mrs. Batcham were with him, Mr. Batcham said to himself, "There is certainly something behind *that!*" and when Mrs. Walter Luff, who is as proper as proper can be, proposed to drive him about the Maidan in her barouche, Mr. Batcham said coyly but firmly that Mrs. Luff must excuse him for asking, but was her husband to be of the party? Some such uncompromising front Mr. Batcham showed to temptation in forms even more insidious than these. I need not say that he never in any case failed to make a careful note of it; and I have no doubt that long before this reaches you the glaring facts will have been confided with inculpating initials to the sympathetic British public through the columns of the *Times* over the bashful signature of Jonas Batcham.

Mr. Batcham saw no reason for concealing his preconceived ideas of Anglo-Indian society from any of the Anglo-Indians he met—our morals embarrassed him as little as he supposed that they embarrassed us. He discussed them with us in candid sorrow, he enquired of us about them, he told us exactly to what extent he considered the deterioration of the ethical sense amongst us was to be ascribed to the climate. He spoke calmly and dispassionately about these things, as an indifferent foreigner might speak about the exchange value of the rupee or the quality of Peliti's ices. He seemed to think that as a subject of conversation we should rather like it, that his investigations would have a morbid interest for us. It was reported that he approached an A. D. C. in uniform with the tentative remark that he believed Simla was a very immoral place, and that the A. D. C. in uniform made with great difficulty three wrinkles in his forehead—it is almost impossible for an A. D. C. in uniform to wrinkle himself — and said with calm surprise, "WE are Simla," subsequently reporting the matter to the Viceroy and suggesting the bastinado. The story adds that the Viceroy said that nothing could be done, because an M. P. was certain to go home and tell. But this is the merest rumour.

Mr. Batcham found the Brownes disappointing in this respect as he found them disappointing in other respects. They were not extravagant, they were not in debt, and Mrs. Browne neither swore nor smoked cigarettes nor rode in steeplechases. Mr. Batcham investigated them until he found them quite hopelessly proper, when he put them down as the shining and praiseworthy exception that proves the rule, and restricted his enquiries to the private life of their neighbours. Thus, driving upon the Red Road in the evening and encountering a smart young pair in a cabriolet, Mr. Batcham would demand, "Who is that lady?"

"That's Mrs. Finsley-Jones," Mrs. Browne would reply.

"And with whom," Mr. Batcham would continue severely, "is Mrs. Finsley-Jones driving?"

"With Mr. Finsley-Jones."

"Oh—ah! and who is that lady in the straw hat on the grey cob?"

"Mrs. MacDonald, I think."

"And the gentleman?"

"Her husband."

"Really! you are quite sure it is her husband, Mrs. Browne. I understood that in India ladies seldom rode with their husbands."

"On the contrary, Mr. Batcham," Helen returned innocently, "horses are apt to be so skittish in India that it isn't really safe to go out without a man, and of course one would rather have one's husband than anybody else."

"Not at all, I assure you, Mrs. Browne. I understand that quite the opposite opinion prevails among the ladies of Calcutta, and I can depend upon the source of my information. Now these two people in the dog cart—they are actually flirting with each other in broad daylight! It is impossible," said Mr. Batcham, with an accent of grave deprecation, "that they can be married."

"Mr. and Mrs. Tubbs," said Helen shortly, "they were married about the same time as we were. Why shouldn't they flirt with each other if they want to?"

"Certainly not," said young Browne, who was driving. "It leads to incorrect ideas of their relations, you see. Fact is, I caught Tubbs kissing his wife in a dark corner of the Maidan by the Cathedral myself the other evening, and it was such a very dark corner that if I hadn't happened to be lighting a cheroot at the time, I wouldn't have believed that Tubbs was Tubbs any more than Mr. Batcham does. Tubbs can't afford a popular misapprehension that he isn't Mrs. Tubbs's husband. I'll tell Tubbs."

"I think," said Helen rebukingly, "that you might have taken some other place to light your cigar in, George."

"Didn't light it. Dropped the match, I was so startled. Last match I had, too. I've got that against Tubbs. Oh, I must speak to Tubbs!"

"If you speak to Tubbs," Mr. Batcham put in prudently, "don't mention my name. I am glad to find myself wrong in this case. But Mr. Banerjee assures me—"

The pony leaped forward under the cut of young Browne's whip, and Mr. Batcham very nearly tumbled out of the back seat. Young Browne didn't apologise. "Do you mean to say," said he in a red fury, "that you have been talking to a beastly baboo about the white women of Calcutta? It—it isn't usual."

It was as much for their own amusement as for their guest's edification that the Brownes asked Mr. Sayter to dinner to meet Mr. Batcham. Mr. Sayter came unsuspectingly, and I have reason to believe that he has not yet forgiven the Brownes. Nobody in Calcutta could hate a large red globe-trotter more ferociously than Mr. Sayter did. And the Brownes failed to palliate their offence by asking anybody else. They were a square party, and Mr. Batcham sat opposite Mr. Sayter, who went about afterwards talking about his recent narrow escape from suffocation.

Mr. Batcham welcomed Mr. Sayter as if he had been in his own house or his own "works." He shook Mr. Sayter warmly by his slender and frigid hand and said he was delighted to meet him—it was always a pleasure to meet representative men, and his young friends had told him that Mr. Sayter was a very representative man indeed, standing almost at the head of his department.

"Oh, goodness gracious!" exclaimed Mr. Sayter, sinking into a chair. "Fancy being talked about like that now."

"I have a thousand things to ask you," continued Mr. Batcham with increasing cordiality, "a thousand questions are surging in my brain at this very moment. This India of yours is a wonderful place, sir!"

"Well," said Mr. Sayter, "I suppose I can't help that. But it isn't as wonderful as it used to be—that's one comfort."

"I'm afraid," Mr. Batcham remarked with seriousness, "that your eyes are blinded. I've met numbers of people out here—people of more than average perception—whose eyes seem to me to be blinded to the beauties of Ind."

"Probably affected by the dust of Ind," put in young Browne. "Will you take my wife in, Mr. Sayter?"

"No," said Mr. Sayter, "it's the perverseness of the Anglo-Indian. He thinks if he talks about the beauties of Ind the Secretary of State will cut his pay."

"And yet," said Mr. Batcham, tucking his napkin into his capacious waistcoat, "the average public official in this country seems to me to be pretty fairly remunerated."

"As a matter of fact," said Mr. Sayter confidentially, looking up from his soup, "they're grossly overpaid. They live in luxury. I am one of them. I live in luxury. I have a servant to put on my boots. In England what action should I be obliged to take in regard to my boots? I should be obliged to put them on myself! And for the misfortune of living in a country where I get my boots put on, I'm paid twice as much as I would be in England, and three times as much as I'm worth. Monstrous, isn't it?"

Mr. Batcham smiled a benign smile of approbation. "I assure you, sir, that is not the way the situation has been represented to me thus far. I hope that before I leave India I may meet other gentlemen who like yourself have the moral rectitude to rise above mere considerations of gain—I may say of plunder —and state the case frankly as it is. With regard to yourself I have no doubt you exaggerate, but I will tell you candidly that I have myself for some time held the same opinion precisely with regard to—with regard to—"

"The Indian services generally. Exactly," responded Mr. Sayter, "and when you get home you mean to bring it under the consideration of Lord Kimberley. Quite so. I wouldn't be too sanguine about popularizing your view among the Europeans out here—the Anglo-Indian is a sordid person—but all the baboos will be very pleased. You will of course endeavour to extend the employment of baboos in the higher branches of the Covenanted service—the judicial and administrative. They come much cheaper, and their feelings are very deeply hurt at being overlooked in favour of the alien Englishman. You could get an excellent baboo for any purpose on earth for thirty rupees a month. And yet," continued Mr. Sayter absently, "they pay me two thousand."

Mr. Batcham looked reflective, and young Browne said, "Cheap and nasty."

"Oh, dear no!" remarked Mr. Sayter, "A nice fat wholesome baboo who could write a beautiful hand—probably a graduate of the Calcutta University. Talking of universities reminds me to add, Mr. Batcham, that the university baboo is not quite so cheap as he used to be. He is still very plentiful and very inexpensive, but his price is going up since the new regulations."

"Regulations!" said Mr. Batcham. "You people will regulate these unfortunate natives off the face of the earth."

"We should love to," replied Mr. Sayter, "but we can't. You

have no idea of their rate of multiplication. These particular regulations were a frightful blow to the baboo."

"May I ask their nature?" Mr. Bateham inquired:

"Oh yes. They were connected with the examinations for degrees. It was thought remarkable for some time how universally the baboos passed them, and how singularly similar the answers were. The charitable put it down to the extraordinary aptitude of the Bengali for the retention of printed matter and the known tendency of his mind to run in grooves. The uncharitable put the other baboos in charge of printing the examination papers under a mean system of espionage. I regret to say that it was only too successful; they caught a whole batch of baboos taking the means of earning an honest living a little prematurely."

"Then what happened?" asked young Browne. "I haven't heard this story."

"I don't remember whether they suppressed that lot of baboos or not. But they put an end to the extra edition of examination papers system. They had the lithographing stone brought into an office where there was only one man, a European, and they shut the shutters and they locked the door—oh, they took stringent measures!—and they had the papers turned off by a coolie, in solemn secrecy, the day before the examination."

"That must have been entirely satisfactory," Mr. Bateham remarked.

"It was not. The baboos passed in great numbers that year and sent in their papers with a smile. Then I believe they stopped up the key-hole and blindfolded the coolie. It made no difference whatever."

"How did they find out?" Helen asked.

"In the end they took to watching this simple, ignorant coolie. And they observed that when he had finished his work he invariably sat down and rested on the lithographing stone. So that he went away charged, one might say, with the wisdom of the examiners, and published himself in the bazar for I dare-say four annas a copy."

"That boy, if he lived in the United States, would rise to be president," remarked Mr. Batcham oracularly.

"He was of great assistance to the B. A.'s of that year. Though I believe they found him rather bony for a satisfactory proof, and they complained that the sense of the questions was a little disconnected."

"Mrs. Browne, have you seen anything of the Tootes lately?"

"Nobody has, Mr. Sayter. Mr. Toote has fever."

"Temperature one hundred and five this morning," said Mrs. Browne. "The third attack this year."

"And the Archie Campbells are going home on sick leave," added Helen. "Poor Mr. Campbell is down with abscess of the liver. There's a great deal of sickness about."

"Not more than usual; it's a deadly time of year," Mr. Sayter remarked. "You heard about Bobby Hamilton?"

"Hamilton seedy?" inquired young Browne. "I saw him riding a fine beast the day before yesterday—he looked fairly fit. Hamilton's a very knowing chap about horses, he's promised to look after a pony for my wife."

"You'll have to get somebody else, I'm afraid."

"Hamilton's not——"

"Yes. Went to the funeral this morning. Fine chap. Aw-ful pity. Cholera."

"And Mrs. Hamilton is at home!" exclaimed Helen.

"With another baby. Yes. Four now, Hamilton told me

last hot weather. He'd been seedy, and I was urging him to take furlough."

"Why didn't he? It might have saved him," asked Helen.

"I believe the fourth baby was the reason. He couldn't afford it. Had to stay and grill, poor chap."

"How very distressing," said Mr. Batcham. "I suppose the widow will be able to live on her pension?"

"She will receive no pension, sir. Mr. Hamilton belonged to the Education Department, which is uncovenanted. In the uncovenanted service it is necessary to live in order to enjoy one's pension, and that is the reason why its departments add so little to the taxes."

"Ah, well," said Mr. Batcham rather vaguely, "you can't have your cake and eat it too. I should consider marriage under those conditions an improvidence, and I don't understand people being ill in this climate. I think it must be largely due to the imagination. So far as *my* testimony is worth anything, I find myself much benefited by it. Thanks, Browne, I'll have Bass. *I'm* not afraid of it."

Young Browne smiled and wistfully drank half the unsatisfactory contents of the long glass by his plate.

"To say nothing," said he, in mournful reference to the climate, "of the magnificent thirst it engenders."

Mr. Sayter joined his hands together at the finger tips and looked at Mr. Jonas Batcham, M. P., from under his eyebrows in a way which was certainly impertinent, oblivious of the kitmutgar at his elbow who patiently offered him iced asparagus.

"I'm perfectly certain," said he, with a crispness in every syllable, "that Mr. Batcham has been benefited by staying six weeks in India. If he stayed six years he would doubtless be more benefited still. I daresay, as he says, we would all be benefited if it were not for our imaginations. It's a climate that leaves only one thing to be desired, and if some people say that's a coffin, that is clearly their imagination. Uncovenanted people have a way of dying pretty freely, but that's out of sheer perverseness to get more furlough. Most of them go for ever because they can't arrange it any other way. And as for cholera, I give you my word not one man in ten dies of cholera out here; they go off with typhoid or dysentery, or in some comfortable way like that, and probably have a punkah the whole time they're ill."

The half-past nine gun boomed from the fort, and Mr. Batcham started nervously. "I don't know why it is," said he, "that one doesn't accustom one's self to hearing guns in India. I suppose it is some association with the Mutiny."

"Oh, we'll have another mutiny," Mr. Sayter remarked; "it's quite on the cards. But you must not be alarmed, Mr. Batcham. It won't be," he added irrepressibly, "till after you go home."

The conversation turned upon light literature, and Mr. Batcham contributed to it the fact that he understood that man Besant was making a lot of money. Helen had been reading the memoirs of Mdlle. Bashkirtseff, and had to say that one half she didn't understand, and the other half she didn't like. "And when," said Mr. Sayter, "does your book come out, Mr. Batcham?"

"I haven't said that I was writing one," Mr. Batcham replied, smiling coyly.

"It isn't necessary," declared young Browne, "we should expect a book from you, Mr. Batcham, as a matter of course."

"Oh, well, I expect I shall have to own to some little account of my experience," confessed Mr. Batcham. "My friends have urged me to do something of the kind. If the illustrations can be got ready, I daresay it will be out in time to catch the spring market."

"Don't forget the illustration of the cobra milking the cow," said George Browne, infected by Mr. Sayter; "it will add a great deal to the interest of the volume without detracting seriously from its reliability."

"No," said Mr. Batcham, "I haven't got a photograph of that, I'm sorry to say. The illustrations will be entirely reproduced from photographs. I've got a beauty of the Taj, taken by magnesium light."

"Have you decided on a title, Mr. Batcham?" Helen inquired, playing with the orange-blossom in her finger-bowl.

Mr. Batcham looked carefully round him, and observed that the kitmutgars had left the room. "Don't mention it," he said. "because somebody else may get hold of it, but I think I'll christen the book either 'My Trot Through India,' or 'India, Its Past, Present, and Future.'"

"Capital!" exclaimed Mr. Sayter, skipping nimbly to hold back the purdah for the exit of Mrs. Browne. "You can't really dispense with either title, and if I were you I should use them both!"

A little later, before Mr. Sayter disappeared into his brougham, exploding a vast yawn among the wreaths of his Trichinopoly, Mr. Batcham shook him warmly by the hand, and re-expressed his gratification at the opportunity of meeting so representative a gentleman, to whose opinions such great importance would naturally attach itself. "Joking apart," said Mr. Batcham, "the candid statement of your views upon many points this evening will be very useful to me."

"I'm so glad!" said Mr. Sayter.

CHAPTER XVIII.

HELEN BROWNE never could be brought to understand that she was not rich with five hundred rupees a month. Every now and then she reduced the amount—reduced it indeed, with the rupee at one and twopence!—to pounds, shillings, and pence, in order to assure herself over again that it was only a little less than the entire stipend of the Canbury rectory, "and we all lived upon that," she would argue, as if she had there somewhat unanswerable. It was to her a source of continual and lamentable mystery that they never seemed to find it convenient to open a bank account—it was so unwise not to have a bank account—and yet there was always what George Browne called a "negative difficulty," always something to be paid first. On the last days of every month when it came to balancing the accounts and finding nothing over, Mrs. Browne regularly cut the bawarchi six pice on general principles, for which he as regularly came prepared. Kali Bagh cooked nothing better than his accounts. Besides this she had her evening gloves cleaned, and saved the price of a ticca dhurzie, which is at least eight annas, every Saturday by doing the family darning, and this, in a memsahib, is saintly. Certainly the Brownes were not extravagant. Helen used to maintain that the remarkable part of it was vegetables being so cheap, but there was probably more force in her reflection that it didn't really matter much about getting a cauliflower for a penny when one's ticca gharries came to three pounds. It was much more curious to observe how exactly every month the Brownes' expenses met their income with perhaps just a trifle now and then to spare, which they might put away if they liked, unreceipted, to be a nest-egg for a comfortable debt in the near future—the fact being that Kasi and Kali Bagh and the rest knew the sahib's *tulab* as well as they knew their own, and were all good at arithmetic to the splitting of a pi. It is perhaps a tribute to the perfection of their skill that they never disturbed Helen's idea that she was very well off. When the rupees disappeared more quickly than usual, she thought of the price of vegetables and was convinced that retrenchments were possible and should soon be effected. Next month Kasi would permit himself to forget various trifling bills, and there would be great prosperity with the Brownes for a fortnight. But invariably there came a time of reckoning when Kasi demonstrated that the income was very nearly equal to the outgo. On the whole Kasi was contented with the sahib's present pay, having great faith in his prospects of promotion. Barring accidents, Kasi's speculations upon the financial future of the Brownes were very perfectly adjusted.

It was the elusive bank account that induced them to listen to the Jack Lovitts, who lived in Park-street in a bigger house than they could afford. "We can perfectly well let you have the top flat," said Mrs. Jack Lovitt at the end of the cold weather, "and it will be that much off our rent besides being a lot cheaper for you. You see we could divide the mallie and the sweeper," said Mrs. Lovitt, enunciating this horror quite callously, "and that would be an advantage. Then we might have one leg of mutton between us, you know, and that sort of thing—save a lot of bazar."

"But should you like to have somebody living over your head?" asked Helen, pondering over the idea.

"Of course not," replied Mrs. Lovitt candidly, "who would? But if we mean to go on leave next year we've got to do something. Jack's eight hundred simply vanishes in our hands. Last month, Helen Browne, our bill from Peliti alone was a hundred and ten—beast! If Jack wouldn't insist on giving ice to his polo ponies I think we might get on. But you can't reason with him about it. He'll come home with a broken neck from that polo one of these days. And we haven't earned anything approaching a decent pension yet, and my complexion's absolutely gone," added this vivacious lady, who liked saying these insincere things to her "young friend Mrs. Browne," who began at this time to be amused by them.

"I've done my little uttermost," Mrs. Lovitt continued. "This nougat is filthy, isn't it? I'll never leave my dear Peliti again!" The ladies were tiffining together in a luxury of solitude. "I've sold three frocks."

"No!" said Helen. "Which?"

"That vieux rose brocade that I got out from home for the Drawing-Room—the more fool I!—and that gray shimmery crêpe that you like; and another, a mouse-coloured sort of thing, with gold bands, that I don't think you know—I've never had it on. Frifri sent it home with a bill for a hundred and fifty if you please—and I gave her the foundation. However, I've been paid for it, and Frifri hasn't, and she can jolly well wait!"

"What did you get for it?" asked Helen.

"Eighty-five—wasn't I lucky? That new little Mrs. Niblit—jute or indigo or something—heaps of money. Lady Blebbins bought the other two for Julia. She's up in Allahabad, you know, where the fact of my having swaggered around in them all season won't make any difference. What a pretty little flannel blouse that is of yours, my dear—I wish I could afford one like it!"

"It cost three eight altogether," said Mrs. Browne, "the dhurzie made it last week. He took two days, but I think he dawdled."

"Three eight's a good deal, I think, for a blouse," returned Mrs. Lovitt, the experienced. "Dear me, what a horrible thing it is to be poor! And nothing but boxes in that upper flat! Three rooms and two bath-rooms, going, going, gone—I wish it were! What do you say, Mrs. Browne? Ninety-five rupees only!"

"It's cheap," said Helen; "I'll ask George."

She did ask George, at the shortest possible intervals for three days, and when the subject had been allowed to drop for a quarter of an hour George asked her. It became the supreme question, and the consideration they devoted to it might have revised the Permanent Settlement or decided our right to occupy the Pamirs.

There were more pros and cons than I have patience to go into, and I daresay they would have been discussing it still, if Mrs. Browne had not thought fit to decline her breakfast on the morning of the third day. Whereat young Browne suspected fever—he hoped not typhoid—but the place certainly smelt feverish, now that he came to smell it—and there was no doubt that it would be an economy to take Mrs. Lovitt's flat, and forthwith they took it.

Moving house in India is a light affliction and but for a moment. The sahib summoned Kasi, and announced to him that the change would be made to-morrow, "and in thy hand all things will be." Kasi received particulars of the address in Park-street, salaamed, saying "Very good," and went away more sorrowful than he seemed, for he was comfortable and mighty where he was, and change was not often a good thing. Besides, he knew Lovitt sahib that he had a violent temper and reprehensible modes of speech—it might not be good to come often under the eye of Lovitt sahib. And he would be obliged to tell the mallie his friend that it would be to depart, which would split his heart in two. However, it was the sahib's will and there was nothing to say, but a great deal to do. Moreover, there might be backsheesh, which alleviated all things.

Next morning the Brownes found themselves allowed one table and two chairs for breakfast purposes, and six coolies sat without, dusty and expectorant, waiting for those. Kasi, at the gate, directed a departing train, each balancing some portion of their worldly goods upon his head, Kasi, watchful and stern, the protector of his master's property. The dining-room was dismantled, the drawing-room had become a floor space enclosed by high white walls with nail marks in them. There was a little heap of torn paper in one corner, and cobwebs seemed to have been spun in the night in half the windows.

"It's pure magic!" Helen exclaimed. "It's to-day week, and I've been asleep," and then "We've been awfully happy here, George,"—an illogical statement to accompany wet eyelashes.

Even while they sat on their single chairs at their single table, which George put his elbows on, to secure it he said, the bedroom furniture decamped with many footsteps, and after the meal was over there was nothing left to testify of them but their hats laid conspicuously on a sheet of paper in the middle of the drawing-room floor. "I suppose," said young Browne, "they think we've got brains enough to carry those over ourselves."

Mrs. Browne put hers on and drove her husband to office. Then she shopped for an hour or two, and finished up by coming to tiffin with me. Then she repaired to Park-street, where she found herself established in the main, with Kasi still superintending, his locks escaping from his turban, in a state of

THEIR HATS LAID CONSPICUOUSLY ON A SHEET OF PAPER.

extreme perspiration. Then she made a dainty afternoon toilet with great comfort, and by the time young Browne came home to tea it was quite ready for him in every respect, even to the wife behind the teapot, in circumstances which, except for the pictures and the bric-a-brac, might be described as normal. And of course, being an insensate sahib, he congratulated his wife—it was prodigious, and all her doing! Kasi was also commended, however, and the praise of his master fell pleasantly on the ear of Kasi, who immediately added another rupee to the amount he meant to charge for coolie-hire. Thus is life alleviated in India; thus do all its material cares devolve into a hundred brown hands and leave us free for our exalted occupations or our noble pleasure. We are unencumbered by the consideration of so much as a button. Under these beatitudes the average Anglo-Indian career ought to be one of pure spirit and intellect, but it is not so—not singularly so.

"What we must be thoroughly on our guard against," said young Browne in the top flat at his second cup, "is seeing too much of the Lovitts. They're not a bad sort if you keep them at a proper distance; I don't believe for an instant there's any harm in little Mrs. Jack; but it won't do to be too intimate. They'll be as troublesome as sparrows if we are."

"There's one thing we'll have to look out for," said Mr. Jack Lovitt in the bottom flat at his third muffin, "and that is being too chummy with the Brownes; they're all right so long as they stay upstairs, but we won't encourage them to come down too often. We'll have Mrs. B. gushing all over the place if we do. They'll have to understand they've only rented the top flat."

"They'll always know what we have for dinner," remarked the spouse in the top flat.

"They'll see every soul that comes to the house," said the spouse in the bottom flat.

"It isn't the slightest concern of theirs," replied the lord upstairs.

"It's absolutely none of their business," returned the lord downstairs.

And they were both "blowed" if they would tolerate the slightest interest in their respective affairs. The Brownes concluded that "perhaps once a month" would be often enough to ask the Lovitts to come up and dine, and the Lovitts thought the Brownes might come in to tea "once in three weeks or so." Before this they had been in the habit of entertaining each other rather oftener, but then they were not under the same roof, with a supreme reason for establishing distance. Mrs. Browne believed that on the whole she wouldn't engage Mrs. Lovitt's dhurzie—it might lead to complications; and Mrs. Lovitt fancied she had better not offer Helen that skirt-pattern —it would necessitate endless discussions and runnings up and down. Mrs. Lovitt deliberately arranged to go up to see Helen for the first time with her hat and gloves on, to make it obvious that the call should be formally returned. Helen sent down a note, beautifully written and addressed, to ask Mrs. Lovitt to come to tea on Wednesday afternoon, at a quarter past five. The ladies left no little thing undone, in fact, that would help to quell a tendency to effusion; they arranged to live as remotely from each other as the limits of No. 61, Park-street, permitted. The Brownes had always the roof and habitually sent chairs up there. "They can't say we haven't rented it," said Helen.

Their precautions not to be offensive to each other were still more elaborate. Mr. Browne ascertained at what time Mr. Lovitt went to office, and made a habit of starting a quarter of an hour earlier. Mrs. Lovitt, observing that the Brownes were fond of walking in the compound in the evening, walked there always in the morning. Neither of them would give any orders to the mallie, whom they jointly paid, for fear of committing an unwarrantable interference, and that functionary grew fat and lazy, while the weeds multiplied in the gravel walks. Helen even went so far as to use the back staircase to avoid a possible encounter at the front door, but young Browne disapproved of this. He believed in abating no jot or tittle of their lawful claims. "Use the staircase freely, my dear," said he, "but do not engage in conversation at the foot of it."

They assumed a bland ignorance of each other's affairs, more discreet than veracious. When Mrs. Lovitt mentioned that they had had a lot of people to dinner the night before, Helen said, "*Had* you?" as if she had not heard at least half a dozen carriages drive up at dinner time; as if she had not decided, she and George, indifferent upon the roof, that the trap which drove off so *much* later than the others must have been Jimmy Forbes's. And they would be as much surprised, these two ladies, at meeting anywhere else at dinner as if they had not seen each other's name inscribed in the peon book that brought the invitations, and remarked each of the other, at the time, "It seems to me we see enough of those people at home."

They were a little ridiculous, but on the whole they were very wise indeed, and the relations that ensued were as polite and as amiable as possible. It was like living on the edge of a volcano, taking the precaution of throwing a pail or two of water down every day or two. And nothing happened.

CHAPTER XIX.

NOTHING happened. Thus for three months, three hot weather months. The punkah wallahs came and ministered to the sahiblok with creakings and snorings that cannot be uttered, much less spelled. The mango-crop was gathered and sold, the *topsy muchies* swam up the river Hooghly, and were caught and cooked in their appointed season. The Viceroy and his shining ones went to Simla, and a wave of flirtation swept over the Himalayas. The shops put up grass-tatties for the wind to blow through, and the customers who went in were much cooler than the coolies who stood outside throwing water over them. The brain-fever bird spoke—he does not sing—all day long in the banyan-tree—"*Ponk! Ponk!*" all day long in the thickest part of the banyan-tree, where nobody can see or shoot him. He comes and stays with the hot weather, a feathered thing accursed. The morning paper devoted itself exclusively to publishing the "Gazette" notices of leave and the lists of intending passengers by P. and O., and week after week the tide bore great ships outward, every cabin occupied by persons connected with more or less disordered livers, going home for three or six or twelve months' repairs. You could count on your fingers the people you knew in the Red Road. Kasi asked for an umbrella; respectfully as a right, it was the *dustur* for the sahib to provide an umbrella. The ayah begged for an umbrella, humbly as a favour; she had far to come and the sun was "*ag kamofik*."* The kitmutgar asked for an umbrella, not because he had the slightest idea that he would get it, but because it was generally more blessed to ask than not to ask. The cholera arrived punctually, and increased the native death-rate, with its customary industry. The Lovitts lost a bearer from this cause, and a valuable polo pony from heat apoplexy. The latter bereavement was in the paper. The oil exuded more profusely still upon the adipose tissue that encloses the soul of a baboo, and Calcutta flamed with the red flowers of the gold mohur tree, panting nightly, when they were all put out, under the cool south wind from the sea.

Neither the Lovitts nor the Brownes left Calcutta; they were among the people you counted on your fingers. There is very little to talk about in the hot weather, and the fact that nothing had happened was discussed a good deal, in the dead privacy of the roof or the lower veranda. Both the top flat and the bottom flat thought it had managed admirably, and congratulated itself accordingly. That nothing should have happened caused them to rise considerably in each other's esteem—there were so few people living under one roof in Calcutta who were able to say it. They told society how agreeable they found it to live with each other, and society repeated it, so that the Brownes heard of the Lovitts' satisfaction, and the Lovitts heard of the Brownes'. Indeed, there came a time when the Brownes and the Lovitts thought almost as much of each other as they did before they lived together.

* Like fire.

It had been an extinct volcano after all, and they stopped throwing water down. Mrs. Lovitt, by degrees, became easily confidential again, and told Helen among other things that edified her, exactly what they were saying at the club about Mrs. Lushington and the General's A. D. C., Mrs. Lovitt's version coming straight from Jimmy Forbes, and being absolutely correct. Helen being without a confidential male admirer upon these matters—husbands kept them notoriously to themselves—had not the wherewithal to exchange; but she borrowed the Lovitts' khansamah to make some cocoanut creams, which was going a great deal further. When the Brownes' pony was laid up with the sun, threatening vertigo, Jack Lovitt took young Browne to office very sociably in his cart; and when the Lovitts ran up to Darjiling on ten days' casual leave, the Brownes looked after "the littlest black and tan in Calcutta," and took it out for a drive every day. They dined and lunched and shopped more and more often together, and Mrs. Lovitt knew exactly how many *topsy muchies* Mrs. Browne got for eight annas.

It was just at this very favourable point that the difficulty about Mr. Lovitt's unmarried sister arose. Mr. Lovitt's unmarried sister had been shipped six months before to an up-country relation, and having made no use whatever of her time in Cawnpore, was now to be transferred to Calcutta as a final experiment. Mrs. Lovitt wanted a room for her unmarried sister-in-law, wanted Helen's dining-room. It was a serious difficulty, and the Lovitts and the Brownes in the plenitude of their confidence and good-will agreed to surmount it by "chumming,"—living together and dividing the bulk of the household expenses—a form of existence largely supported in Calcutta.

In the beginning, chumming lends itself vastly to expansion, and the Brownes and the Lovitts expanded to the utmost verge.

They forgot the happy result of past discretions; they became a united family, no longer a top and a bottom flat. They pooled their domestic resources—the soup-plates were Mrs. Lovitt's, the dessert-knives were Mrs. Browne's. They consulted each other's tastes pressingly. They had brisket always on Saturday night because "Jack" liked cold brisket for breakfast on Sunday morning, and mutton twice a week because young Browne had a weakness for caper sauce. Mrs. Lovitt sent away her cook—a crowning act of grace—and Kali Bagh reigned in his stead. It was all peace and fraternity, and the sahibs sat together in long praise of each other's cigars every evening, while the memsahibs upstairs discussed their mutual friends and sank deeper into each other's affections. Indeed, in little Mrs. Lovitt's Helen had absolutely no rival except Jimmy Forbes, the black and tan, and Mr. Lovitt.

They saw a good deal of Mr. Forbes naturally, and the interesting and unique position in the house occupied by that gentleman was revealed to Helen with all the force of an Anglo-Indian experience. He was nearly always there, and when he hadn't been there he was in the habit of giving an account of himself as having been elsewhere. It was expected of him, and much beside. Helen decided that he couldn't be described as a "tame cat" in the family, because the position of a tame cat is an irresponsible one, and Mr. Forbes had many responsibilities. If Mrs. Lovitt's racquet went "*fut*" * it was Jimmy who had it restrung for her. When a new theatrical company came sailing up from Ceylon, Jimmy went on its opening night to report, and if it were good enough to waste an evening on, he took the Lovitts—generally both of them—later. If the roof leaked, or the servants misbehaved, Mrs. Lovitt complained to Jimmy quite

* To ruin.

as often as to Jack, and Jimmy saw to it. When Mrs. Lovitt wanted some Burmese carvings, Jimmy arranged it at the jail, where the captive Burmese carve, and when that lady decided that she would like to sell her victoria and buy a cabriolet, Jimmy advertised it in *The Englishman* and made the bargain. In fact Mr. Forbes relieved Mr. Lovitt of more than half the duties pertaining to his official position, of which kindness the latter gentleman was not insensible. Nor could anybody say that little Mrs. Lovitt was. She nursed Jimmy Forbes when he was ill, scolded him when he was imprudent, and advised him on the subject of his clothes. I don't know that she ever put his necktie straight, but she never would allow him to wear anything but blue ones, and made a point of his throwing away all his high collars—the turned down ones suited him so much better. She did not overload him with benefits, but at Christmas and on his birthday she always gave him some little thing with a personal association, a pair of slippers, some initialled handkerchiefs, a new photograph of herself, generally taken with the littlest black and tan in Calcutta.

Thus they made no secret of their affection; it had the candour of high noon. They called each other Jimmy and Jenny with all publicity. When Jimmy went home on three months' leave, Jennie told all her friends that she was simply desolated. She declared to Jimmy and to the world that she was a mother to this young man, and no mother could have walked and danced and driven more self-sacrificingly with her son. Mrs. Lovitt was at least three years younger than her "Jimmy-boy," but that, in cases of adoption, is known to be immaterial. In periods of absence they wrote to each other regularly twice a week, and Jimmy never forgot to send kind regards to Jack. Their manner to each other was conspicuous for the absence of anything foolish or awkward or constrained—it was above embarrassment, it spoke of a secure footing and an untroubled mind, Mrs. Lovitt lectured Mr. Forbes, and Mr. Forbes rebuked Mrs. Lovitt with a simplicity and good humour that produced a kind of astonishment in the spectator, who looked about her in vain for a formula of criticism. "No," Mr. Forbes would say, "you'd better not call on Mrs. Lushington. It's all right for me to go, of course, but I'd rather you didn't know her." And Mrs. Lovitt would poutingly acquiesce. When Tertium Quiddism takes this form, what is there to say?

Mrs. Lovitt's official lord, at all events, found very little to say. He liked Forbes himself extremely—capital fellow—awfully clever chap—and admitted him into full communion as a member of the family in good and regular standing, with a placidity which many husbands doubtless envied him. The gentlemen were not brothers or even brothers-in-law, the relation was one too delicately adjusted to come under any commonly recognised description; but there was a kind of fraternity in it which Mrs. Lovitt seemed to establish, with tacit limitations which established themselves. The limitations were concerned with impropriety—in the general sense. It is certain that there were no occasions *a deux* when Mr. Forbes felt out of it with Mr. and Mrs. Lovitt—they had no privacy to speak of which Jimmy was not welcome to share. In family matters Mr. Lovitt treated Mr. Forbes much as a valued Under-Secretary. The two men were calling upon me one Sunday, and I inquired of Mr. Lovitt whether his wife were going to Mrs. Walter Luff's concert for the East Indian Self-Help Association. "'Pon my word," he said, "I don't know. Forbes will tell you." Mrs. Lovitt had frequent occasion to mention these amicable conditions to her friends. "My husband thinks the world of Jimmy Forbes," she often said, "and Jimmy is perfectly devoted to him." In moments of intimacy after tiffin with Mrs. Browne, she was fond of comparing the two. "Jimmy is a good deal the cleverer," she would say judicially, "but Jack is much the better tempered, poor dear, and his looks leave *nothing* to be desired, in my opinion. But then I always did spoil Jack."

When Miss Josephine Lovitt arrived, tall and vigorous, with a complexion fresh from the school-room, full of bubbling laughter, and already made fully aware of herself by six months' diligent spurning of nice little subalterns, who thought her a Juno of tremendously good form, these ladies had further confidences. Mrs. Lovitt initiated them by asking Helen if she didn't think it would be just the thing for Jimmy, and in the discussion which followed it appeared that Mrs. Lovitt had often tried to marry Jimmy off—she was sure he would be much happier married—but hitherto unavailingly. No one knew the trouble she had taken, the efforts she had made. Mrs. Lovitt couldn't understand it, for it was only a matter of picking and choosing, and Jimmy wasn't shy. "I've argued it out with him a score of times," she said, "but I can't get the least satisfaction. Men are queer animals."

Helen agreed that Mr. Forbes ought to be married. It was so much her opinion that she had to be careful not to argue too emphatically. It seemed to Mrs. Browne that there were particular as well as general grounds for approving such an idea, and Miss Josephine Lovitt struck her also as its brilliant apotheosis. "Josie's a nice girl," declared Mrs. Lovitt, "and a great deal cleverer than she pretends to be. And Jack would like it above all things. But it's too nice to hope for," and Mrs. Lovitt sighed with the resignation that is born of hope deferred.

Helen reported the matter duly to George, who laughed in

a ribald manner about Mrs. Lovitt's intentions, and would hear nothing of the advisability of the match, as men never will. So she was not encouraged to suggest anything of co-operation on her own part. Indeed, she was hardly conscious of such an idea, but the married woman's instinct was already awake in her, and she was quite prepared to do anything she could to further Mrs. Lovitt's benevolent design. It should be furthered, Helen thought, in the interests of the normal and the orthodox.

Opportunities did not immediately occur, because Mrs. Lovitt took them all herself. She gave tennis parties at the Saturday club, and made up sets so that Mr. Forbes and Miss Lovitt played together. When Mr. Forbes sang "The Bogie Man" to them all after dinner she made Josephine play his accompaniment to save her "rheumatic" finger-joints. Josephine might teach Jimmy "Halma"—she was much too stupid to learn—she would talk to Mr. Browne. All this quite shamelessly, rather with an air of conscious rectitude, of child-like *naïveté*. It was the old thing, Jimmy Forbes thought, over his peaceful private cigar; it amused her to do it, it always had amused her to do it. Before he had generally resented it a good deal; this time he resented it too, by Jove, but not so much. After all, why should he resent it—deuced bad policy; it only encouraged the little woman to go on with this sort of game. And for the first time in Mr. Forbes's dawning experience of womankind it occurred to him that it might be advisable under some circumstances not to sulk. He wouldn't sulk—he would teach the little woman a lesson. It wouldn't be a bad thing to do. Besides, Miss Lovitt was rather amusing, and no fool either; she wouldn't misunderstand things. And Mr. Forbes finished his cigar with the conviction that such an experiment would be

JOSEPHINE MIGHT TEACH JIMMY "HALMA."

absolutely safe so far as the girl was concerned—of course, he was bound to think of the girl—and more or less agreeable.

A little later Helen confided to George that she really wouldn't be one bit surprised if something came of it; Jack Lovitt remarked to his wife that Forbes seemed rather taken with Josie, and he was quite prepared to give them his blessing; and Mrs. Lovitt replied that it *would* be lovely, wouldn't it, but she was afraid it was only temporary, adding rather vaguely that Jimmy Forbes wasn't a bit like other men. On the whole it wouldn't be unsuitable, but it was a pity Josie was so tall—she overtopped him by about a foot—a tall woman and a little man did look so idiotic together. That evening Mrs. Lovitt accompanied "The Bogie Man" without any reference to her rheumatic finger-joints.

It was at this juncture—when any lady of discretion living in the same house would have been looking on in silent joy, without lifting a finger—that Helen found herself yielding to the temptation of furthering matters, so successfully, you understand, was Mr. Forbes making his experiment. Here a little and there a little Mrs. Browne permitted herself to do what she could, and opportunities occurred to an extent which inspired and delighted her. She discovered herself to be a person of wonderful tact, and the discovery no doubt stimulated her, though it must be said that circumstances put themselves very readily at her disposal. Mrs. Lovitt, for one thing, had gradually retired from the generalship of the situation, becoming less and less sanguine of its issue as Helen became more and more hopeful. She even had a little confidential conversation with Josephine, in which she told that young lady that though Jimmy was a dear good fellow and she had always been able to depend upon him to be kind to any friends of hers, she was afraid he was not a person to be taken altogether *seriously*. Josie would understand. And Josie did understand quite well.

As to Mr. Forbes himself, his experiment had succeeded. There was no doubt whatever that the little woman had been taught a lesson; anyone could see that she had learnt it remarkably well. Yet he continued to instruct her, he did not withdraw the experiment. He found it interesting, and not exclusively in its effect upon Mrs. Lovitt. Miss Josephine found it interesting too. She thought she would like to hand Mr. Forbes back to her little sister-in-law, to hand him back a little damaged, perhaps. This was doubtless very naughty of Miss Josephine, but not unnatural under the circumstances. It was only, after all, that she did not make a good cat's paw.

And thus it went on, to be brief—for this is not a chronicle of the affair of Jimmy Forbes and Mrs. Lovitt's sister-in-law, the which any gossip of Calcutta will give you at great length and detail—until the Brownes asked Miss Josephine Lovitt and Mr. Forbes to go with them to see Mr. Wylde de Vinton, assisted by a scratch company, perform *Hamlet* in the opera house, on a Saturday evening. Hitherto Mr. Forbes's Saturday evenings had not been his own, they had been Mrs. Lovitt's. She had established a peculiar claim to be amused on Saturday evenings—they were usually consecrated to long talks of a semi-sentimental order, which Jack Lovitt could not possibly have understood even if he had been there. Therefore when Mr. Forbes showed Mrs. Lovitt Helen's note and stated his intention of accepting, it was in the nature of a finality.

I am not interested in deciding whether it was from purely conscientious motives that Miss Josephine Lovitt, having discovered Mr. Forbes to have sustained considerable damage, refrained from handing him back to Mrs. Lovitt. All I wish to establish is that the Brownes did not leave No. 61, Park-street until quite three weeks after the engagement was announced.

MISS JOSEPHINE LOVITT REFRAINED FROM HANDING HIM BACK TO MRS. LOVITT.

Mrs. Lovitt was obliged to wait until they found a house. And of course their going had nothing whatever to do with dear Josie's engagement—Mrs. Lovitt made that match, and was very proud of it. The incident that brought about their misunderstanding with the Brownes was the merest trifle, Mrs. Lovitt would tell you if you knew her well enough, the merest trifle. They, the Lovitts, had asked the Honourable Mr. Justice Lamb of the High Court to dinner on, say, Friday of next week. His lordship was suffering very much from the weather when the invitation came, and declined it, fabricating another engagement as even their lordships will. Mrs. Browne and Mrs. Lovitt had then reached that point in the development of the chumming system—hastened a little by circumstances—when one thinks it isn't absolutely necessary for those people to concern themselves in *all* one's affairs, and the circumstance was not mentioned. As it happened, therefore, the Brownes two days later invited Mr. Justice Lamb to dinner on the same Friday, the old gentleman being a second cousin of young Browne's, and in the habit of dining with them once in six months or so. The thermometer having gone down a few degrees, his lordship, who was a person of absent mind, accepted with much pleasure, putting the note in his pocket-book so that he wouldn't forget the youngster's address.

"We have a man coming to dinner to-night," Helen remarked casually at breakfast, and Mrs. Lovitt was of course not sufficiently interested to inquire who it was, if Mrs. Browne didn't choose to say. The man came, ate his dinner with a good conscience and a better appetite, and being as amiable as he was forgetful, mentioned particularly to Mrs. Lovitt how sorry he was not to have been able to accept her kind invitation of last week.

It was a little thing, but Mrs. Lovitt foresaw that it might lead to complications. And so the Brownes departed from No. 61, Park-street, not without thanksgiving.

CHAPTER XX.

FOR the furtherance of a good understanding between the sahibs and the Aryans who obey them and minister unto them, the Raj * has ordained language examinations. This was necessary, because in war, contract-making, or the management of accounts, neither a Ghurka nor a Bengali will comprehend you if you simply swear at him. He must be approached through a rudimentary medium of imperative moods and future tenses. Therefore the institution of the Higher and the Lower Standard, and much anguish on the part of Her Majesty's subalterns. The Raj attaches rather more credit to the former of these examinations, but afterwards the difference is nominal—you forget them with equal facility.

It might be respectively pointed out, however, that the Government of India has done nothing in this direction to stimulate intercourse with the native population among memsahibs. In fact the Government of India does not recognise memsahibs in any way that is not strictly and entirely polite. And so the memsahib "picks up" Hindustani—picks it up in her own simple artless fashion which dispenses with all ordinary aids to the acquirement of a foreign tongue. She gathers together her own vocabulary, gathers it from the east and the west, and the north and the south, from Bengal and Bombay, from Madras and the Punjab, a preposition from Persia, a conjunction from Cashmere,

* Government.

a noun from the Nilgherries. She makes her own rules, and all the natives she knows are governed by them—nothing from a grammatical point of view could be more satisfactory than that. Her constructions in the language are such as she pleases to place upon it; thus it is impossible that she should make mistakes.

The memsahib's Hindustani is nevertheless not perfectly pure, entirely apart from questions of pronunciation, which she regulates somewhat imperiously. This is because she prefers to improve it by the admixture of a little English; and the effect upon the native mind is quite the same. It really doesn't matter whether you say, "That's *bote atcha hai khansamah-gee*," * or "This is very *carab*, † you stupid *ool-ka-beta*," ‡ or use the simple Hindustani statements to express your feelings. The English may adorn them, but it is the Hindustani after all that gives vitality to your remarks. "*Chokee lao*," means "bring a chair," but if you put it, "bring me a *chokee lao*," the meaning of the command is not seriously interfered with, beside convincing you more firmly that you have said what you wanted to say. I suppose Mrs. Browne talked more Hindustani to Kali Bagh than to anybody else, and one dinner's dialogue, so to speak, might be like this:

"*Kul ka* # mutton, how much is there, Kali Bagh?"

"*Ha, bus hai, hazur.*" ‖

"Then you may *irony-stew do*, ^ and undercut beefsteak *muncta*, ◊ and mind you find an *atcha wallah*. ‡ Onions fry *ka sat, sumja?*" ↕

* Very good, worthy Khansamah.
† Bad.
‡ Son of an owl.
\# Of yesterday.
‖ Yes, there is enough, your honour.
^ Give an Irish stew.
◊ I want.
‡ Good one.
↕ Therewith, do you understand?

"*Ha, hazur! Bote atcha wallah miliga.** *Ecpuddin kawasti?*" †

"Oh, you can plum-pudding, *do*—a *chota wallah*, and *cabadur bote* plenty *kismiss*." ‡

"*Brunndi-sauce ka sat?*" #

"*Na.* Put into whiskey-shrab. *Brunndi burra dom hai.* ‖ And *dekko*, curry *hazri na muncta*, tiffin *muncta*."

This last statement is to the effect that curry does not want breakfast, wants tiffin, but the heathen mind never translates the memsahib literally. It picks the words it knows out of her discourse and links them together upon a system of probabilities which long application and severe experiences have made remarkably correct. Then it salaams and acts. The usually admirable result is misleading to the memsahib, who naturally ascribes it to the grace and force and clearness of her directions. Whereas it is really the discernment of Kali Bagh that is to be commended.

Considering the existence of the Higher and Lower Standard there is less difference between the Hindustani of Anglo-Indian ladies and Anglo-Indian gentlemen than one would expect. The sahib has several choice epithets that do not attach themselves to the vocabulary of the memsahib, who seldom allows her wrath to run to anything more abusive than "Son-of-an-Owl," or "Poor-kind-of-man," and the voice of the sahib is in itself a terrible thing so that all his commands are more emphatic, more quickly to be obeyed. But he is pleased to use much the same forms of speech as are common to the memsahib, and if he isn't understood he will know the reason why. The same delicate autocracy

* I will find.

† And for pudding?

‡ Take care to put plenty of raisins.

With brandy sauce?

‖ Brandy is a large price.

pervades the sahib's Hindustani as characterises most of his relations with his Indian fellow-subjects. He has subdued their language, as it were, to such uses as he thinks fit to put it, and if they do not choose to acquire it in this form, so much the more inconvenient for them. He can always get another kitmutgar. The slight incongruities of his system do not present themselves to the sahib. He has a vague theory that one ought not to say *tum* * to a Rajah, but he doesn't want to talk to Rajahs —he didn't come out for *that*. So that my accuracy need not be doubted I will quote the case of Mr. Perth Macintyre, and I am quite sure that if Mr. Perth Macintyre were to be presented to the Nizam of Hyderabad to-morrow—an honour he would not at all covet—he would find nothing better to say to him in Hindustani than "*Atcha hai?*" †—the formula he would use to a favourite syce.

Mrs. Browne had a great aptitude for languages. She had brought her German prizes with her, and used to look at them with much satisfaction when the problem of conquering Hindustani was new to her, and she thought it would be a matter of some difficulty. She had ambitious ideas at first, connected with a grammar and a dictionary, and one January afternoon she learned a whole page of rules for the termination of the feminine. Mrs. Macdonald found her at it, and assured her earnestly that she was "going the wrong way about it." "With all you have to do," declared Mrs. Macdonald, "you'll never get to the end of that book, and when you do you'll have forgotten the beginning. Whatever is the difference to you whether ghoree is the feminine for horse, or what the plural is! They're all gorahs! Now I picked up Hindustani in the ordinary way. I listened, and

* You (familiar).

† Are you well? (familiar).

whenever I didn't know a thing I asked my ayah what its name was—and in two months I spoke the language *fluently*. So will you, but never with a grammar; a grammar won't help you to order dinner. Neither will a dictionary—you won't find 'hoss-nallis' in a dictionary. That's Hindustani for 'horse-radish.' It's awfully funny, how like English the language is in some words?"

"Is it?" said Helen, "I hadn't noticed that. It must be quite easy to learn, then."

"Oh, *quite!* For instance, where we say 'stable,' and 'coat,' and 'beer,' they say 'ishtable,' and 'coatee,' and 'beer-shrab.' And the Hindustani for 'kettle' is 'kettley,' and for 'bottle,' 'botle.' Oh, it's not a difficult language!"

One does not cling to a manual of Hindustani in the face of the protestations of one's friends, and Mrs. Browne found herself induced to abandon hers before the terminations for the feminine were quite fixed in her mind. One might just as well acquire the language in a less laborious way. So she paid diligent attention, for one thing, to ordinary Anglo-Indian conversation, which is in itself a very fair manual of Hindustani. There is hardly any slang in Anglo-India, the tongue of the gentle Hindu supplies a substitute for that picturesque form of expression. It permeates all classes of society, that is, both Covenanted and Uncovenanted classes; and there are none so dignified in speech as to eschew it. Mrs. Wodenhamer uses it, and the missionaries' wives. It is ever on the tongue of Kitty Toote; I have no doubt it creeps into the parlance of Her Excellency. Therefore it cannot be vulgar. Only this morning, Mrs. Jack Lovitt in the course of ten minutes' conversation in my drawing-room simply scintillated with it. She wanted to know if it was pucca that we were going home for good next hot weather, and remarked that it was a pity we had the house on a long bundabust,* it was always such a dick and worry to get rid of a lease. One of her kitmutgars had been giving her trouble—she was afraid he was a bad jat of man—he was turning out a regular budmash.† He attended to his hookums ‡ very well, but he was always getting into golmals # with the other servants. Had I heard the gup about Walter Toote's being in trouble with his Department? Awful row on, Mrs. Lovitt believed. And had I been at Government House the night before? It was getting altogether too gurrum ‖ for nautches now. As for her, she had been up every blessed night for a week with Mrs. Gammidge's butcha ^—awfully bad with dysentery, poor little wretch—and was too done to go. It was quite time the season was over, and yet they had three burra khanas ◊ on for next week.

It will be evident that a very limited amount of intercourse of this sort will assist tremendously toward a self-satisfying acquaintance with Hindustani. There is a distinct flavour of the language about it. But this lingers only in India. We leave it when we sail away from the Apollo Bunder,‡ where it attaches itself to the first new-comers. It belongs to the land of the kitmutgar; it forsakes us utterly in Kensington.

Mrs. Browne found it very facilitating, and if she did not finally learn to speak like a native she speedily learned to speak like a memsahib, which was more desirable. In the course of time young Browne forgave her the agonies her initiation cost him. They began early in the morning when Helen remarked that it was a very "atcha" day, they continued at breakfast when

* Agreement.
† Blackguard.
‡ Orders.
\# Rows.
‖ Hot.
^ Offspring.
◊ Big dinners.
‡ The Bombay jetty.

she asked him if he would have an "unda"* or some "muchli"† or some "tunda beef,"‡ and it went on at intervals from five o'clock till bed-time. It was her impression, poor dear thing, that she was humorous in this—it was not for six whole months that she learned how Anglo-India sanctions Hindustani for grim convenience only, declining to be amused by it in any way whatever, and has placed its own stamp upon such time-established expressions as are admissible. More than these are recognised to come of vanity and the desire of display, and Anglo-India will have none of them. In the meantime Mrs. Browne trespassed daily, smiling and unaware. At first her George received these pleasantries with a pained smile. Then he looked solemn, then severe. When Mrs. Browne's lapses had been particularly flagrant a chill fell upon their intercourse which she was puzzled to understand. Whereupon she tried to dissipate it by the jocular use of more Hindustani, which made young Browne wriggle in his chair. They arrived at a point where it was obviously impossible to go on. It did not occur to young Browne to propose a separation, though he had shocking liver that day, but he arose suddenly and said he'd be hanged if he'd stand being talked Hindustani to any longer. Thereat Mrs. Browne, being a person of tender feelings, wept. Whereat Mr. Browne, being a man of sentiment in spite of liver complications, was instantly reduced to nothingness and suppliance, when explanations of course ensued, and Helen was made acquainted with most of the information in this chapter. In the upshot, whether Mrs. Browne never spoke a word of Hindustani again, as she proposed, or spoke it all day long for a year and nothing could be sweeter, as he proposed, I have never been made aware.

* Egg. † Fish. ‡ Cold beef.

CHAPTER XXI.

IT would be improper to pretend to chronicle even the simple adventures of a memsahib without a respectful reference to their clerical side. The reference will be slight; but it must be made, if only in answer to Aunt Plovtree's communication upon the subject, in which she took the trouble to remark particularly how curious it was that Helen's letters said so little about parish matters or a clergyman. One might almost fancy, said Aunt Plovtree, that such things did not exist in India; and it is highly inadvisable that these chapters should produce a similar impression. Helen replied to her aunt that on the contrary there were several churches scattered about Calcutta, with clergymen attached to all of them, also an Archdeacon and a Bishop. Some were higher than others—the clergymen she meant—and she believed that a number of them were very nice. She didn't know any of the clergymen themselves yet; but she had met one or two of the wives of the junior chaplains, and one she thought an awfully sweet woman. The Archdeacon she didn't know by sight, the Bishop she had seen once at a distance. They—the Brownes—were not quite sure which parish they belonged to yet; but when they found out she would be sure to mention anything connected with it that she thought would interest her dearest Aunt Plovtree. Doubtless Mrs. Plovtree thought that this left something to be desired, and if my chapter should provoke the same opinion I can only deplore without presuming to question it.

The Government of India provides two medical departments for the benefit of its servants: one for the body and one for the soul. The Government of India has the reputation of being a hard taskmaster, but its liberality is not questioned here, unless one cavils at being obliged to pay one's own undertaker. It has arranged, educated, graduated, and certificated assistance in all cases of bodily and spiritual extremity free of charge, assuming, however, no ultimate responsibility, except towards the higher grades of the Covenanted Ones. To them, I believe, it guarantees heaven; but it is difficult to obtain accurate information upon this point, especially as that state is apt to be confounded out here with the rank and privileges of a Knight Commander of the Order of the Star of India.

It is, of course, a debatable question—I speak here of the senior chaplains; the junior chaplains suffer an almost prohibitive baby-tax, which, to a junior chaplain, is a serious financial consideration, and his pay is not luxurious—but I have always understood that the spiritual service of the Raj is not such an excessively bad thing. I know that comparatively few of its members are of this opinion, and I have no doubt that the peculiarly agreeable absence of theological controversy in India is due to the fact that the energy of reverend gentlemen is largely occupied in popularising a different one. Still it remains the lay idea that the chaplains of the Government of India are in their father-in-law's house. The term of service is brief, and during its course the reverend servant may claim to write his sermons and proclaim the example of the wicked man for three years comfortably in a hill station, where his clerical liver need never compel his clerical temper to spend itself unbecomingly upon kitmutgars. His pay is moderate, but as high probably as could be considered prudent in view of the undesirability of encouraging worldliness in a spiritual department, and it is not written in his contract that the beady simpkin shall enhance his little dinner parties.

"Pegs, claret, and beer for a junior chaplain," remarked one of Calcutta's spiritual advisers to me once; "but sherry is expected as well of a senior chaplain, and even curaçoa!" He spoke ruefully, for he was a senior chaplain, and given to hospitality. The reverend brotherhood are eligible for three months' privilege leave every year upon full pay, and three years' furlough during service on half pay. In addition to which they do not scruple to hold "retreats," also doubtless upon full official allowances, though their cardinal features may be fish and eggs. They enter into their reward early, and it is a substantial one—three hundred a year, and such pickings as offer themselves in England to reverend gentlemen with a competency. Neither is the exercise of faith required of them in regard to it; it is in the bond. In this respect it is obvious that the Indian vineyard offers a distinct advantage over others, where the labourers are expected to be contented with abstract compensations to be enjoyed after their decease. Popularly they are known as "padres," which is a Portuguese survival more respectable than any other, and a demi-official tag which admits its owner to society. It ought to be mentioned that the Indian padre does not move in the atmosphere of feminine adoration which would be created for him in England; there are too many other men for that. Doubtless the more attractive of the junior chaplains, sent out, as it were, in cotton wool, miss the little attentions of the ladies of the parish at home, but then they have their polo ponies and their pegs.

There were various reasons why Mrs. George Browne had been compelled to write to her inquiring aunt that as yet she had not the pleasure of any clergyman's acquaintance. The padres are official, for one thing, and one does not approach an official in India—especially if one is a commercial—without some appropriate excuse. When the Brownes wanted to be married a reverend gentleman married them, and did it very well—as they always do in the cathedral—for I was looking on. If either of them had since required to be buried he would doubtless have done that with the same ability, despatch, and desire to oblige. He might also in the future be applied to with propriety in connection with a christening. If the Brownes' water-pipes leaked the Brownes would with equal and similar propriety request the Municipal Engineer to mend them and they would be mended, but the Municipal Engineer would probably not consider himself naturally drawn within the circle of the Brownes' amicable social relations in consequence. Mrs. Brown would not call upon Mrs. Municipal Engineer to assure her that they were well mended. The spiritual official also discharges his duty as specified, and one would have an equal hesitation, generally, in interpreting it too broadly. And, indeed, with only the forms and papers relating to the nuptial, baptismal, and burial business of the capital upon his hands the Calcutta cleric may claim to be overburdened.

His cemetery work alone would keep a hill padre from all sloth and fatness.

Bien entendu, the missionary padres are different. The missionary padres are not official. I have no doubt the Government would interfere to prevent their being eaten if the Bengali baboo were carnivorous; but he is not, he has no fleshy tastes; he prefers an inglorious diet of rice, fried sweetmeats and mango chutney, to even a stalled chaplain, beside whom a missionary padre is lean and tough. Moreover, the Bengali baboo was never designed for the shedding of blood. So that the Government has really no responsibilities toward the missionary padres. It will educate and sanitate the baboo, but it leaves his salvation to private enterprise, undertaking nothing on behalf of the *entrepreneurs*.

The missionary padre receives his slender stipend from the S. P. G. or from some obscure source in America. It is arranged upon a scale to promote self-denial, and it is very successful. He usually lives where the drains are thickest and the smells most unmanageable, and when we of the broad river and the great Maidan happen to hear of his address, we invariably ejaculate, "What a frightfully long way off!" The ticca gharry is not an expensive conveyance, but the missionary padre finds himself better commended of his conscience if he walks and pays the cost of his transportation in energy and vitality, which must be heavy in the hot weather and the rains. For the rest, he lives largely upon second-class beef and his ideals, though they don't keep very well either in this climate. Those who come out celibates remain celibates if not by force of conviction by force of circumstances. The expensively home-bred young ladies of Anglo-India are not for missionaries! Whereas those who are married are usually married to missionary ladies of similar size and complexion labouring in the same cause. Covenanted chaplains, on the contrary, with the prospects I have mentioned, may be yoked together with the *débutante* of any season. So there is this further difference, that while the official padre's wife looks like any other memsahib, the missionary padre's wife looks like the missionary padre. I believe that chaplains sometimes ask missionary padres to dinner "quietly," and always make a point of giving them plenty to eat. And I remember meeting a married pair of them at the Brownes', a Mr. and Mrs. Week. Young Browne had known Mr. Week at school before his vocation appeared to him. He was an undersized young man, high-shouldered, very hollow-chested, and wore his long hair brushed back from his high forehead, almost, one might say, behind his ears. She was a little white woman in a high dress, and wore her locks, which were beginning to thin, in a tiny knot at the very back of her crown. It was in the hot weather, and they spoke appreciatively of the punkah. They had no punkah, it seemed, either day or night; but the little wife had been very clever, and had made muslin bags for their heads and hands to keep off the mosquitoes while they were asleep. We couldn't ascertain that either of them had ever been really well since they came out, and they said they simply made up their minds to have sickness in the house during the whole of the rains. It was either neuralgia or fever that season through, and neither of them knew which was worst. I asked Mrs. Week inadvertently if she had any children. She said "No," and there was a silence which Helen explained afterwards by telling me that Mrs. Week had lost her only baby from diphtheria, which they attributed to a certain miasma that "came up through the floor."

Young Browne tried to make the conversation, but it invariably turned to some aspect of the "work," and left him blundering and embarrassed, with no resource except to beg Mrs. Week to have another slice of the joint. They knew little of the Red Road or the Eden Gardens, where the band plays in the evening; they talked of strange places — Khengua Puttoo's Lane—Coolootollah. Mrs. Week told us that her great difficulty in the zenanas lay in getting the ladies to talk. They liked her to come, they were always pleased and polite, but they seemed interested in so few things. When Mrs. Week had asked them if they were well, and how much of a family they had, and how old the children were, there seemed to be no getting any further, and she could *not* chew betel with them. Mrs. Week said she had tried, but it was no use. She loved her zenana ladies, they were dear things, and she knew they were attached to her, but they were provoking, too, sometimes. One day last week she had talked very seriously to them for nearly an hour, and they had seemed most attentive. Just as she was going away one of them—an old lady—approached her, with cast-down eyes and great reluctance, wishing to speak. Mrs. Week encouraged her to begin—was she at last to see some fruit of her visits? And the old lady had said "*Eggi bat*," would the memsahib please to tell them why she put those shiny black hooks in her hair?

Everybody laughed; but Mrs. Week added gravely that she had shown them the use of hairpins, and taken them a packet next day, to their great delight. "One never can tell," said Mrs. Week, "what these trifles may lead to."

And Mr. Week had been down in the Sunderbunds, far down in the Sunderbunds where the miasmas are thickest, and where he had slept every night for a week on a bench in the same small room with two baboos and the ague. Mr. Week had found the people very much interested in the joys of the future state; their attention only flagged, he said, when he referred to the earthly preparation for them. Mr. Week was more emaciated than clever. He spoke with an enthusiastic cockney twang of his open-air meetings and discussions in Dhurrumtollah, of the anxiety with which the baboos wished to discuss the most recondite theological points with him. "Yes," said Mr. Perth Macintyre, "the baboo is a great buck-wallah." * There is reason to fear that the lay community of Calcutta is rather inclined to consider the baboo's soul an unproved entity.

Returning to the senior and junior chaplains, it is delightful to see the natural man under the Indian surplice. At home the padre is an order, in India he is an individual. He is not suppressed by parish opinion, he is rather encouraged to expand in the smile of the Raj, which is above all and over all. He is official, joyous, free, and he develops happily along the lines which Nature designed for him before ever he turned aside into the crooked paths of theology. It is seeing by these lights that we say so often of an Indian padre, "What an excellent politician, broker, soldier, insurance agent he would have made?"

Being now, as one might say, a sheep of some age and experience and standing in the community, I have agreeable recollections of many shepherds. Most of them have long since retired upon pension, while the flock is still wistfully baaing over the bars toward the west. Doubtless the reunion will not be long deferred. It will take place at Bournemouth, and we will talk of the debased value of the rupee. For one, I should like to see Padre Corbett again—he would be able to express himself so forcibly on the subject of the rupee. Padre Corbett, it is my certain belief, entered the Church because there was no practicable alternative. He looked facts in the face in a

* Talker.

business-like manner, shook his big square head over them, smoked a farewell pipe to the sturdy *bêtises* of his youth, and went in for orders under the advice of a second cousin in the India Office. Then he came out to minister to the soul of Tommy Atkins in Murshidabad, where it is very hot, and whether it was the heat of Murshidabad, or the atmosphere of military discipline there, Padre Corbett got into the way of ordering Tommy Atkins to come to be saved and not to answer back or otherwise give trouble about it, that I remember him by. Padre Corbett never lost the disciplinary air and ideas of Murshidabad. As he marched up the aisle of peaceful St. Ignatius in Calcutta behind his choir boys, there was a distinct military swagger in the rear folds of his surplice, and he put us through our devotional drill with the rapidity and precision of a field-marshal. "Fours about! *Trot!* you miserable sinners!" he gave us to understand at the beginning of the Psalms, and the main battalion of St. Ignatius in the pews, following the directing flank under the organ came on from *laudite* to *laudite* at a magnificent pace. The sermon was a tissue of directions and a statement of consequences; we were deployed out of church. We bowed to it, it was quite befitting. We were not Tommy Atkinses, but we were all officially subordinated to Padre Corbett in a spiritual sense; in the case of an archangel from Simla it would be quite the same, and he was perfectly entitled to "have the honor to inform" us that we would do well to mend our ways. This sense of constituted authority and the fitness of things would naturally lead Padre Corbett to the chaste official glories of the archdeaconry. Indeed, I'm not sure that it didn't.

The Rev. T. C. Peterson, too, once of St. Pancras. I wonder in what rural corner of South Devonshire Padre Peterson to-

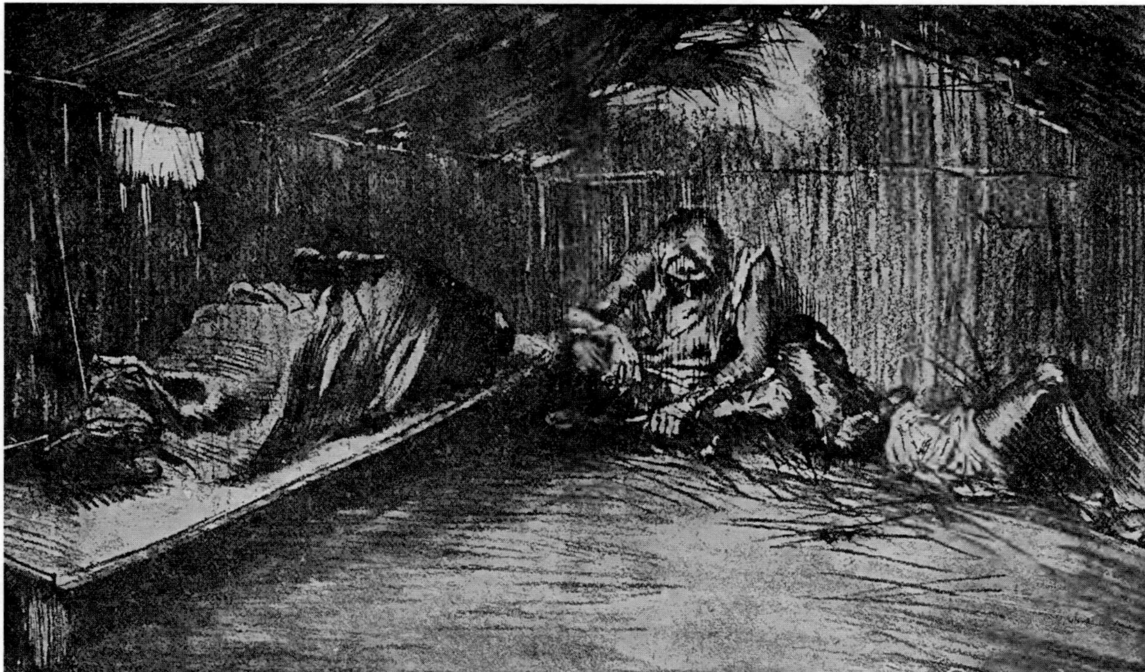

MR. WEEK SLEPT ON A BENCH IN THE SAME SMALL ROOM, WITH TWO BABOOS AND THE AGUE.

day entertains Dorcas meetings with innocently amusing accounts of domestic life in India! He was always by way of being amusing, was Padre Peterson; he had a fine luminous smile, which he invariably took with him when he went out to dine. He was kindly and unostentatious, he lived simply and quietly, giving a little of his money to the poor and putting a great deal of it into the Bank of Bengal pending a desirable rate of exchange. Padre Peterson was every inch a padre; there was nothing but ecclesiastical meekness in *his* surplice of a Sunday; and even his secular expression, notwithstanding the smile, spoke of high ideals and an embarrassed compromise with week-day occupations. He had a humble, hopeful way of clasping his hands and sloping his shoulders and arranging his beard over his long black cassock, especially when he sat at meat, which reminded one irresistibly, though I admit the simile is worn, of an oriel apostle in stained glass. He was seriously happy, and he made old, old Anglo-Indian jokes with his luminous smile in a manner which was peculiarly maddening to the enlarged liver of Calcutta. He would have hesitated to employ coercion even as a last resort with his flock of St. Pancras. He was no shepherd with a cracking whip, he would go before rather, and play upon the lute and dance and so beguile the sheep to follow. His amiability was great; he was known to "get on" with everybody. Nobody knew precisely why Padre Peterson always got everything he wanted, but it was obscurely connected with the abounding charity for sinners in general, and official sinners in high places in particular, which was so characteristic of him. He could placate an angry Under-Secretary, and when an Under-Secretary is angry India quakes and all the Lieutenant-Governors go to bed. The finances in St. Pancras were never in better hands. St. Pancras had a new organ, a new font, and new beams and rafters all through in Padre Peterson's day. If new graves and gravestones had been as urgently required then as they are now, Padre Peterson would have found the money and had the thing done at the lowest contract rates. A remarkable man in many ways, and now that I think of it, he's dead, quite a long time ago.

Others I seem to remember best in some secular connection. Padre Jenkins, whose pony won the Gymkhana Cup at the Barrackpore races of I can't remember just what year; Padre MacWhirter, who used to say very truly that he made golf what it was in Alipore; Padre Lewis-Lewis, who had for five years the most charming manners and the best choir in Calcutta. But there is no reason why I should count them over to you. Long since they have disappeared, most of them, with their little flat black felt hats on their heads and their tennis racquets in their hand, into the fogs of that northerly isle whither in the end we all go and whence none of us return. This chapter is really more of an apology to Mrs. Plovtree than anything else.

Mrs. Plovtree will be grieved, however, and justly so, that I have not said more about the Indian bishop. The explanation is that I have never known a bishop very well, as I have never known a Viceroy very well. Even at my own dinner-table I have never permitted myself to observe a bishop beyond the point of admiration. Some day in Bournemouth, however, I will write a thoughtful essay on the points of similarity, so far as I have noticed them, between Indian bishops and other kinds, and sent it to the *Guardian*, where Mrs. Plovtree will be sure to see it; but it is not considered wise in India to write critical estimates of bishops or of any other heads of departments until after one retires. I might just say that the bishop, like the Viceroy, is a foreign plenipotentiary. He does not rise from the withered ranks of the Indian service, but, like the Viceroy, comes out fresh from the culling hand of the Secretary of State. He divides with the Viceroy certain Divine rights, divinest of which is the right not to care a parrot's eyelash for anybody. In consequence the bishop holds his venerable head high and dines where he pleases. Certain of the Raj-enthralled of Calcutta find the independence of a bishop offensive. In me it provokes a lively enthusiasm. I consider the episcopal attitude even more valuable than the episcopal blessing, even more interesting than the episcopal discourse. And I agree with Mrs. Browne, who thinks it must be lovely to be a bishop.

But neither for our spiritual pastors and masters are times what they were. There was a day, now faded, with all the rollicking romance of John Company Bahadur, when two honest butts of golden crown madeira a year helped to alleviate the sorrows of exile for King George's chaplains in India—the present Secretary of State would probably see them teetotallers first! The mails come out in a fortnight, the competition-wallah overruns the land, the Rajah studies French. India is not what it was, and another of the differences is that the padres buy their own madeira.

I saw a priest of Kali, wrapped in his yellow chudder, sit hugging his knees under a mahogany tree to-night beside the broad road where the carriages passed rolling into the "cow's dust" of the twilight. A brother cleric of the Raj went by in his victoria with his wife and children, and the yellow robed one watched them out of sight. There was neither hatred nor malice nor any evil thing in his gaze, only perhaps a subtle appreciation of the advantages of the other cloth.

CHAPTER XXII.

HAVING suited themselves with the furnished house of a junior civilian, who had suddenly decamped before heat apoplexy and gastric complications, the Brownes settled down, if the expression is not too comfortable, to wait for the rains. I should dislike any misunderstanding on the point of comfort. It is not too much to say that the word is not understood in Calcutta. We talk of *aram* here instead, which means a drugged ease with heavy dreams.

The Brownes stored their furniture in the godowns of the other man, and had *aram* nevertheless in contemplating his, which was ugly. *Aram* is cheap—the price of a cup of coffee and a long veranda chair—and seductive; but I was annoyed with Helen Browne for accepting the other people's furniture so pacifically. It seemed to me that she was becoming acclimatised too soon. There is a point in that process where a born British gentlewoman will live without antimacassars and sleep on a charpoy; but I do not wish to be considered a morbid modern analyst, so this need not be enlarged upon. The other people's furniture, moreover, would have been entertaining if it could have talked, to so many people it had been let and sub-let and re-let and leased, always with the house, since it left Bow Bazar, where it was originally bought outright by an extravagant person secondhand. It had never belonged to anybody since: it had always been a mere convenience—a means of enabling people to give dinner parties. No one had ever regarded it, or mended it, or kept it any cleaner than decency required. It was tarnished, cracked, frayed, soiled; it included tables with white marble tops, and bad chromo-lithographs and dusty bunches of dried grasses which nobody had ever taken the trouble to eliminate. In the cold weather certain people had paid five hundred rupees a month for the privilege of living with it; in the hot weather certain other people had lived with it for nothing, to keep the white ants out. Withal it was typical Calcutta furniture—a typical part of the absurd pretence that white people make of being at home in this place.

The rains are due, as all Calcutta knows, on June the fifteenth. That is the limit of our time of pure grilling. We know it is written upon our foreheads that we must turn and writhe and bite the dust in the pain of the sun to that day; but on that day we expect that the clouds will come up out of the east and out of the west and clothe the brazen sky, and interpose between us and the dolour of India. It is what we call a pucca bandobust, arranged through the Meteorological Department, part of the bargain of exile with the Secretary of State. For so many years of active service we get so much pension and so much furlough, and we are to be rained upon every fifteenth of June for three months.

Therefore when the sun arose upon the fifteenth of June of this current year of the Brownes, and marched across the sky without winking, the Brownes were naturally and properly aggrieved together with the Bengal Government and all Calcutta. When one has defined the very point and limit of one's endurance, it is inconsistent and undignified to go on enduring. The ticca-gharry horses were so much of this opinion that they refused too, and dropped down dead all up and down Chowringhee, as a preferable alternative—those that were driven. The more prudent gharry wallah drew up in the reeking shade of some great building—it was cooler in the streets than in the stables—and slept profoundly, refusing all fares till sundown; and the broker-sahib, who spends his life upon wheels, changed horses four times a day. On the night of the fifteenth of June young Browne got up stealthily and deftly turned a jug of water over a hole in the floor through which a punkah rope hung inert. There was a sudden scramble below, the punkah rope sawed convulsively, and young Browne, with a ghastly smile, put out the glimmering candle and went back to bed. It is a popular form of discipline in Calcutta, but as applied by young Browne it bore strikingly upon the weather.

The Maidan cracked and split, and even the broad leaves of the teak-wood tree hung limp and grey under the powder of the road. The crows had nothing to say all day, but hopped about with their beaks ridiculously agape, while the sun blazed down through the flat roofs of Calcutta, and made Mrs. Browne's chairs and tables so hot that it was a surprise to touch them. At the same time it drew up the evil soul of the odour of the bazars, the "*burra krab* * smell," as Kipling calls the chief characteristic of Calcutta, and cast it abroad in all the city. The Brownes squandered sums upon Condy's fluid wholly disproportionate with their income vainly, for nothing yet known to pharmacy can cope with that smell. It grew hotter and hotter, and sometimes the south wind failed, and then the smell became several smells, special, local, individual, though the frangi-panni tree leaned blooming on its spiky elbows over every garden wall, and made them all sweet and langorous and interesting and truly

* Very bad.

Eastern. The smells were not of great consequence; one gets accustomed to the smells as one gets accustomed to the curries. Mrs. Browne declared, too, that one could put up with the weather, and the cholera, and sunstroke—one didn't particularly mind even having one's house turned inside out occasionally by a dust-storm. The really trying things—the things one hadn't reckoned with beforehand—were that one's envelope flaps should all stick down; that the pages of one's books should curl up; that the towel should sting one's face; that the punkah should stop in the night. Even under these greater afflictions we are uncomplaining up to the fifteenth of June. But the sixteenth passed over these Brownes, and the seventeenth and the eighteenth, and many days more, and still the dusty sun went down in the smoky west, and against the great red glow of his setting the naked beesties ran like black gnomes with their goat skins on their hips, slaking the roads that were red too. . . . And a mile and a league all round about the city the ryot folded his hands before his baking rice-fields, not knowing that men wrote daily in the *Englishman* about him, and wondered in what way he had offended Lakshmi that for so many days she should withhold the rain!

. . . .

A shutter banged downstairs at three o'clock in the morning, there came a cool swishing and a subsiding among the fronds of the date-palms, the gold mohur trees raised their heads and listened—it was coming. Far down in the Sunderbunds it was raining, and with great sweeps and curves it rained further and further inland. Calcutta turned more easily upon its pillow, and slept sound and late, the punkah-wallah slept also with impunity, and when the city awoke in the morning the rains had come.

Mrs. Browne professed to find a great difference and novelty in the rains of India. She declared that they came from lower down, that they were whiter and greyer, that they didn't refresh the earth, but beat it and sat upon it, that there was quite an extraordinary quality of moisture about them. I believe every new-comer makes similar observations. To the rest of us, it has been obvious for so many years that during July, August, and September a considerable amount of water descends upon Bengal, that we have ceased to make original remarks about it. But Bengal certainly gets very wet, and Mrs. Browne's observations as the time went on, and the floods abated not, were entirely excusable. Every day it rained, more in the morning and less in the evening, or less in the morning and more in the evening. The garden became a jungle, the English flowers that had died a puzzled death in May, sent up hysterical long shoots; one could see the grass growing. An adjutant sailed in from the mofussil * marshes, trailing his legs behind him, to look for frogs on the Maidan. He stood on one leg to look for them, upon the bronze head of Lord Lawrence, and his appearance, with his chin buried thoughtfully in his bosom, was much more sapient than that of the administrator underneath. In the evening he flew back again, and then the frogs were at liberty to express their opinion of him. They spoke strongly, as was natural; one of them, in the tank of Ram Dass Hurrymunny, barked like a pariah. The crickets did their concerted best to outvoice the frogs, the cicadas reinforced the crickets, and all the other shrill-voiced things that could sing in the dark, sang in such a wheezy heaving eternal monotone, that Mr. and Mrs. Browne, sitting damply behind their open windows, were quite reduced to silence.

* Country.

They were planting the little green rice shoots in the mofussil, they wanted it all and more; but Mrs. Browne in Calcutta was obliged to look in the newspapers for the assurance that she ought to be thankful for quite so much rain. It seemed to Mrs. Browne that all her relations with the world were being submerged, and that she personally was becoming too wet. She found it an unnatural and unpleasant thing that furniture should perspire; and when in addition to the roof leaking, and the matting rotting, and the cockroaches multiplying, the yellow sunset and the blue sea of her nicest water-colour mixed themselves up in a terrible and crumpled and impossible manner, Mrs. Browne added tears to the general moisture, and thought the very fabric of her existence was dissolving. Besides that, the Rev. Peachey came unglued out of his blue plush frame, and Aunt

HE STOOD UPON ONE LEG ON THE BRONZE HEAD OF LORD LAWRENCE.

Plovtree developed yellow spots. Moreover, a green mould sprouted in the soles of their shoes, fresh every morning, and Helen's evening dresses and gloves "went," as she expressed it in writing to Canbury, "all sorts of colours." To pass over the fact that centipedes began to run in their playful zigzag way across the floor, and young Browne killed a snake in the veranda, which he was not indisposed to believe a cobra. Helen thought there was no room for doubt about it, and, as a matter of fact, one hardly ever hears of a snake being killed in Calcutta that is not a cobra. The harmless varieties have a remarkable facility in keeping out of the way.

All over India it was raining, coming down hard on the marginless plains, on the great slopes of the Himalayas, on the great cities where the bunnias hive gold in the bazars, on the little thatched brown villages where the people live and die like harmless animals, with the memory that once or twice they have had enough to eat.

But more than anywhere it seemed to rain in Calcutta, where only about six feet of solid ground intervenes between the people and the bottomless miry pit. So that it is telling the literal truth to say that Calcutta was soaked through and through, dripping, reeking, pestilentially drunken with water. Infinite deeps below, infinite sources above, between the two a few macadamised roads, and an inadequate supply of gutters and drain-pipes. And yet it is not recorded that at any time Calcutta has succumbed to the rains, and sunk swamped into herself.

Nevertheless, at first it was a few degrees cooler, and, to borrow a phrase from the press, there was a slight increase in social activity. People began to give dinners. There are people in Bengal whom all the manifestations of Providence and of Nature together would not prevent giving dinners. They find it agreeable to feel the warming, drying influence of the various forms of carbon prepared by the khansamah in company. They talk of appointments, promotions, and the Lieutenant-Governor, and they chatter as if the ague were already upon them, about how much more sociable Calcutta is in the rains than in the cold weather—you get to know people so much better.

Then there were days when it didn't rain; it shone. Early in the morning it shone with a vague and watery brilliance in the sky, and a curious white gleam over the earth. Later the shining was hot, and straight, and strong, and then Calcutta steamed, and one saw a parboiled baboo at every corner. Later still the sun went down over the river, and then one saw hundreds of parboiled baboos everywhere; and on the Maidan, driving about in carriages, a few score of the very whitest people on earth. The Brownes were as white as anybody. Privately Helen thought her complexion much more interesting than it used to be, and coveted a barouche to lean back and look languidly bored in like the few burra memsahibs that devotedly stayed in Calcutta. It was impossible to be languid in a tum-tum, which is an uncompromising vehicle, not constructed to encourage poses.

Behind their stubby little country-bred, Mr. and Mrs. Browne, taking the air, saw a Calcutta that never revealed itself to any globe-trotter, and which you will not find described in the printed experiences in cloth, at 7s. 6d., of Jonas Batcham, for instance. They saw the broad Maidan laid out in lakes and rivers, with a theatrical sun, set in purple and gold, dissolving in each of them, and all the spaces between a marvellous lush-green, where the horses sank to their fetlocks. Floating over it they saw a gossamer white pall that consisted of water and bacilli in a state of suspension, and hung abreast of the people. Calcutta has a saving grace, known to her Anglo-Indians as the Casuerina-avenue. You can lose your soul in the infinite filmy shadows of the marching trees. Even the Indian sunlight, filtering through their soft dead green, becomes a delicate thing. The Brownes saw this ranged before them, misty and wonderful in the evening, hiding the last of the glow in its plumy nearer branches, and piling up soft clouds of dusk as it stretched further away. They saw the fort and all the pillared façade of Chowringhee, with its monuments and palaces and praying places yellow against a more and more empurpled sky, and the grey spire of the cathedral rising in its green corner of the Maidan behind a cluster of trees and a brimming lake, just as it might do in England. Calcutta sits close beside her river, and there are no miles of teeming wharfage between her and it. The great ships lie with their noses against the bank, and the level road runs beside them. Thus, by a wise provision of the municipality, people who live in Calcutta are able to drive down every day and see for themselves that it is possible to get away. For this reason the Brownes loved the close ships and all the populous river, lying under the wraith of the rains—the faint outlines of the crowding masts, with the sunset sky behind them as far as they could see; the majestic grey ghost of the old East Indiamen at anchor, with her "state cabin" full of dates from Mocha; slipping towards them solitarily out of the unreality the dipping red-brown three-cornered sail of an Arab dhow. Eloquently always the river breathed of exile and of home-going, sometimes with her own proper voice, sometimes with the tongue of a second mate from Portsmouth, or the twang of a negro cook from Savannah, full of airs and superciliousness. It depended on where you lived yourself when you were at home.

On a corner of the Maidan a number of mad young Englishmen played football; in another place there was a lively sale of goats for sacrifice. An erection of red and gold paper, like a Chinese pagoda, still wobbled about the biggest tank in propitiation of its god. Calcutta emptied itself on its wide green acres. The Brownes met a smart turnout with a thoroughbred, driven at a spanking pace by a pucca Chinaman, who leant forward nonchalantly with his pigtail streaming out behind. They met a fiery pair in a mail-phaeton, with two anxious syces behind, and driving on the high seat a small, bold, brown lady, all in green and pink gauze, tinselled, bareheaded, wearing her iniquity as lightly as a feather. They met a big roomy barouche, with two servants on the box, two more behind, and an ayah inside, all in attendance upon a tiny white mite of a belati baby. A small British terrier met them, regarded them, sniffed them, wagged his tail and followed them. They were not personal friends of his, but they were sahibs, and his countrymen; they would understand his lost estate, a sahib's dog; he could confide himself to their good feeling and hospitality pending explanations. And so the stubby little country-bred trotted down the river road till he came to a place where the road widened—where, beside an octagonal erection with a roof, a great many other stubby little country-breds and slender Arabs and big Walers stood very quietly between their shafts with drooping heads; and here he turned, almost of his own accord, and trotted in amongst them until he found comfortable standing room, when he stopped. This was Calcutta's place of pleasure. Behind the octagonal erection, where presently the band would play, stretched those

Eden Gardens which the photographers reproduce so effectively, and the globe-trotters buy so abundantly. Here we have the elements of the most romantic municipal scenery—tall palms and red poinsettias, a fine winding artificial lake with a beautiful arched artificial bridge, realistic artificial rocks cropping out of the grass, and a genuine Burmese pagoda of white chunam, specially constructed for the gardens, in the middle of it all. The pagoda runs up into a spire, or a lightning conductor, or something of that nature; and on the top of this a frolicsome British tar once placed an empty soda-water bottle upside down. I think the native municipal commissioners regard this with some pride as a finial ornament; certainly nobody has ever taken it down. And that is as well, for the soda-water bottle gives, one might say, the key to the design of the place, which might otherwise puzzle the stranger. I should not omit to say that the gardens are illuminated with electric light, as such gardens of course should be. The people walk up and down under the electric light, looking at each other; the young men go in among the carriages and talk to the ladies they know. Calcutta makes a violent attempt to distract itself. On this particular evening the Brownes also came to distract themselves—it becomes a habit in time.

The electric light sputtered and fizzled over the crowd of standing carriages. Helen thought it darkened the black circle round young Browne's eyes; and he asked his wife apprehendingly if she were feeling chilled or anything—she looked so white. The damp, warm air clung to their faces. A man in a ticca gharry said to a man in the road that it was damned muggy. Several people in the carriages near heard him say this—it was so quiet. The crowd of carriage-tops gleamed motionless, the horses stood dejectedly on three legs, and under every horse's nose a cotton-clad syce "bitoed"* on the ground with his chin on his knees. A peddling native thrust up a round flat bouquet of pink and white roses that smelt of "Jockey Club." "*Jao!*" said young Browne.

Presently the band played a gay and lightsome air, very sad to hear, from an opera long superseded at home, and with the playing of the band the general depression seemed to thicken and close down. There are people in Calcutta who, even for distraction's sake, cannot stand selections from the *Mikado* so near the end of the century. One by one the carriages began to roll away. Perhaps along the river road there would be a breath of air. The band played a medley, all sorts of things, and then "The Land o' the Leal." I saw the MacTaggarts drive off. "*Syce!*" said Mr. Perth Macintyre; "*buttie jallao! Gur ko!*" † . . . The last of the pink flush faded out of the sky behind the ships. The air grew sodden and chill, a little raw breeze crept in from the east. Young Browne took off his hat to "God Save the Queen," and then "I think we ought to hurry him a little," said Helen, referring to the stubby little country-bred. "It's going to rain."

It was in this month of August, I remember, that we lost a partner of the firm, in a sad though not unusual way. He died, as a matter of fact, from a little Calcutta mud which rubbed itself into his elbow one afternoon when he was thrown out of his brougham. Tetanus the doctors called it, and they said he would have had a better chance if he had been thrown out of his brougham at another time of year. He was buried, poor man, in seven inches of water; and Mr. Perth

* Sat on his heels.

† "Light the (carriage) lamps. To the house!"

Macintyre had two months' fever after attending the dripping funeral.

It would be an affectation to write about Mrs. Browne's experiences and to omit a chapter on at least one phase of the weather; but I could have told you in the beginning that it would not be amusing.

CHAPTER XXIII.

IF you have not entirely forgotten your geography you will know that against the eternal gold and blue of the Indian sky, across and across the middle of the land, there runs unevenly a high white line. You will remember it better, perhaps, as "the trend of the Himalayas," and it may have a latter-day association in your mind with imprudent subalterns and middle-aged ladies who consume a great many chocolates and call each other "my dear girl." Out here we never forget it for a single instant; it survives the boundaries of our native counties, and replaces in our imaginations every height in Europe. We call it "The Snows," and the name is as little presumptuous as any other. It is very far off, and the more like heaven for that reason; moreover, that way Simla lies, which is heaven's outer portal, full of knights and angels. They are distant and imperturbable, the Snows, we can only gaze and wonder and descend again to earth; we have only the globe-trotter's word for it that they do not belong to another world. It is the brown outer ranges that we climb, the heaving brown outer ranges that stand between the Holy of Holies and the eye of the profane, the unbeliever, the alien. Because these brown outer ranges are such very big mountains it is our pleasure to call them "The Hills"—if you talked of spending three months in the mountains it would not be clear that you didn't mean Switzerland. Here we perch our hill-stations, here once in every year or two we grow fat and well-liking, here on the brink of a literal precipice the callow subalterns and the *blasé* married ladies flirt.

It was by the merest accident, which I helped to precipitate, that the Brownes went to the Hills in September. A planter in the Doon * had committed suicide—acute dyspepsia—whose business was in our hands, and somebody had to go to see about it. The junior partner wanted to go, but the junior partner had just come out from England weighing fourteen stone, and I got Mr. Perth Macintyre to persuade him that it was absolutely necessary to spend two months of the rains in Calcutta if he wished to recover his figure. Thus to the Brownes also came the hope of the clean breath of the Hills. I went myself down to Howrah station after dinner to add my blessing to their luggage, but the train was gone. A fat baboo of Bengal told me so, with a wreath of marigolds round his neck. I thought, looking at him, how glad they must be to have turned their faces toward a country where men eat millet and chupatties,† and are lean.

* Valley. † Native cakes of flour and water.

Kasi was there too. Kasi travelled "intermediate," that is to say sitting on the floor, quite comfortably, in a wooden box, iron-barred down the sides to let in light and air. Before the train started Kasi had unrolled all the rugs and pillows, had made ready soap and towels and brushes, and had left the sahib who had been very troublesome all day, and the memsahib who had already unjustly accused him of having forgotten seven things, with nothing to do but to go to bed and to rise again. Then he returned to his own place, where his own kind buzzed about him with flat baskets of sticky brown balls and fried sweetmeats to sell. Kasi regarded them indifferently and bought nothing; the kinship was only skin-deep, the lime-marks upon their foreheads were different, he could not eat from their hands. Secretly, when the shadow of none fell upon it he took from a little brass box his betel solace, then as the train whistled he unwound the ten yards of his turban, wrapped his red chuddar * about him, and disposed himself on the floor to dream of the profit there might be when the sahib took a journey.

In the morning a dry coolness blew in at the windows. It had been raining, it would rain again; but here in Behar the earth had been needy, and her face had grown lovely with the slaking of her great thirst. The rain had washed the air and the sun had dried it; to these dwellers in Calcutta it seemed that they were already on the heights. All night long they had been going through the rice country, where the pale green shoots stood knee-deep in the glistening water for miles around, now they rolled through a land where the crops waved tall with sprouting ears—maize and millet and wheat. The little villages were almost

* Cloth worn over shoulders.

lost in them. High over the grain the ryot's sons kept watch and ward against the thieving parrots in little open thatched houses stuck on the top of a long pole or in the fork of a dead tree. They were perched up there to be safe from the leopard's spring; the leopards like a maize-fed ryot's son. They could give warning, too, if the zemindar's servant came that way, to ask an extra tax for the wedding expenses of his master's second daughter. The little villages seemed of kindly disposition; here was a precarious crop that wanted shade, and upon this field every man had set his bed, one beside another, so that it was covered. They were at ease, the little villages, the crops throve, there would be enough for the zemindar if they pretended to be *very* poor; nobody would starve that year, and perhaps Malita or Alanga would add a new silver bangle to her wedding portion.

The Brownes were too utterly poor for the railway restaurants. They brought a tiffin-basket. Young Browne designed the tiffin-basket, a Chinaman designed the price. It was as big as a small trunk; it would just go under the seat. There was room in it for everything that has yet been thought of in connection with a civilized repast. I believe Mrs. Browne is now using it as a china and linen closet. It held ten rupees' worth of tinned stores among other things, and a kerosene stove. Mrs. Browne filled the rest of it up economically with bread and butter and cold meat, and young Browne added as an after-thought half-a-dozen pints of champagne. It was a modest Anglo-Indian tiffin-basket, and they drew it forth with much joy in the morning, having the carriage to themselves. It was seven o'clock and the train had stopped. Servants were running about the platform with cups of tea and slices of toast for the *chota hazri* of people who hadn't brought tiffin-baskets. "Just for curiosity, George," said Helen, "ask how much they are charging?"

Young Browne, in the unconventionality of his pyjamas,* leaned out of the window. "Hi, you!" he called, "*dom kitna?*" †

"Aht anna, sahib!"

"Good gracious!" cried Mrs. Browne. "*Eight* annas for a cup of tea and two bits of toast! The tiffin-basket *is* a saving, dear!"

"Oh, it is!" responded Mr. Browne, "for the other meals. But now that I think of it, I want my chota hazri *now*, don't you? Hi-ups kitmutgar! *lao chota hazri* and *jeldi karo!*" ‡

"One could so easily boil the water, dear," objected Mrs. Browne.

"For the other meals. But we can't cook our chota hazri. Everything's at the bottom. We shouldn't get it ready till midnight. The fact is," said young Browne decisively, "we ought to have brought a kitmutgar—that would have been a saving if you *like!*" And as the steaming tea came through the window and the price went out, "I don't think it's so very much," said young Browne.

That is the way they began. The precise number and extent of the economies effected by the tiffin-basket will never be recorded, but I believe they drank the champagne.

I doubt either your information or your gratification at being told that they changed at Mogulsarai. Mogulsarai is on the map, but you will not find it there because you will not look—which I do not say censoriously; it is quite enough that Anglo-Indians should be obliged to remember the names of such places. They are curiously profane, with their crowded little roofs and

* Night garments worn by men in India. † "Price, how much?"
‡ "Bring a little breakfast, and be quick about it!"

their mosque-towers; and they are very hot. The Brownes' train lay on a side-track baking, as they entered it, four coolies bearing the tiffin-basket. The place grilled almost silently, black and white and grey with converging railway lines encumbered with trucks; an engine moved about snorting painfully, and nearly naked men ran in and out under the carriages smiting the wheels. They rolled out of the place and on for an hour, then over the bridge of the Ganges and past some old fortifications, and out of the windows they saw Benares, Benares the impressively filthy, trailing her skirts and her sins in her great sacred river, but fair, very fair indeed, with the morning sunlight on the faces of all her gods, and the morning sky behind the minarets of Aurungzebe.

It was the middle of the night before they reached Lucknow, where they awoke thirsty. A wide, lighted, orderly station platform, railway guards walking about in white duck and gold buttons, a single dissipated-looking little subaltern promenading with his hands in his pockets. There was no ice, and young Browne sleepily abused the first railway official that passed the window. "A big station like this, and the ice allowed to run out in such weather! The thing ought to be reported."

"It's in weather the like o' this, sir, that the ice *diz* run out," suggested the guard. "Tickets, sir!"

Lucknow, with her tragedy still upon her lips, her rugged walls still gaping in the white moonlight up yonder, her graves still tenderly remembered—and the Brownes' bitter complaint of Lucknow was that they found no ice there! Ah, little Brownes! I write this of you more in sorrow than in anger; for I know a soldier's wife whose husband's name you might have read graven on a Lucknow tablet in the moonlight that night, and when I remember all that she has told me, I find it grievous that you should even have been aware that there was no ice in Lucknow!

In the morning they were rolling through a lightsome country, all gay fields and gravelly river-beds, with billows of sunlit air coming in at the windows, an hour from Saharanpora. A blue hill stood like a cloud on the edge of the horizon, the Brownes descried it simultaneously and laughed aloud together. It was so long since they had seen any elevation greater than their own roof, or a palm-tree, or an umbrella. They got out at Saharanpore, and Kasi got out at Saharanpore, and the bundles and the boxes and the bags got out at Saharanpore. They were all as dirty as they could possibly be, but the people who did not get out at Saharanpore looked at them enviously, for they had the prospect of being dirtier still. Arrived at the place of the dâk-bungalow, and the solace of unlimited ablutions, Mrs. Browne could not imagine in what respect she had ever found a dâk-bungalow wanting. Could anything be more delightful than that they should have it entirely to themselves! Between her first dâk-bungalow and this one Mrs. Browne had made steps towards the solitary Calcutta ideal. On this occasion she pulled down all the chicks,* and told the solitary box wallah who had outspread his wares in the veranda against her arrival to "Jao, jeldi!"

Here they tarried till the following day, when the blowing of a trumpet aroused them at what they considered an excessively early hour of the morning. It was their trumpet; they had bought the exclusive right to it for twelve hours. It belonged to the dâk-gharry that was to take them from Saharanpore to Dehra,

* Venetian blinds.

"a distance," as any guide-book will tell you, of "forty-two miles." If you could see a dâk-gharry you would probably inquire with Mrs. Browne if there wasn't any other way of going. There is no other way of going. There are large numbers of places in India to which there is no other way of going. And if one had answered you thus, you would have said that if you had known that you wouldn't have come. Mrs. Browne said that when she saw the travelling-carriage of this Orient land of dreamy luxury, but she didn't particularly mean it, and neither would you.

In appearance the Browne's dâk-gharry was a cross between a sun-bonnet and a blue hearse. This may be a little difficult to imagine; but I don't appeal to your imagination, I state facts. It was the shape of a hearse, and you were supposed to lie down in it, which completed the suggestion. To counteract the gloomy apprehension of this idea, it was painted blue inside and out—distinctly a *foncée* blue. This superficial cheerfulness was accentuated by shutters in the back and sliding doors at the sides, and the whole thing was trimmed from the roof with canvas wings. The top would take as much luggage as the hold of a ship—a small ship. Inside there was nothing at all, and a place to put your feet. Kasi condoned this austerity with rugs and pillows, and took his seat beside the driver, with whom he conversed as affably as his superior social position would admit. The two Brownes were carefully extended inside like modern mummies; four native persons of ambiguous appearance and a persuasive odour fastened themselves on behind. The driver cracked his whip, and the two meek brown spotted down-trodden horses stood promptly upon their hind legs pawing the air. They came down in time, and then they began to back into the dâk-bungalow dining-room. Dissuaded from this they walked across the road with the intention of putting themselves in the ditch; and finally, after a terrific expenditure of language on the part of the driver, they broke into a gallop, which brought each of the recumbent Brownes inside to a right angle by the action of some mechanical principle containing a very large element of alarm. This was not at all a remarkable demonstration. It is the invincible *dustur* of every animal in the dâk-gharry business, and is perfectly understood, locally. The animals attached to the Brownes galloped their three miles and arrived reeking at the next dâk-stable without another thought of anything but their business. In the meantime the local understanding spread to the Brownes, who specified it afterwards with liniment.

To this impetuous way of going it was a relief, Mrs. Browne told me afterwards, to hang one's feet out of the door. The picturesque conduct of the fresh dâk-ponies every three or four miles displayed novel forms of vice, interesting to the uninitiated. They bit and strove and kicked, and one of them attempted to get inside. Helen said it was very wearing to one's nerves. But when they had accomplished the little earthquake of starting there were compensations. The road was green and shaded, as it would be in England; squirrels frisked from one trunk to another, silvery doves with burnished breasts cooed in the bamboo branches, and ever the gracious hills drew nearer and a little nearer.

"These are only the Siwalliks," remarked young Browne, in a pause of their jubilant conversation. "Wait till you see the Himalayas on the other side! The Siwalliks are only rubble. They're rapidly crumbling away."

"If they were in England," replied Mrs. Browne, watching the little topmost turrets grow greener, "we wouldn't admit that they were rubble. And I don't believe they'll crumble away very soon."

"In a few æons," returned Mr. Browne superiorly. "It won't matter to us. We're getting regularly up amongst them. This is the beginning of the pass."

They had journeyed four hours and had come to a little white bungalow perched high upon the flank of the nearest hill. Here the khansamah had a red beard, and swore by it that the sahib had not forwarned him; how should there be beef and potatoes! Milk and moorghy might be, but eggs no—the eggs were a little bad.

"For that saying, son of the Prophet," said young Browne, "backsheesh will be to you. In Bengal there is no true talk regarding eggs. And now hasten with the milk and the warmed moorghy curry of the traveller of yesterday, and dekko, Kasi, tiffin-basket, lao!"

Broad is the road that leads over the Mohun Pass, and beautiful are the summits that look down on it, but it cannot be climbed with the unaided strength of horses. It was dull driving but for the sunset behind the hills, when they put oxen on in the bad places; and still duller when the sulky, long-haired black buffaloes lent a leg; but there was a certain picturesqueness in being pulled by the three varieties of beasts at once, especially when a gang of road-coolies turned in and pushed behind.

They had always the trumpet, too, which enlivened the whole of that part of Asia. And wild white balsams grew high on the rocks, and naked little children, in blue necklaces, played about the road.

There was the blackness of a tunnel, and then the vision of a fair valley mightily walled in, with the softness of evening still in her face, and the smoke of her hearth-fires curling up to a purple sky. They rattled across a quarter of a mile of dry river-bed full of stones, and were in Dehra, Dehra Doon, where all the hedges drop pink rose-petals, and the bul-bul sings love songs in Persian, and the sahib lives in a little white house in a garden which is almost home.

CHAPTER XXIV.

IN Dehra the Brownes were within sight of the promised land, not always but often. Sometimes it lay quite hidden in some indefinable matted cloud-region of the sky, and then the last of the September rains came pelting down the Doon. Sometimes it thrust only a shoulder out of its cloud garments, and sometimes white fleeces swept over it from morning till night. But there were other days when the clouds sailed high above it, trailing their shadows after them, and then indeed the Brownes could climb to it by a winding road that began at their very feet. The road ascended to Mussoorie, which twinkled white on a spur above them seven thousand feet up, and twelve miles off. It would have been perfectly easy and practicable for them to go to Mussoorie; so easy and practicable that they didn't go. When young Browne had looked after the planter's tea-bushes, and put a headstone to his grave, and settled his bills and written home to his people the details of his affairs, there were eight days over. Mussoorie, the particular paradise of "quiet" people and retired old gentlemen who mean to die in the country, was an insignificant achievement for eight days. The Brownes surveyed the great brown flanks of the hills and burned for a wider conquest. They would go to Chakrata, high in the heart of the Himalayas to the west, half way to Simla. They would ride on horseback all the way up and down again to the railway station at Saharanpore; it would be more than a hundred miles—an expedition, as young Browne remarked, that they could dine out on for weeks when they got back to Calcutta. His own statement of their equipment for the journey is succinct. "We shall want," said he, "two ponies, two syces, and an ekka. The ekka will take the luggage, bedding, Kasi, and the tiffin-basket. The ponies will take us, and the syces will come along behind. Let us go and hire them."

They drove out the long shady main road of Dehra, creeping always upward to Rajpore, upon this business, and on the way Mr. Browne explained to Mrs. Browne the natural history, character and antecedents of the "bazar tat." "They run small," said young Browne, "mostly ears and tails. They have a tendency to displace objects to the rear of them, and a taste for human flesh. They were born and brought up in the bazar, and their morals are unspeakable. But you can't get morals at any price in the bazar; they are too expensive to be sold there. And there's no real harm in the bazar tat, if you only keep away from his heels and look a bit spry when you get on."

Mrs. Browne asked, with concealed anxiety, if there were no donkeys. She was accustomed to a donkey, she said; she could ride one really rather well, and if George didn't mind she would so *much* prefer it. But George answered in a spirit of ribaldry. The only donkeys in India, he said, belonged to the dhobies, and were permanently engaged in taking home the wash. By that time they had arrived. It was only a sharp elbow of a narrow mountain road, Rajpore, with its tumble-down houses, overhanging it on both sides, and it was quite empty. "There aren't any horses here!" Helen remarked with disparagement.

"Wait," returned her husband. Then, with really no particular emphasis, he said, "Gorah!" * to Rajpore.

* Horse!

"*Ha, hazur!*"

"*Good* pony, sahib!"

"Here iz, memsahib—here iz!"

Rajpore human on innumerable pairs of brown legs, turned suddenly into the best and most spacious of its ground floors, dragging thence Rajpore equine hostile on four, wearing an aggrieved expression above clinging strands of country grass. They came, and still they came, from above trotting down, from below trotting up. A human being of sorts was usually attached to them, but Rajpore was obviously inhabited by ponies. No other census would have been worth taking there. Mrs. Browne was surrounded by ragged turbans and man-eaters. With Mr. Browne's anxious hand upon her arm she felt herself precipitated in every direction at once. "I can't keep out of the way of *all* their heels, George," she exclaimed in the voice of the tried woman, and then George backed her carefully against a wall, drew a semicircle round her with a diameter of five feet, and forbade man or beast to cross the line. Then they proceeded to a choice.

"Here iz, hazur! Good nice thin wallah, memsahib *kawasti!*" *

"Thanks," said Helen; "he's a diagram! I want a fat one."

"Look, memsahib! This one *bote* plenty fat. *Rose, rose,* tarty bun'nles ghas *khata!*" †

"He's a baote-tamasha-wallah," remarked young Browne. "Look at his eye, Helen. He also appears to have kicked all his skin off his fetlocks. For you I should prefer the diagram."

Finally it was the diagram for Helen, who commanded that

* For the memsahib.

† Day by day he eats thirty bundles of grass!

an unreasonable quantity of food should be given to it under her eyes, and remained until it was finished. "If she isn't fatter after that," she said with satisfaction, "it's her own fault." Young Browne selected the veritable charger of Rajpore. He wore his mouth and nose carefully tied up in rope, and might be relied upon at all points so long as that one remained secure. "They're not much of a pair," said young Browne, "but in *your* animal, dear, I don't mind sacrificing both speed and appearances."

"To safety. Yes, dear, you are *perfectly* right." And Mrs. Browne, whose sense of humour was imperfectly developed, regarded her husband with affection.

Thereafter it became a question of an ekka, and Rajpore had ekkas bewildering in their variety and in their disrepair. If you have never seen an ekka it will be difficult for you to understand one. The business ekka does not stand about to be photographed, and therefore you must be told that, although it appears to rest mainly on the horse's back, it has two wheels generally, one on each side. There is a popular saying that no sahib likes a one-wheeled ekka, and though it is a popular saying it is true. The vehicle will do prodigious distances with one wheel, but it is anticipating Providence to engage it on that basis. An ekka is rather like a very old two-storied birdcage tilted up and fore-shortened, with a vaulted roof, and it runs in my mind that the roof is frescoed. The upstanding little posts at the four corners are certainly painted red and yellow; they are carved also, like the rungs of certain chairs. I know that the ekka-wallah sits in the upper story smiling upon the world. An ekka-wallah always smiles; his is a life of ease. I know too that there are bulgings above and protuberances below, and half a yard of dirty sacking, and seven pieces of ragged rope, and always room for something else; but at this point my impression becomes a little confused, and I cannot state with assurance which end is attached to the horse. That, however, is a matter of detail. The real point is that the Brownes found an ekka apparently two feet square, which contracted to carry their luggage, bedding, tiffin-basket, and Kasi up to Chakrata and down to the plains for the sum of three rupees per diem, which was extortionate. But the *pulthans* * were moving down, and the sergeants' wives would require many ekkas. They could afford to wait for the sergeants' wives. In expectation of these ladies the ekka market was a solid unit and the Brownes succumbed before it.

Next day they left Dehra, dropping the first of its October rose-leaves. Thinking of the planter in his grave, Helen wondered how he could have been so indifferent as to close his eyes wilfully and intentionally on such a place. It was the morning, there was a sweet and pungent gaiety in the air, the long road they had to travel stretched before them in the pleasaunce of leaf-checkered sunshine. Little striped squirrels played on the boles of the trees—they were English-looking trees—that met over their heads. Young Browne thanked God audibly that they were out of the region of palms and plantains.

Tiny green fly-catchers swung on the rushes of an occasional pool, pink-breasted ring-doves sidled out of their way, thieving parrots flew by sixes and sevens screaming up from the *kharif* crops.† Very green were the *kharif* crops, with the rain still about their roots, surging up under the lowest branches of the trees as far as these travellers could see before them. But for the teeming luxuriance of everything, the sense of breadth and

* Regiments.

† Cold weather crops.

brightness and the caressing sun, it might have been a road in Devonshire. But for the wayfarers too. There were neither smocks nor gigs; the ryot went by, chiefly dressed in his own brown skin, urging his lean oxen; all the gentle cows had curious humps between their shoulders. And here by the wayside they saw the tiny dome of a battered white praying place, and there the square slab of a Mahomedan tomb.

The sun grew hot as they scrambled with the road down to the bridge across a broad river bed full of round white stones and boulders, with a narrow shallow brown stream hurrying along the middle. Further away it trickled into the Jumna; here it played with pebbles and crabs, but now and then in the rains it brought the boulders down from the mountains swirling, and threw stones at the Department of Public Works, and shook the bridges. Looking one way as they crossed the bridge, it was a piled-up picture, the blue hills massed behind, the big white stones huddled and stranded in the glistening grey sand, the foolish little stream in the middle. Looking the other, the picture went to pieces, the hills sloped further away, the sky came down, the big stones rounded themselves into little ones, and spread indistinguishably far. Either way it was beautiful in the crisp Indian sunlight; it had a gay untroubled life, like porcelain.

After that there were miles of irresponsible curving, weedy road, that led them sometimes past the sirkar's* sarl forest, and sometimes past a little village gathered together under a mango-tree, but oftenest it straggled through wide, sunny, stony country, full of pale half-tints, where only wild grasses grew. Such tall wild grasses, purple and yellow and white, bending and tuft-

* Government's.

ing above their heads on either side of the way. "They would make Aunt Plovtree happy for life," Helen said. They would indeed, and many another estimable lady resident in Great Britain. It was a sorrowful waste that they should be growing there far from the solemn interiors that yearned for their dusty charms. Helen was so much of this opinion that she dismounted and gathered a bunch, compelling her husband to do the same, to send by parcel post to Aunt Plovtree. She flicked the flies off the Diagram's ears with them for three miles, then she lost a third of them in a canter, and young Browne arranged that the rest should be carefully forgotten at Kalsi dâk-bungalow. He was of opinion that in undertaking an ascent of nine thousand feet on a bazar tat in India you couldn't be expected to gather and preserve wild grasses for your aunt in England.

CHAPTER XXV.

ALL night long the Jumna purred in their ears, rolling over the stones at the bottom of the shady hill, whereon the Raj had built a travellers' rest. Looking out through the dewy branches in the morning, they saw the Doon lying under its mists at their feet, with the ragged Siwalliks on the other side—already they had begun to climb. Already, too, there was the mountain scent in the air—that smell of wet mossy rock and ferns and running streams and vigour—and this, as they set forth upon the Himalayas, with their faces turned upwards, took possession of their senses and made them altogether joyous. The Rajpore charger sniffed the wind with his Roman nose as copiously as circumstances would permit, and snapped viciously at young Browne's trousers with his retreating under-lip. The Rajpore charger must have been at least twelve hands high, and fat out of all proportion. His syce and proprietor, Boopbal—

probably thirteen years old, wearing a ragged cloth jacket, a dhoty, and an expression of precocious iniquity, was very proud of him. The syce attached to Helen's pony was visibly abased by the contrast, and Helen herself declared loudly against the injustice of being expected to keep up under the circumstances. Mrs. Browne's mount had only one idea of going, and that was to imitate the gait of her distinguished friend in front at a considerable distance to the rear; and there is no doubt that it must have been trying invariably to come up puffing, to the reproaches of a waiting lord, complacent in his saddle. "If you could ride behind for awhile and beat it," suggested Helen; "it doesn't seem to mind me." But young Browne thought that was quite impossible. There was one thing they *might* do, though—at Saia they might get her a spur! "George!" cried she, "do you think I would use a spur?—horrid, cruel thing, that you never can tell when it's going in!" with ungrammatical emotion. "But we might change ponies for a bit, if you like."

"We might," said young Browne, reflectively, "but I don't think that I should feel justified in putting you on this one, my dear; his rage and fury with his nose are awful."

"But, George, I should like to ride *beside* you!"

"Not more than I should like to have you, dear. But I think, since I can't have that pleasure, what a satisfaction I take in the knowledge that you are *safe.* Do you feel disposed to trot?"

"*I* do," returned Mrs. Browne, with plaintive emphasis; "but you'll have to start, please. What is the matter with this animal?"

The Diagram was neighing—long, shrill neighs of presagement, with her ears cocked forward. "Something's coming," said young Browne. "*Dâk-wallahata!*" * remarked Boophal. A faint jingling on the far side of the nearest curve; the dâk-wallah had rounded it, and was upon them, at a short, steady, unrelenting trot. The dâk-wallah, all in khaki, had charge of Her Majesty's mails. There was no time for a salaam. He wore bells at his waist for premonition, and a spear over his shoulder for defence. These hills were full of *janwas* † without special respect for Her Majesty's mails. On he went, jingling faint and fainter, bearing the news of the mountains down into the valleys, a pleasant primitive figure of the pleasant primitive East. Young Browne liked him particularly. "What a decent way of earning one's living!" said he.

The hills began to round out nobly before them now. The road took great sweeps and curves, always penetrating and climbing, and a low stone wall made its appearance running along the outer edge. Over the wall they looked down upon a hurrying river and tree-tops; but the hill-sides towered straight up beside them, lost in sarl, and oak, and mosses, and shadows. They had climbed a very little way. The stillness seemed to grow with the sunshine. Only now and then a jungle-fowl stirred, or a hoo-poe cried, or they heard the trickling of a tiny stream that made its ferny way down the face of the rock to the road. Underneath the warm air lay always the cool scent; strange flowers bloomed in it, but did not change it; it was the goodly smell of the mountains, and Helen, respiring it, declared that it was the first time her nose had been the slightest pleasure to her in India. They turned to look back—the hills had grown up around them and shut them in; they were upon the solitary, engirdling road, with its low stone parapet below unknown

* The postman comes. † Animals.

heights, above unknown depths, insisting always upwards round the nearer masses to hills that were greater, further, bluer. It was the little parapet, Helen decided, that made it look so lonely. It must have taken quantities of people to build the little parapet along such mighty curves, and now they had all gone away down the road, and it seemed as if none of them would ever come back.

After the dâk-wallah the *jogi* * with his matted hair and furtive eyes. He asked nothing of the Brownes, the jogi, he extracted pice from his own people, for the good of their souls; the souls of the Brownes were past paying for; besides, it was so unlikely that a sahib would pay. And after the jogi came a score of black, long-haired, long-horned buffaloes, and a man seated upon an ass driving them. The buffaloes had evidently never seen anything approaching a Browne before, for they all with one accord stood quite still when they came within twenty yards of these two, and stared with the stolidly resentful surprise that never strikes one as an affectation in a buffalo. There were so very many buffaloes and so very few Brownes and so little room for any of them that the situation was awkward. "Keep close behind me and stick to the inside," young Browne enjoined his lady. "They *have* been known to charge at things they don't understand, but they take a good while to make up their minds."

"Do let's try to squeeze past before they make them up," said Helen nervously; but as the Brownes circumspectly advanced each of the small syees ran out from behind his pony's heels, and laying hold of the buffaloes by any horn, ear, or tail that came nearest, jostled them intrepidly out of the way. And

* Religious beggar.

there was a deeper humiliation to come. As they took their right of way at a trot with what dignity they might, a buffalo calf, a highly idiotic baby bull, overcome by the dazzling appear-

HE ASKED NOTHING OF THE BROWNES.

ance of the Rajpore charger, turned round and trotted after him and would not be denied. In vain young Browne smote him upon the nose, in vain he who sat upon the ass abused with a loud voice the ancestors of all buffaloes, the little bull fixed upon the charger a look which said, "Entreat me not to leave thee," and lumbered steadfastly alongside. Already the little bull's mamma, smelling desertion from the rear, had looked round inquiringly—she was in process of turning—she was after them horns down, tail straight out, and she was coming fast! There was very little time for reflection, but it occurred irresistibly to both the Brownes that the little bull's mamma would not be likely to put the blame upon the little bull. There was nothing for it but flight, therefore, and they fled; promiscuous and fast, for even the ponies appeared to understand that it was an unpleasant thing to be pursued by an enraged female buffalo for the restitution of maternal rights. First the flying Brownes, neck and neck exhorting each other to calmness, then the bleating calf that chased the flying Brownes, then the snorting cow that chased the bleating calf, and, finally, he upon the ass who chased them all, with shouts and brayings to wake the mountain-side. It was a scene for the imperishable plate of a Kodak: there was hardly time to take it with the imagination. As his ideal departed from him the calf fell back into the hands, as it were, of his mother and his master; and young Browne, glancing behind, declared with relief that they were both licking him.

They stopped to rest, to consume quantities of bread and butter and hard-boiled eggs, to ask milk of an out-cropping village. Milk was plentiful in the village, cool creamy buffaloes' milk, and the price was small, but from what vessel should the sahib drink it? All the round brass bowls that held it were sacred to the feeding of themselves, sacred to personalities worth about four pice each; and the lips of a sahib might not defile them. The outcast sahib bought a new little earthen pot for a pice, breaking it solemnly on a stone when they had finished; and even mixed with the taste of fired mud the buffaloes' milk was ambrosial.

On they went and up, the trees shelved further down below and grew scantier above; upon the heights that rose before them there seemed to be none at all. Down where the river was evening had fallen, and all the hills behind stood in purple, but a little white cluster still shone sunlit in a notch above them. Boophal pointed it out. "*Tin cos*," * said Boophal. They hastened on at that, all six of them; they rounded a last flank, rattled over a bridge with a foaming torrent underneath, and found themselves clinging, with several fowls, oxen, and people, to the side of the gorge the torrent made. The dâk-bungalow sat on a ledge a hundred feet or so further up, and the Brownes felt this to be excessive. They climbed it, however, and entered into peace at the top. There was a khansamah and two long chairs, there would be dinner. The Diagram, unsaddled and fed, folded herself up like a chest of drawers for repose; but the charger roamed up and down seeking something to kick, and all night long at intervals they heard him chewing in imagination the cud of the buffalo calf, neighing, yawning, biting his under-lip.

Next day they saw what the creeping road had conquered, and what it had yet to conquer. It was no longer question of climbing the great hills, they were amongst the summits, they walked upon the heights, behind them slope after outlying slope rose up and barred the way that they had come; and yet the parapeted road, with its endless loops and curves insisted upward, and the little military slabs that stood by the mountain-side told them that they had still eighteen, seventeen, sixteen miles to follow it before they came to Chakrata, whence they

* Three miles.

should see the Snows. Helen found it difficult to believe that the next turn would not disclose them, that they were not lying fair and shining beyond that brown mountain before her to the left—it was such a prodigious mountain, it must be the last. But always the belting road sloped upward and disappeared again, always behind the prodigious brown mountain rose a more prodigious brown mountain still. They had astounding, soul-stretching views, these Brownes, but always around and behind them; before them rose ever the bulk of a single mountain, and the line of the climbing girdling road.

When God gave men tongues, he never dreamed that they would want to talk about the Himalayas; there are consequently no words in the world to do it with. It is given to some of us, as it was given to these Brownes, thus to creep and to climb up into the heart of them, to look down over their awful verges and out upon the immensity of their slopes, to be solitary in the stupendous surging, heaving mountain-sea that stands mute and vast here upon the edge of the plains of India. Afterward these people have more privacy than the rest of the world, for they have once been quite alone in it, with perhaps a near boulder and a dragon-fly. And their privacy is the more complete because there is no password to let another in—language will not compass it. So they either babble foolishly, or are silent.

The Brownes, in the fulness of their hearts, babbled foolishly. They wondered whether the white speck near the top of the mountain across the ravine was a cow or a house, and in either case how it held on. They wondered what the curious blood-red crop could be, that lay in little square patches far below them on the lower slopes where people had tiny farms. They wondered how cold it was up there in the winter—it was jolly cold now when you faced the wind. They found ox-eyed daisies and other

Christian flowers growing in clefts of the rock, and they gathered these rejoicing. They implored each other to "keep to the inside" in places where the low stone wall had been washed away, and neither of them dared to look over. And they had an adventure which to this day Mrs. Browne relates as blood-curdling.

It was in rounding an old sunny corner in silent disappointment at again failing to find Chakrata. Young Browne, riding first, noticed a loose pebble rattle down the side of the rock. Mrs. Browne insists that she did not notice the pebble, and I don't know that it is important to her evidence that she should. But she certainly noticed the leopard, so carefully that she never will be *quite* sure it wasn't a tiger. She saw it rise from its four legs from a ledge of rock above young Browne's head and look at young Browne. Mrs. Browne is naturally unable to give anyone an accurate idea of her emotion during the instant that followed, but she was perfectly certain that it did not occur to young Browne to transfix the animal with his eye, and he had nothing else. Neither it did, but the situation did not find Mr. Browne entirely without presence of mind notwithstanding. Raising his whip in a threatening manner Mr. Browne said "Shoo!" and whatever may have been the value of that expletive in Mr. Browne's mouth under ordinary circumstances, in Mrs. Browne's opinion it saved his life on that occasion. For without even an answering growl the leopard turned and trotted into the thicket quickly, as if she had forgotten something.

"Did you see that, Helen?" inquired her husband, turning in his saddle.

"I sh-should think I did?" exclaimed Mrs. Browne. *W-w-w-wait* for me, George!" And as the Diagram came up alongside, young Browne received several tearful embraces, chiefly upon his arm, in the presence of the syces. "I told you you ought to have a g-g-gun, darling, and you *wouldn't* be advised," Mrs. Browne reproached him hysterically. "It's all very well to laugh, but thin-thin-think of what *might* have been!"

"It's awful to think of what might have been if I had had a gun," said young Browne solemnly. "In the excitement of the moment I should have been certain to let it go off, and then she would have been down on us, sure. They hate guns awfully. Oh, we may be thankful I hadn't a gun!"

CHAPTER XXVI.

PRESENTLY they met a wonderfully pretty lady with red cheeks, such red cheeks as all the Miss Peacheys had in Canbury, being swung along in a dandy on the shoulders of four stout coolies. The red cheeks belonged to Chakrata; they were within half-a-mile of it then; they would see it before the sun went down. The road zig-zagged a bit and climbed more steeply, narrowing hideously here and there. The khuds became terrific. Young Browne dismounted and walked at his wife's bridle, pushing her pony close to the mountain-side. The precipices seemed to shout to them.

There was a last outstanding brown flank; the road hurtled round it, over it, and then with the greeting of a mighty torrent of wind that seemed to come from the other side of the world it ran out upon a wide level place, where a band played and five hundred soldiers, in Her Majesty's red, wheeled and marched and countermarched, it seemed to the Brownes, for pure lightheartedness. That was the end; there, grouped all about a crag or two, was Chakrata. There across a vast heaving of mountains to the horizon—mountains that sank at their feet and swelled again and again and again purple and blue—stood the still wonder of the Snows.

"They aren't real," said Helen simply, "they're painted on the sky."

The Brownes followed a path that twisted through Chakrata, and in course of time they came to a little out-cropping wooden diamond-paned chalet, with wide brown eaves that overhung eternity and looked toward the Snows. It was a tiny toy dâk-bungalow, and English dahlias, red and purple and yellow and white, grew in clumps and thickets tall and wild around it. Here they entered in and demanded a great fire and a cake; while a grey furred cloud, flying low with her sisters, blotted out the Snows, and darkness, coming up from the valleys, caught them upon the mountain-top.

Distinct and unusual joys awaited them in the morning. The fire had gone out for one thing, and they shivered luxurious shivers at the prospect of getting up without one. They enjoyed every shiver and prolonged it. How little one thought of being thankful for that sort of thing in England, Helen remarked, with little sniffs at the frosty air; and young Browne said "No, by Jove," and how one hated the idea of one's tub. Oh, delightfully cold it was, snapping cold, squeaking cold! Helen showed her hands blue after washing them, and they tumbled through their respective toilettes like a couple of school children. It was so long since they had been cold before.

At breakfast the butter was chippy, and that in itself was a ravishing thing. At what time of year, they asked each other, would butter ever stand alone without ice in Bengal. And their fingers were numb—actually numb; could anything have been more agreeable, except to sit in the sun on the little veranda, as they afterwards did, and get them warm again! There, without moving, they could watch that magical drifted white picture in the sky, so pure as to be beyond all painting, so lifted up as to be beyond all imagination. A ragged wallnut-tree clung to the edge of the cliff; the wind shook the last of its blackening leaves; the vast, wheeling sky was blue and empty, except of the Snows, and the dahlias had trooped to the verge to look, so that the sun shone through their petals with the light of wine. It is their remoteness, their unapproachableness, that make these Himalayan Snows a sanctuary. From the foot of man anywhere they are prodigiously far off, so that they look to him always the country of a dream just hanging above the world he knows, or if he be of prayerful mind, the Habitation of the Holiness of the Lord. And since it is permitted to us that by mountain and by valley we may journey to look upon the Snows, even from very far off, our souls do not perish utterly in India, and our exile is not entirely without its possession.

The Brownes had only two days in Chakrata, which they employed chiefly as I have mentioned—sitting in the sun devout before the Himalayas, or ecstatically blowing upon their fingers. They made one expedition to see a pair of friends whom the merciful decree of Providence had recently brought up from the Plains for good, and found them laying in coal and flour for the winter, which made them quite silent for a moment with suppressed feeling. "I hope," said young Browne flippantly, to conceal his emotion, "that on the event of other stores giving out you have plenty of candles. They are sustaining in an emergency."

And as they made their thoughtful way on pony-back to the brown wooden chalet, Helen observed upon her riding habit some clustering spots of white, that multiplied and thickened, and she gathered them up between her fingers with a delighted cry. "George, dearest, look! We're being *snowed on*—in India!"

All of which was doubtless very trivial, but they were not remarkable people, these Brownes; from the first I told you so.

THE SNOWS.

And though they found this journey of theirs brimful of the extraordinary, the unparalleled, there was really only one remarkable thing about it, which was the dignified and self-reliant conduct of the ekka. The ekka had always gone before, overflowing with their goods and crowned with Kasi in cross-legged pomp. They had traced its wavering progress by ends of ravelled rope, and splinters of wood, and scraps of worn-out leather which lay behind in the road to testify of it; and grave as had been their apprehensions, they had never overtaken it in a state of collapse. Invariably when they arrived they found the ekka disburthened, tipped up under a tree, the ekka pony browsing with a good conscience, Kasi awaiting with an air which asked for congratulation. How it held together was a miracle which repeated itself hourly; but it did hold together, and inspired such confidence in young Browne that he proposed, when she tired of the Diagram, to deposit Mrs. Browne in the ekka also. This, however, was declined. Mrs. Browne said that she had neither the heart nor the nerves for it; in which case, of course, an emergency would find her quite anatomically unprepared.

Leaving the Snows with grief, therefore, they left the ekka with trusting faith. There had been a hitch in the process of packing, examination, consultation. The sahib, inquiring, had been told that one of the wheels was "a little sick." It was an excellent ekka—an ekka with all the qualities; the other wheel was quite new, and you did not often find an ekka with an entirely new wheel! But the other was certainly a little old, and after these many miles a little sick. Young Browne diagnosed the suffering wheel, and made a serious report; there were internal complications, and the tire had already been off seven times. Besides, it wouldn't stand up; obviously it was not shamming, the *purana chucker** was taken bad, very bad indeed. Its cure could be accomplished, however, with wet chips and a hammer—and time. If the sahib would permit, the ekka would follow in half an hour.

So the Brownes departed gaily, and an hour and three-quarters later the ekka tottered forth also, with Kasi and the ekka-wallah walking lamentably alongside exchanging compliments upon the subject of the wheel. They travelled three miles and an hour thus, and then the wheel had a sudden relapse, with signs of dissolution; while young Browne's dressing-case, which happened to be on top, shot precipitately first into space and then into the topmost branches of a wild cherry-tree growing three thousand feet down the khud. The ekka pony planted his feet in the road-bed and looked round for directions; the ekka-wallah groaned and sat down. "And the sahib, O, my brother-in-law!" exclaimed Kasi, dancing round the ekka.

"The sahib is in the hand of God!" returned the ekka-wallah piously. "To-day I have been much troubled. I will smoke." And while the Brownes, at Saia, remotely lower down, grew chilly with vain watching in the shadows that lengthened through the khuds, the weary ekka leaned peacefully against the mountain wall, the ekka-wallah drew long comfort from his hubble-bubble, and Kasi reposed also by the wayside, chewing the pungent betel, and thinking, with a meditative eye on the wild cherry-tree below, hard things of fate.

Nevertheless, without the direct interposition of Providence, the ekka eventually arrived, and there was peace in one end of the dâk-bungalow, and the crackling of sarl branches, and the

* Old wheel.

simmering of tinned hotch-potch. In the other end was wrath, and a pair of Royal Engineers—a big Royal Engineer and a little Royal Engineer. To understand why wrath should abide with these two Royal Engineers in their end of the bungalow, it is necessary to understand that it was not an ordinary travellers' bungalow, but a "Military Works'" bungalow, their very own bungalow, for "Military Works" and "Royal Engineers" mean the same thing; and that ordinary travellers were only allowed to take shelter there by special permission or under stress of weather. By their proper rights, therefore, these Royal Engineers should have had both ends of the bungalow, and the middle, and the compound, and the village, and a few miles of the road north and south—and a little privacy. If these ideas seem a trifle large, it becomes necessary to try to understand, at least approximately, what a Royal Engineer is, where he comes from, to what dignities and emoluments he may aspire. And then, when we have looked upon the buttons which reflect his shining past, and considered the breadth of his shoulders and the straightness of his legs, and the probable expense he has been as a whole to his parents and his country, we will easily bring ourselves to admit that he is entirely right in considering himself quite the most swagger article in ordinary Government service in India. We may even share his pardonable incredulity as to whether before his advent India was at all. And certainly we will sympathise with the haughtily impatient expletives with which he would naturally greet pretensions to circumscribe his vested rights in the Himalayan mountains on the part of two absurdly unimportant and superfluous Brownes.

The Brownes in their end heard the two Royal Engineers kicking the fire logs in theirs, and conversing with that brevity and suppression which always marks a Royal Engineer under circumstances where ordinary people would be abusively fluent. Apparently they had command of themselves, they were Royal Engineers, they weren't saying much, but it was vigorous the way they kicked the fire. The Brownes were still as mice, and absorbed their soup with hearts that grew ever heavier with a grievous sense of wrong inflicted not only upon their neighbour but upon a Royal Engineer!

"As a matter of fact, you know," said young Browne, "we've no business here. I think I ought to go and speak to them."

"We've got permission," remarked Mrs. Browne feebly, "and we were here first."

"I'm afraid," said young Browne, "that we have the best end, and we've certainly got the lamp. Maybe they would like the lamp. I think I ought first to go and see them. After all, it's their bungalow."

Young Browne came back presently twisting the end of his moustache. It was an unconscious imitation of the Royal Engineers acquired during their short and embarrassed interview.

"Well?" said Helen.

"Oh, it's all right. They don't particularly mind. They accepted my apology—confound them! And they *would* like the lamp—their's smokes. They're marching, like us, down to Saharanpore, inspecting the road or something, and fishing. No end of a good time those chaps have."

"What are their names?"

"Haven't the least idea—they're Royal Engineers."

"Well," returned Mrs. Browne disconsolately, "what are we to do when you give them the buttic?"

"Go to bed," returned her lord laconically.

Mrs. Browne prepared, therefore, for repose, and while Mr. Browne yielded up the lamp there reached her from the other end of the bungalow the ineffable condescension of a Royal Engineer, who said "Thanks awfully."

They were gone in the morning; the Brownes heard from the khansamah that the burra-sahibs had departed at daylight, and the very burra of the burra-sahibs rode a white horse. The Brownes were glad these particularly burra-sahibs had gone; they found they preferred to be entertained by the Military Works Department in the abstract. "They probably mean to ride a long way to-day, starting so early," said Helen hopefully. "We won't find them at Futtehpore." It was unreasonable in the Brownes; they had no grievance against these Royal Engineers, and yet they desired exceedingly that somewhere, anywhere, their ways should diverge; and there is no doubt whatever that the Royal Engineers would have heartily recommended a change of route to the Brownes. Unfortunately there was only one, and it lay before them unravelling down among the hills to Futtehpore. It was such glorious cantering, though, that these inconsiderable civil little Brownes on their bazar tats, all agog with their holiday, almost forgot the possible recurrence of the Royal Engineer. He became a small cloud on the horizon of their joyous day; he would probably vanish before evening. So that the sun shone and the doves cooed and the crested hoopoe ran across the path, of what import was a Royal Engineer—or even two? So the Brownes rode valiantly down among the hills, she upon her Diagram and he upon the charger of Rajpore, and when they really went with wings and glory, the syce-boys running behind attached themselves to the tails of the Diagram and the charger of Rajpore respectively, relieving their own legs and adding greatly to the imposing character of the

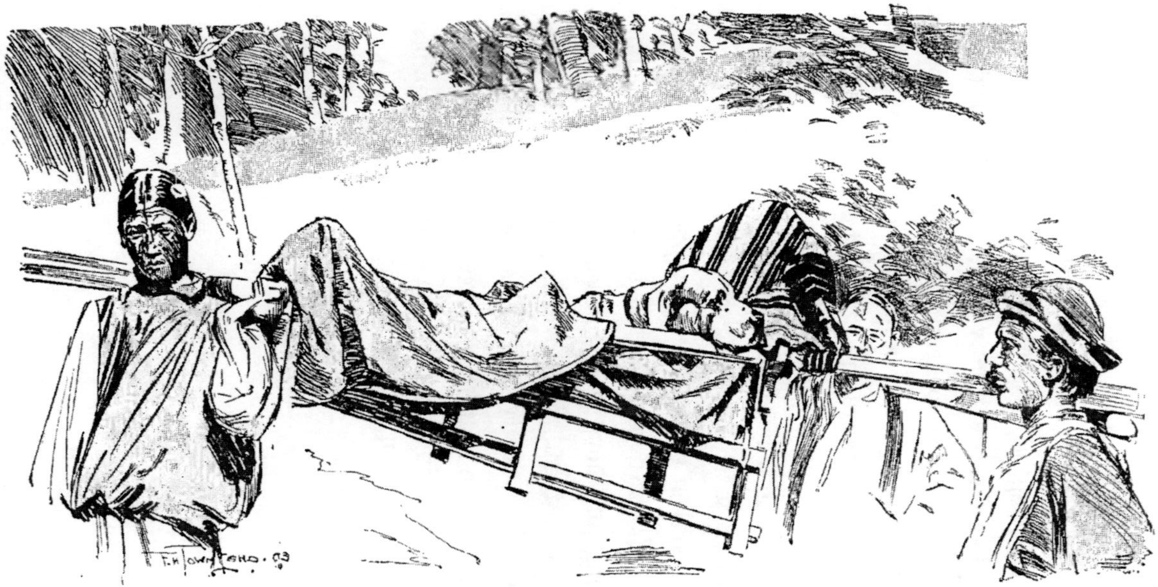

LIVER COMPLICATIONS—WE ALL COME TO IT.

cavalcade. And so they went down, down, where purple-veined begonias grew beside the course of the springs, and tall trees fluttered their ghostly white leaves over the verge, and orchids bloomed on dead branches up overhead. As they went they met an invalid being taken to Chakrata for change of air and scene. He rode in a dandy evidently made for his special accommodation, carried by two coolies; and a chuprassie attended him, a beautiful chuprassie with a red sash and a medal. The invalid looked at the Brownes in a way that asked their solicitude, but he made them no salutation because he was only a big brown and white mastiff, and besides, he didn't feel up to promiscuous conversation with strangers who might or might not be desirable. But when young Browne stopped the chuprassie and the coolies, and called him "old fellow" and asked him where he was going and how he had stood the journey, he gave young Browne a paw and a depreciating turn of his head over the dandy which distinctly said, "Liver complications. We all come to it. Your turn next hot weather. This country isn't fit for a Christian to live in!" and one more homesick alien passed on to look for his lost well-being in the Hills. Mrs. Browne hoped he would find it, he was such a dear dog.

CHAPTER XXVII.

THE Brownes had left the sunset behind them red upon the heights when they reached Futtehpore, but there was still light enough for them to descry a white horse from afar, browsing in the compound, and they looked at each other in unaffected melancholy, saying, "They're here." If they wanted further evidence they had it in the person of the khansamah, who ran forth wagging his beard, and exclaiming that there was no room—how should there be any room for these Presences from without, when two Engineer-sahibs had already come! Among his other duties one Engineer-sahib had to report the shortcomings of this khansamah. Should it be written among them that the Engineer-sahib was rendered uncomfortable in his own house! Ah, that the Presence could be persuaded that there was another bungalow five miles further on, which the Presence knew perfectly well there was not.

"Khansamah," replied young Browne, "two sahibs do not require four apartments and all the beds. Go and make it right; and, look you, bring a long chair for the memsahib that thy back be not smitten," for by this time the heart of George Browne, of Macintyre and Macintyre's, Calcutta, had waxed hot within him by reason of Royal Engineers.

The khansamah returned presently and announced that the Presences might have beds, but a long chair—here the khansamah held his back well behind him that it should not be smitten—he could not give, for the burra Engineer-sahib sat upon the one, and the chota Engineer-sahib sat upon the other. Yes, they could have something to eat, when the Engineer-sahibs had dined; but there would not be time to prepare it before—the Engineer-sahibs had commanded dinner in one hour. He would see if a fire was possible—it might be that the Engineer-sahibs required all the dry wood. It was presently obvious that they did, and as young Browne and Kasi struggled unavailingly with an armful of green sarl and a year-old copy of the *Overland Mail*, that gentleman might have been overheard to remark roundly in the smoke and the gloom, "*Damn* the Engineer-sahibs!"

Next morning the white horse was still in the stable when young Browne stepped out upon the veranda, and the Royal Engineer stood there smoking with his hands in his pockets, his legs describing a Royal Engineering angle. He said "Morning!" with a certain affability to young Browne, who made a lukewarm response.

"Think of getting on to-day?" inquired the R. E.

"Oh, yes," Mr. Browne replied. "We must. We're due at Saharanpore Friday."

"Aw! same with us. Bagshiabag to-day, Kalsia to-morrow, Saharanpore Friday."

"Exactly our programme," said young Browne with firmness.

"Aw! Hown' for'tchnit!"

"Is it?"

"Well, yes, rather. Y'see it was all right at Saia, and it's all right here, but at Kalsia there'll be Mrs. Prinny of the 97th, and Mrs. Prinny's got baby, and baby's got nurse. That'll be rather tight, *waoun't* it?" and the Royal Engineer removed a cigar ash from his pyjamas.

"Now if either of us should push on to Kalsia to-day," he continued insinuatingly.

There was a pause.

"It's awkward for *us*, y'see," continued the R. E., "because we're fishing."

"How far is it?"

"'Bout twenty-six miles."

"H'm! Rather long march for a lady."

"Oh, yes—it would be *long*," responded the Royal Engineer with an irresponsible air, "but then think of that awful nurse an' baby."

A quarter of an hour later the Brownes were off again. Crossing a bridge they passed the two Royal Engineers sitting upon one of the buttresses examining their fishing tackle. "We're going to see if we can manage it," remarked young Browne. "Good morning."

The larger and finer of the Royal Engineers looked up. "Aw," said he, "mustn't over-do it, y'know."

"We won't," returned young Browne.

As a matter of fact they didn't. Arrived at Bagshiabag, Mrs. Browne declared herself very nearly dead, the Diagram had been more diagrammatic than usual. She would rest, and "see" if she felt equal to going on.

"I'm blowed if you shall," said her lord, "not for all the R. E.'s in Asia." So they peacefully put up in their choice of ends this time, and made an impartial division of the furniture, and after tea went for a walk. It was the very last station on the edge of the hills; the plains began at their very feet to roll away into unbroken, illimitable misty distances. Bagshiabag—the King's garden—the palm-fringed plains that were doubtless fair in the King's sight. The Brownes looked at them sorrowing; it requires an Oriental imagination to admire the King's garden from an inside point of view.

"We must start early to-morrow," said young Browne regretfully. "It will be hot."

Returning they found the two Royal Engineers refreshing themselves under a mango-tree in the compound, surrounded by everything that appertained to the establishment, and wearing an expression of god-like injury. "We didn't get on, after all," said young Browne, as he passed them with what countenance he could. The Royal Engineers looked at him and smiled a rectilinear smile. "No," they said. It was not much to say, but there was a compulsion in it that awoke the Brownes before daylight next morning and put them in their saddles at sunrise. By ten o'clock the last blue ridge had faded out of the sky-line, by eleven they were in Kalsia—not Kalsi of the Doon—in the midst of a great flatness. The ekka with the tiffin basket was behind upon the road. They would wait there till it came, and then make up their minds about pushing on to Saharanpore. The ady with the nurse and baby was no fiction; she was coming by dâk-gharry at three o'clock, the khansamah said. And could the Presence give him any tidings of the Engineer-sahibs who were on the way? He had been in readiness for the Engineer-sahibs these three days. The Presence could give him no tidings whatever of the Engineer-sahibs. He thought very likely they were dead. Numbers of people had died in India in the last three days, and the Presence assuredly did not wish any talk of the Engineer-sahibs. "What is there to eat?" asked the Presence. And if there was only milk and eggs and chupatties—the sahibs generally bringing their own food to this place—then let it be served instantly, to be in readiness when the ekka should appear. And it was served. But the khansamah had lived a great many years upon the earth, and, moreover, he had privately questioned the syce-boys, so that he knew of the coming of the Engineer-sahibs. He knew, too, that it would not be good, either for his temporal or his eternal happiness, that the Engineer-sahibs should find four people and a baby in their house when they arrived. Therefore the khansamah, being full of guile as of years, sent an open-faced one privily to the turning of the lane into the road, who gave word to Kasi and to the ekka-wallah that the sahibs—the Browne sahibs—had gone on to Saharanpore, and they were by no means to tarry at Kalsia, but to hasten on after. Believing this word, Kasi and the ekka-wallah, while the Brownes famished upon the veranda, were drawing ever nearer to Saharanpore.

It is difficult to make a meal of eggs and milk and chupatties, but the Brownes found that it could be done, even when because of anger it is the more indigestible. They found an unexpected and delightful solace, however, afterward in Saharanpore. The place was full of the southward bound, a regiment was on the move, all Mussoorie had emptied itself in dâk-gharries upon the station. Nevertheless, Kasi the invaluable had intrigued for a room for them, a room that opened upon a veranda, with a lamp in it, and a smoking dinner. Kasi was the more invaluable for being conscience-stricken at having swallowed false talk. And there is no Military Works bungalow in Saharanpore, which is a station built primarily and almost wholly for the use of the general public. The joy of these unregenerate Brownes, therefore, upon seeing a white horse vainly walk up to this veranda and hearing a hungry voice, the voice of the Royal Engineer, vainly inquire for rooms and dinner, was keen and excessive.

"They've funked the baby after all!" said young Browne,

"thinking we wouldn't. Now they'll become acquainted with the emotions of the ordinary travelling public in a congested district. Hope they'll enjoy 'em as much as we did, Nellie. I'm going to have a bottle of beer."

And if the Royal Engineer outside in the dark, where it was getting chilly, could be susceptible to a note of triumph, he heard it in the pop of the Pilsener with which on this occasion Mr. George Browne fortified his opinion of Royal Engineers at large.

CHAPTER XXVIII.

YOU might have read in this morning's *Englishman*, in the list of passengers booked per P. and O. steamer *Ganges*, sailing 3d April, "Mr. and Mrs. Perth Macintyre and Miss Macalister, for Brindisi." Miss Macalister is a niece of the Perth Macintyres. She has been out two years and a half, and, so far as her opportunities are concerned, we have nothing to reproach ourselves with. For the first time in fifteen years we have attended the subscription dances to take her, and did not shirk the fancy dress ball, Mr. Perth Macintyre going as Falstaff, for her sake. At our time of life this is a great deal of exertion for a niece, and I consider, if such things are possible, Mr. Perth Macintyre's deceased sister ought to have felt gratification at what we did. Nevertheless, I have not had occasion to mention Miss Macalister before, and it is only in connection with her return-ticket that I mention her now. It represents an outlay which we did not expect to be obliged to make.

We are due in England about the 1st of May, when we will endeavour to find the warmest south wall in Devonshire—I shiver at the thought—and hang ourselves up on it. As the summer advances and the conditions of temperature in Great Britain become less severe, we will make an effort to visit the parental Peacheys in Canbury, if neither of us have previously succumbed to influenza; in which case the box of chutneys and guava jelly that the Brownes have charged us to deliver will be sent by luggage train. The survivor—we expect there will be at least a temporary survivor—is to attend to this.

It will make a difference to the Brownes, our going, the difference of a junior partnership; and although I hope I have a correct idea of the charms of our society, I fully expect that their grief at our departure will be tempered by this consideration. Some one of our administrators is always being quoted in the newspapers as having called India "a land of regrets." It is to be feared, however, that the regrets are felt exclusively by those who are going. The satisfactions of retirement are obscure, and the prospect of devoting a shrunken end of existence to the solicitous avoidance of bronchitis is not inviting. Whereas it is always to somebody's profit that an Englishman leaves India, and he is so accustomed to the irony of the idea of being his own chief mourner, that he would suspect the deeply-afflicted at his going of more than the usual manœuvres to obtain his shoes. The Brownes are very pleased, undisguisedly very pleased, though Mrs. Browne has condoled with me sincerely, in private, on the subject of Miss Macalister; and we quite understand it.

There is nothing, on the other hand, to mitigate our regret at parting with the Brownes, which is lively. I may not have been able to make it plain in these few score pages, but I like the Brownes. They are nice young people, and my advice has been so often useful to them. As the wife of the junior partner in Macintyre and Macintyre's, Mrs. Browne will be obliged to depend upon her own for the future; but I am leaving her a good deal to go on with, and a certain proportion of our drawing-room furniture as well, which she will find equally useful. I inherited it myself from Mrs. J. Macintyre; it has been a long time in the firm. Further, we have put off sailing for a fortnight so that I can be godmother in person to the Browne baby, for whose prospective future I knitted fifteen pairs of socks this last cold weather; and that I consider the final proof of our regard.

If it is necessary to explain my interest in these young Brownes, which you, I regret to think, may find inexplicable, it lies, I dare say, as much in this departure of ours as in anything else. Their first chapter has been our last. When you turn down the page upon the Brownes you close the book upon the Perth Macintyres, and it has been pleasant to me that our story should find its end in the beginning of theirs. If this is not excuse enough, there is a sentimental one besides. For I also have seen a day when the spell of India was strong upon my youth, when I saw romance under a turban and soft magic behind a palm, and found the most fascinating occupation in life to be the wasting of my husband's substance among the gabbling thieves of the China bazar. It was all new to me once—I had forgotten how new until I saw the old novelty in the eyes of Helen Browne. Then I thought of reading the first pages of the Anglo-Indian book again with those young eyes of hers; and as I have read I have re-written, and interleaved, as you see. It may be that they will give warning to some and encouragement to others. I don't mind confessing that to me they have brought chiefly a gay reminder of a time when pretty little subalterns used to trip over their swords to dance with young Mrs. Perth Macintyre also, which seems quite a ludicrous thing to print—and that has been enough.

I think she will avoid the graver perils of memsahibship, Mrs. Browne. I think she will always be a nice little woman. George and the baby will take care of that. With the moderate social facilities of the wife of a junior partner in Macintyre and

Macintyre's, she will not be likely even to make the acquaintance of the occasional all-conquering lady who floats on the surface of Anglo-Indian society disreputably fair, like the Victoria Regia in the artificial lake of the Eden Gardens. As to the emulation of such a one, I believe it is not in the power of circumstances to suggest it to Mrs. Browne. Besides, she is not clever, and the Victoria Regia must be clever, clever all round, besides having a specialty in the souls of men.

Nevertheless, Mrs. Browne has become a memsahib, graduated, qualified, sophisticated. That was inevitable. I have watched it come to pass with a sense that it could not be prevented. She has lost her pretty colour, that always goes first, and has gained a shadowy ring under each eye, that always comes afterwards. She is thinner than she was, and has acquired nerves and some petulance. Helen Peachey had the cerebral placidity and good temper of one of Fra Angelico's piping angels. To make up, she dresses her hair more elaborately, and crowns it with a little bonnet which is somewhat extravagantly "chic." She has fallen into a way of crossing her knees in a low chair that would horrify her Aunt Plovtree, and a whole set of little feminine Anglo-Indian poses have come to her naturally. There is a shade of assertion about her chin that was not there in England, and her eyes—ah, the pity of this!—have looked too straight into life to lower themselves as readily as they did before. She has come into an empire among her husband's bachelor friends, to whom she will continue to give gracious little orders for ten years yet, if she does not go off too shockingly; and her interests have expanded to include a great many sub-masculine ones, which she discusses with them in brief and casual sentences interspersed with smiles that are a little tired. Without being actually slangy she takes the easiest word and the shortest cut—in India we know only the necessities of speech, we do not really talk, even in the cold weather.

SHE HAS FALLEN INTO A WAY OF CROSSING HER KNEES IN A LOW CHAIR THAT WOULD HORRIFY HER AUNT PLOVTREE.

Domesticity has slipped away from Mrs. Browne, though she held it very tightly for a while, into the dusky hands whose business is with the house of the sahib. She and young Browne and the baby continue to be managed by Kasi with a skill that deceives them into thinking themselves comfortable, and Helen continues to predict with confidence that next month there will be a balance in her favour instead of Kasi's. On the contrary, the accounts will show that the Brownes have had all they wanted to eat and drink, that the dhoby has been paid, the memsahib has had a rupee's worth of postage stamps, and there is one anna and six pieces to pay to Kasi.

It was a very little splash that submerged Mrs. Browne in Anglo-India, and there is no longer a ripple to tell about it. I don't know that life has contracted much for her. I doubt if it was ever intended to hold more than young Browne and the baby—but it has changed. Affairs that are not young Browne's or the baby's touch her little. Her world is the personal world of Anglo-India, and outside of it, except in affection of Canbury, I believe she does not think at all. She is growing dull to India, too, which is about as sad a thing as any. She sees no more the supple savagery of the Pathan in the market-place, the bowed reverence of the Mussulman praying in the sunset, the early morning mists lifting among the domes and palms of the city. She has acquired for the Aryan inhabitant a certain strong irritation, and she believes him to be nasty in all his ways. This will sum up her impressions of India as completely years hence as it does to-day. She is a memsahib like another.

Her mother still occasionally refers to the reports of the Society for the Propagation of the Gospel that reach them in Canbury, and freely supposes that the active interest her daughter took in Indian Missions has increased and intensified in India. In reply, Helen is obliged to take refuge in general terms, and has always discreetly refrained from mentioning the prejudice that exists in Calcutta against Christian cooks.

I hope she may not stay twenty-two years. Anglo-Indian tissues, material and spiritual, are apt to turn in twenty-two years to a substance somewhat resembling cork. And I hope she will not remember so many dead faces as I do when she goes away—dead faces and palm fronds grey with the powder of the wayside, and clamorous voices of the bazar crying, "*Here iz! memsahib! Here iz!*" . . .

So let us go our several ways. This is a dusty world. We drop down the river with the tide to-night. We shall not see the red tulip blossoms of the silk cottons fall again.

THE END.